D0305676

# IRELAND, EUROPE AND THE WORLD

Writings on a new century

# IRELAND, EUROPE AND THE WORLD

Writings on a new century

DAN O'BRIEN ～

*Gill & Macmillan*

Gill & Macmillan Ltd
Hume Avenue, Park West, Dublin 12
with associated companies throughout the world
www.gillmacmillan.ie

© Dan O'Brien 2009
978 07171 4664 2

Type design by Make Communication
Print origination by Carole Lynch
Printed and bound by in Great Britain by
MPG Books Ltd, Bodmin, Cornwall

This book is typeset in Linotype Minion.

The paper used in this book comes from the wood
pulp of managed forests. For every tree felled, at least
one tree is planted, thereby renewing natural
resources.

A CIP catalogue record for this book is available
from the British Library.

5 4 3 2 1

*For Karine*

# CONTENTS

# PREFACE

This book was originally intended as a straightforward collection of articles and essays from the past decade, grouped into six broad thematic chapters, with a newly written essay to introduce each one. While it remains a collected works, it grew in scope in the six-odd months between conception and completion (from late 2008 to May 2009) as the introductory essays expanded—in large part to take account of the extraordinary changes the world was undergoing during those months. The new material makes up almost one third of the book and, I hope, gives added topicality, as well as helping to join the dots contained in the previously published material in each chapter.

The content of the volume reflects my professional and personal experience, with three of the six chapters examining Ireland, two dealing with European matters and one on global affairs. On gathering the material together, it came as little surprise that roughly half of the essays and articles I have written over the past decade were on Irish issues. A working life spent abroad has never dulled my interest in my country of origin. Whenever distraction overcame the instinct to keep one eye cast homeward, it was never long before events drew it back. Ireland has been an interesting place in recent times by any standards, and even those with no native attachment to the country have had cause to look curiously at goings-on there: the process of European integration has been halted in its tracks not once, but twice by Irish voters; the island has experienced the highs and lows of a peace process that has been tortuous, unpredictable and not always peaceful; mass immigration has taken place rapidly and with almost unique social harmony; and, in the mid-1990s, an explosion of economic growth, the like of which had never before occurred in a developed country, ignited almost from the blue before spectacularly consuming itself.

The opening chapter deals with Irish politics and society. The former has changed far too little over decades, and where change has taken place, it has mostly had undesirable consequences. The current crisis has demonstrated just how incapable the country's parochial political system is of governing in a fast-moving and highly internationalised context. Thankfully, Irish society functions far better, and despite much gushing talk about its transformation in recent years, it appears to me to be remarkably unchanged—something that is not at all bad. The second chapter considers economic matters. This was in some ways the easiest chapter to write, and in others the most difficult. Like all Irish people, at home and around the world, I have watched in horror as the economy has plumbed depths not seen in a developed country in living memory. Much is now uncertain. But there is still cause for optimism, even if a great deal will have to change before stable and sustainable prosperity is enjoyed. The crash landing of the Irish economy, made all the more violent by international developments, is affecting Ireland's place in the world. Chapter III reflects on the country's positioning and posture in relation to its most important allies and an integrating Europe. Within weeks of the publication of this book, a second referendum on the Lisbon treaty is due to be held. Another 'No' vote would place Ireland squarely in the path of a historical dynamic of enormous power and momentum. I sincerely hope that nobody has to find out the hard way how dangerous it is to be on the wrong side of history.

These three chapters, taken together, come to a clear conclusion: without constitutional, institutional and administrative reform, Ireland is destined—at best—to return to the mediocrity and underperformance of most of the post-independence era. Such reform would require the embracing of change to a degree we have not managed before. The last two inflection points in Irish history came in the late 1910s and the late 1950s. Perhaps, a half-century on from the last, the current crisis will produce another. It is up to the Irish people. Many other peoples have little or no means of influencing their future. We are fortunate to have more than most. If we do not rise to the challenge, we will have nobody but ourselves to blame.

The second half of the book ranges further afield, reflecting where I have lived and worked. For a decade I have had the good fortune to be paid to watch Europe—its countries and Union—and write about it. For most of the previous decade I lived in four European capitals and worked in the foreign service of the European Commission. These experiences and my fascination with the continent are reflected in this volume. But much travel beyond the old continent's borders and a stint at the United Nations have, I hope, prevented excessive Eurocentrism. So, too, has a decade at the Economist Intelligence Unit. There, staying in a European silo has never really been an option—editorial meetings over the years have covered an extraordinary array of topics: from the clan system in the horn of Africa to religious extremism in the Indonesian archipelago; from border disputes in Latin America and southeast Asia to the risks of nuclear weapons proliferation on the Indian subcontinent and in northeast Asia; from near-perpetual crisis in Japan's banking system to perpetual strife in the Middle East. It would be an understatement to describe my time there as horizon-broadening.

Chapter IV takes a wide angle on Europe: its enormous and enduring influence on the world; its geopolitics; its big countries' historical trajectories; its stronger-than-acknowledged economy and some of its collective delusions. Chapter V tries to make sense of the continent's extraordinary experiment in political and economic integration. Despite its importance and uniqueness, the European Union sends most people into a deep stupor. There are very good reasons for this, and I hope I have avoided them all. The broadest of brush strokes are used and mind-numbing Eurotrivia have been expunged. The chapter attempts to answer three questions: what the entity does; what it is likely to do in the future; and what the risks are to its continued existence. The final chapter deals with issues pertaining to all, or at least most, of the world. Some big trends are considered, including the rise of developing countries and the relative—if overstated—decline of the west. The chapter also contains a (somewhat obligatory) discussion of the implications of economic globalisation. There are good reasons to be optimistic about our world's prospects, most notably the declining propensity to violence, but there is also cause to fear for the future. Both sides are weighed. Perhaps unwisely at the current juncture—when the world is changing more rapidly than at any time in my life—some predictions are made. The conclusion, which to a degree chimes with that of the first half of the book on Ireland, is that international society must adapt its institutions to manage its evolving circumstances. If the world is to continue to become more open and interconnected, much will have to change in the way it governs its affairs.

Dan O'Brien
London
22 May 2009

# ACKNOWLEDGMENTS

My colleagues at the Economist Intelligence Unit deserve particular acknowledgment and thanks. I owe a debt to more of them than can be mentioned here. Special thanks go to those who gave views on aspects of this book, particularly Anjalika Bardalai and Erica Fraga, whose comments on their native countries—India and Brazil, respectively—were insightful, considered and greatly appreciated. Laza Kekic's capacity to get to the nub of the matter has always made him the most challenging of interlocutors. I have enjoyed working with him immensely. Robert Ward knows Asia profoundly, and his thoughts on that continent helped a great deal. I also wish to acknowledge Charles Jenkins, Andre Astrow and Robin Bew. It has been a pleasure to work with them all.

Over the years I have interviewed, met and engaged with political leaders, business people, civil servants, policy-makers and thinkers. It has been an extraordinary privilege to have learnt from so many people who know so much. Their knowledge, views, opinions and insights have enriched my thinking immeasurably and I am indebted to a great many of them. More specifically, a good number of people who do not wish to be named here gave feedback on drafts of the content of this book. I am sincerely grateful to them for their time and thoughts, their help in weeding out inaccuracies and their knocking down of some of my sillier notions.

A large number of people took time to read entire chapters. Four did so for Chapter 1. Hugo Brady of the Centre for European Reform in London contributed to the chapter in many ways, all of which are deeply appreciated. David Gwynn Morgan, an Englishman in Ireland and legal academic, offered detailed comparative perspectives on constitutional matters, and at short notice. Bill Kissane, an Irishman in England—at the London School of Economics—shared his knowledge, and decades of thinking on Ireland in its international context. Maurice Manning, who is, among many other things, a political scientist and past political practitioner, encouraged a bolder stance on some issues and added real perspective on a number of others.

On Chapter 11, Colm Harmon, director of University College Dublin's Geary Institute, shared many ideas on policy and economics. There are few people anywhere who better understand the point at which both meet.

Danny McCoy, now Director General of the Irish Business and Employers' Confederation, gave sound judgments both at the beginning and at the end. Terry Neill, formerly managing partner with Accenture Ireland and now, among other things, a member of the governing board of the London Business School, applied his fine business mind to the chapter, helping to keep it (and me) focused. Jim O'Leary, a one-time financial services economist, and now an academic at NUI Maynooth and regular commentator, made many incisive comments and exposed weaknesses in argument and logic.

On Chapter III, Daniel Keohane of the European Union Institute for Security Studies in Paris gave enthusiastic support and shared ideas of real worth. Ben Tonra, Jean Monnet Professor of European Foreign and Security Policy at UCD, caused me to think again on less measured opinions, resulting in some significant alterations which made the chapter a lot less disjointed. Michael O'Sullivan, author of *Ireland and the Global Question*, made a number of excellent and thoughtful suggestions on aspects of the chapter that required deeper analysis.

On Chapter IV, William Horsley's strong views stiffened my spine where it needed stiffening. His knowledge of Europe is deep and wide after many years reporting for the BBC from the continent. John Hulsman of the German Council of Foreign Relations in Berlin is an American who understands Europe, enjoys its wonders, but sees its flaws. His comments made me do more rethinking than I had anticipated. Joseph Quinlan, Chief Market Strategist at Bank of America in New York and part-time academic who specialises in Europe–US economic ties, made numerous excellent suggestions. Pawel Swieboda, founder and director of demosEUROPA in Warsaw and Poland's chief negotiator during his country's EU accession talks, is one of the great Europeans of his generation. His thoughts and insights were invaluable.

On Chapter V, James Bergeron, an academic lawyer now with the US navy in Naples, made hugely intelligent comments on legal and security issues that I valued immeasurably. Zaki Cooper is an increasingly rare creature in London—a pro-European Briton. He offered detailed perspectives from his perch directing Business for New Europe. Brendan Halligan, president of the Institute of International and European Affairs in Dublin, added his worldly perspectives and thoughts, which, combined with his encouragement, were enormously appreciated. John Peet, Europe editor at *The Economist*, pulled me up on many half-formulated ideas and made some great suggestions.

On Chapter VI, Ettore Greco, Director of the Institute of International

Affairs in Rome and one of the most objective analysts I have ever had the good fortune to work with, saved me from a number of embarrassing oversights. Daniel Franklin, executive editor at *The Economist*, offered penetrating thoughts on an early draft. Fred Tanner, Director of the Geneva Institute of Security, pointed out some big gaps and omissions and suggested ways of plugging them. All errors and omissions that remain are mine and mine alone.

I also wish to thank Gill & Macmillan's publishing director, Fergal Tobin, and acknowledge his patience and forbearance as I struggled to complete the volume during a period that became the most challenging of my professional life. Thanks also to all at Gill & Macmillan for their efforts in making up for time lost by me.

Beyond the many professional associates and acquaintances who assisted on this project, many personal friends and family helped both directly and indirectly. Ivan Cooper and I have been debating the state of the world since we were kids and he has kept me in the loop on Irish affairs over the years. Seamus Taggart is a true cosmopolitan and one-time Shanghai resident whose hospitality in that city and thoughts on China fed into the discussion of that country in Chapter VI. Liam Gowan's love of debate, often late into the night around the table in Ranelagh, has been stimulating and great fun. Unlimited and effusive thanks go to my mother, Una, for support throughout this project, during far more important ones and during everything I have done over a lifetime. Appreciation also goes to Brian, Siobhan, Tom, Catherine and Eleanor, all of whom have always been supportive. So, too, has Basile, as only a child can. His playfulness and irrepressible good humour are a constant joy. Most of all, thanks to Karine, the light of my life, to whom this book is dedicated. Her support, her patience and, above all, her love sustain me. I hope they always will.

*Chapter* 1 ～

# MODERATE SOCIETY, INTROVERTED PSYCHE AND THE CURIOUS CASE OF HIBERNIAN POLITICS

*'Your representative owes you, not his industry only,*
*but his judgment; and he betrays instead of serving*
*you if he sacrifices it to your opinion.'*

EDMUND BURKE

## INTRODUCTION

When interviewing and interacting with politicians over time, those from Ireland have stood out from their counterparts elsewhere. They have done so as often as not for good reasons. Almost all exhibit a humility that is too often lacking in the more pompously self-important elsewhere. They do not demand deference and are usually open and frank. Whereas in most democracies many political leaders do not canvas on doorsteps[1] and have little interaction with voters, Irish elected representatives could never be accused of being aloof from their constituents. Despite frequent allegations, they are relatively unvenal, particularly compared to southern Europe, where some elected representatives can be astonishingly blatant in private about their involvement in politics for their own self-enrichment. Irish politicians are, on average, a pretty civic-minded bunch and, in order to survive in multi-seat constituencies, are among the hardest-working anywhere. The political class's avoidance of pandering to or inflaming anti-immigration sentiment has been to its great credit—in no other European country have politicians been as restrained. The essential decency and 'connectedness' of elected representatives in Ireland has been a real strength over almost a century of independence and has been among the main reasons that the country has enjoyed near-unique social stability.

Yet for all the positives about Irish politicians, the calibre of the average elected representative far from matches that of his counterparts in similar countries. Irish politicians' professional backgrounds only rarely prepare them for leading and managing large organisations. They tend to have no inter-national experience and most have little more than shallow knowledge of what goes on outside the country. It is rare for an Irish politician to be attuned to policy debates, and too many have only a tenuous knowledge of their brief. There are, of course, some exceptions—knowledgable, thoughtful politicians who think laterally and are policy literate. But the thinkers too often become overwhelmed by the demands of constituency politicking, and frequently complain of being little more than 'messenger boys' for their constituents (one never hears this complaint made by politicians in any other country). I recall once discussing with one such politician his interest in other countries' experiences of tackling pockets of persistent urban poverty. His efforts to read up on the issue, he said, were overwhelmed by the day-to-day demands of his constituents. After a period he shrugged, lamenting that he had to devote time to pressuring the local authority to cut the grass in the constituency's parks, and to be seen to do so. He lost his seat at the subsequent election and has left politics.

## THE RISING COST OF PAROCHIAL POLITICS

Until recently, and over more than a decade and a half, the ill effects of these weaknesses had been masked by spectacular economic success. But it is increasingly obvious, as depression takes hold, that inspirational political leadership counted far less for the good years than a favourable inter-national environment, structural economic factors, policy decisions made decades ago, good timing and plain luck. It is equally clear that much of the current crisis is self-inflicted, owing to some truly bad decisions (such as gross mismanagement of the public finances) and much complacency (including the insistence of government that the property boom would not and could not end).

The costs of political parochialism are rising as the world changes. In the past, when economies and societies were far more self-contained, an inward-looking political class was not such a hindrance. Ireland, for instance, came through the 1930s relatively well, avoiding political upheaval, economic collapse and the scourge of hyperinflation. But the world changed in the second half of the 20th century, as an ever increasing amount of human activity took place across borders. However, as Ireland and its political class remained inward looking, the country excluded itself from the post-war boom. Action was taken and direction changed only when decline became so acute in the second half of the 1950s that there was little choice. But whatever the sins of the post-independence generation of leaders at that time, they were ones more of omission than commission. The next generation more proactively wreaked havoc on the economy from the late 1970s. Despite this, lessons were not learnt. At time of writing in early 2009, the second fiscal crisis in a generation threatens the solvency of the state.

Good government matters more, not less, in today's world, as its role has widened over the decades (the role of the state is discussed in Chapter IV). Now, efficient and nimble government counts more than ever. For any country to thrive, it needs proactive leaders who understand the complexities of modern government; are qualified, able and willing to manage large organisations; can recognise and exploit opportunities; identify threats on the horizon and react to them; do not make elementary errors; and can articulate and explain the reasons for change when it is needed. As the Irish political class remains focused on well maintained park-lawns, the shortcomings of the system are becoming greater. How the weaknesses of the Irish system can be remedied, or at least mitigated, is the central long-term challenge for Ireland.

## IRELAND'S IRON LAW OF INERTIA

There will be great difficulties in rising to these challenges. Inertia hinders change everywhere. In Ireland it is an iron law. The protracted failure to deal with clerical child abuse, the unwillingness to address the decades-long inadequacies in the way the Irish language has been taught, and the slow-motion policy responses to chronic recessions of the 1950s, 1980s and today are just some of the examples. There are three big reasons for this inertia that now threatens the country's future: the constitutional framework, social partnership and a society that shows little interest, and is often resistant to, new ideas and new ways of doing things.

When colleagues or foreigners have asked me to explain Irish politics over the years, I have found that beginning with the institution that is most different from every other country is the best starting point as it helps explain so much else. The Irish electoral system is effectively unique and produces a unique political class.[2] Positively, the politicians that emerge from it are plugged into their local communities. But it is also the main reason for the relatively low calibre of Irish elected representatives.[3] Publicans, local solicitors, school teachers and the occasional GP simply do not have the expertise and experience to deal with the complexities of modern government in a highly internationalised setting. This is compounded by the absence of any incentive for those representatives to be agents of change. Politicians who live or die politically by addressing local concerns exclusively do not gain a jot by proposing healthcare reform, the adoption of best practice in public budgeting or the honing of diplomatic focus. In other countries, whether a first-past-the-post electoral system or a list system is used, politicians are insulated from immediate local issues. This can cause its own problems, but it allows space to think, learn, discuss and formulate ideas. Such systems also create different paths to career advancement for politicians. Getting ahead for an aspiring politician in most countries is about showing the party leadership that he can be useful. And that means being able to generate and articulate ideas for change at all levels of government—local, regional, national and international. In Irish politics, as one elected representative put it, 'it is better to keep your mouth shut'.[4] As European and global issues become increasingly important for Ireland, a voting system that produces locally minded and locally focused politicians who keep their heads down, rather than standing up and leading, comes at an ever higher cost. (Other aspects of the constitutional framework which inhibit effective and proactive government are discussed below.)

## ANTI-SOCIAL PARTNERS

Social partnership in recent decades has added to the power of inertia, having expanded over two decades to place Ireland among the most cor-poratist states in Europe. In many ways the partnership process suits Irish society and its way of doing things, given the absence of class cleavages and a non-confrontational and consensus-orientated political culture.[5] In this, Ireland's political culture is close to the arc of small Northern European states stretching from the Netherlands to the Nordics. Such a partnership framework can bring benefits if it facilitates change by the forging of con-sensus. In its early years, in the late 1980s, it did just that. But partnership structures can be costly if they hinder change. There is often a very fine line in any partnership mechanism. Lobby groups in a free society have every right to articulate their interests and have their voices heard. However, if they 'capture' the policy-making process, they cross the line. And Ireland's version of social partnership without doubt crossed that line during the boom years. Much of the increase in public spending was accounted for by public sector pay and the implementation of necessary reforms was blocked because interest groups exercised vetoes within the partnership structures.

Much of the blame for this lies with government. It determines on which side of the line any partnership process is located as it is the arbiter among interest groups, who can hardly be blamed for seeking to extract as much as possible from the process—that is, after all, their *raison d'être*. But the current crisis will determine whether partnership is appropriate for Ireland. If the partners can educate and lead their respective memberships to take the very tough choices necessary, and then ensure their members stick to the terms agreed, the mechanism will demonstrate its worth. At time of writing in May 2009, there seems no prospect of this happening. In effect, Ireland's social partnership model has failed its only real test in 20 years and is hindering, not helping, the search for solutions to a crisis it played a considerable part in creating.

## POLITICAL CHICKEN, SOCIETAL EGG

How any country reacts to challenges depends not only on its political leadership, but also on its society, and how the two interact. Three big things stand out about Irish society in *relative* terms: one of these is its introspection and limited interest in ideas (the others are political moderation and a deep respect for rules, both of which are discussed below). But before going on to discuss this, it may be useful to make two broad comments on how analysis of Irish society and social change is conducted. The first is the introspective tendency to 'auto-exoticism', as described so well by a Dutch academic, Joep Leerssen. Irish self-fascination is not productive and contributes to extremes of sentiment—hubris during the tiger years when Ireland knew best and self-loathing now as some believe the country is worst for everything. The truth is that all countries are unique. There is nothing uniquely unique about Ireland.

The second point, which may appear partially to contradict the former, is that for all the talk of how the economic boom changed Ireland, what is really surprising is how much stayed the same. If Ireland is genuinely different from its peer countries, it is in this regard. Family remains central to Irish life, illustrated not least by one of the highest birth rates in Europe[6] and a still very low divorce rate.[7] For all the talk of 'tip-toeing back to the pews', most people never left them in the first place—weekly church attendance elsewhere in Europe is higher only in Malta and Poland.[8] How leisure time is enjoyed is another example. The GAA has gone from strength to strength, despite perennial fretting that Irish culture is on the verge of being Anglicised or globalised to death, and alcohol consumption—which remains among the highest in Europe—is still central to social life despite greater awareness of health risks. That Irish society has retained much of what is good, while enjoying new-found prosperity, led us at the Economist Intelligence Unit to rank Ireland first in the world in a 'Quality of Life' index in 2004.

## THE INCURIOUSNESS OF THE IRISH MIND

The most striking aspect of the reaction in Ireland to that Quality of Life index was the hostility it engendered (my colleagues were taken aback). Of the acres of coverage it received, almost no one attempted to analyse the reasons we had ranked Ireland above all other countries. A considerable proportion of the reaction was dismissive, despite those taking such a view being patently unfamiliar with the work they were making such sweeping judgments on.[9] This was not entirely unexpected and brought to mind the reaction to a survey of political and cultural discourse on Ireland by Stephen Howe, a British academic. The book, *Ireland and Empire*, quite apart from being encyclopaedic, rigorous, and quite simply the best such survey I have read on the subject was, to boot, broadly sympathetic and was in no way condescending or patronising as works on small countries by writers from big countries can be. Yet a Trinity College academic who reviewed the book was outraged.[10] Howe was guilty of 'an astounding arrogance and contempt for almost all of the most prominent scholars of modern Ireland'. Unable to contain his outrage, the reviewer felt obliged to level the same charge a few lines later; the book was 'characterised by an astounding metropolitan arrogance'. Howe's real crime for this reviewer was to dare to intrude into his cosy world and challenge it with different opinions and perspectives.

Despite enormous changes in education, communications and incomes, it is difficult to avoid the conclusion that the Irish mindset remains introverted and hostile to new ideas. Such an opinion is not lightly made and certainly not based on the mere anecdotes described above, but on cross-country evidence. Take the press and publishing. According to Eurostat, 17% of Irish households used the Internet to read newspapers and magazines in 2008.[11] Among the 27-member bloc, only Bulgaria and Romania—by far the most impoverished and under-educated countries—had lower levels. Perhaps even more important than the press are books. Of the established members of the EU, the number of titles produced per million people was the lowest among the 14 countries surveyed, according to one report from 2001.[12] The lack of curiousness is reflected in the Europe-wide Eurobarometer polls. These show that Irish respondents' knowledge of the EU is frequently among the lowest of the established members of the bloc,[13] which is particularly surprising given that the country has held seven referendums on Europe involving months of campaigning and debate. No other electorate has been exposed to the issues so many times and in such a concentrated way.

Demand for ideas appears at least as weak as demand for knowledge. John Coakley, a political scientist, has provided a good survey of opinion poll data on Irish anti-intellectualism and intolerance of ideas.[14] Buttressing his findings are the observations that there is no tradition of think tanks in Ireland, levels of innovation are far below rich-world levels (as measured by patenting activity[15]), there is only one daily newspaper that offers a forum for ideas from non-staff journalists,[16] and that during the course of the 20th century, no democracy was less affected by radical political ideas.[17] I begin and end this essay with quotes from Edmund Burke not only because they nicely and appropriately bookend the discussion therein, but because he is by a very great distance the most influential political thinker ever to come from Ireland. Despite this, he is quoted and cited far less in Irish political discussion and debate than in many other countries. Alexis de Tocqueville, a French thinker-artistocrat who wrote on his travels in Ireland and in the US the early 19th century, has suffered the same fate. His rich writings on Ireland are not only unread, but largely unknown, in stark contrast to the US, where his masterwork— *Democracy in America*—is known to every educated American to this day and is frequently referenced in the media and elsewhere.

## MODERATION, TOLERANCE AND THE MYTH OF THE LAWLESS IRISH

If a demand for change, and ideas on how to affect change, do not bubble up from society, and if the structures of leadership do not drive needed change from the top, chronic inertia is the result. In most societies, stasis often eventually leads to explosions of frustration. Ireland has been very different in this regard. It has enjoyed near unique social and political stability since the Civil War—in no other country has the pecking order of the three largest parties remained unchanged over seven decades. The conventional view that emigration provided a safety valve for Irish society— those who were not prepared to tolerate stagnation left—explains it in part, but does not come close to explaining it all (many other countries have experienced both emigration *and* political upheaval, notably in southern Europe).

Many countries have images of themselves that are entirely at odds with reality. One of Ireland's is the self-image that it is a nation of inveterate rule-breakers. This is a myth. Crime rates[18] and the prison population are low[19] by both international and European standards; serious social unrest has been very rare, occurring mainly as a result of spillover from Northern Ireland; drivers are relatively careful, with fatalities on the roads lower than the European average;[20] and taxpayers are among the most compliant— the Irish black economy accounts for an estimated 15% of the formal economy, below the average for developed countries, and far below the level for developing countries.[21] The willingness to adhere to rules reflects a strong sense of community, society and nation. Europe-wide polls show Irish people's pride in their nation to be unusually strong, rates of charitable giving are by some measures the highest in the world[22] and the NGO sector is strong and vibrant. The GAA, which is most notable in this regard, is a truly unique organisation in its membership, presence in every nook and cranny of the country, and its level and range of activities. Such an institution could not exist, never mind thrive, in a society where people do not share a respect for and commitment to each other.

The perception that Ireland is, or was, unusually intolerant of outsiders (rather than ideas) is another self-image that does not stand up to scrutiny once one takes even a cursory look at the rest of the world. Much of this is because there is a tendency to equate social conservatism with intolerance. This is far too simple. Most societies in human history have been socially conservative, with strong pressure to adhere to given norms on family structure and social conduct, but their willingness to tolerate others' ways has varied enormously. Ireland until recently was a very socially conservative society by European standards, and, as argued above, it continues to be intolerant of ideas. But it has always been tolerant of minorities. By today's standards of inclusiveness and celebration of diversity, of course, Ireland (from independence to relatively recently) was a cold house for those who did not share the religion, race, outlook and aspirations of the majority. But to judge the past by today's standards is unfair and unwise—far better to judge them against their peers elsewhere at the time.

Ireland's travelling community certainly suffered neglect, but it was never persecuted, something which happened to gypsies even in countries with some of the most entrenched democratic values. In Switzerland—the oldest democracy in the world—Jenisch gypsies endured persecution for centuries and up until as recently as 1973 the state sanctioned a private organisation's forced taking of Jenisch children from their parents. In Sweden, involuntary sterilisations of gypsy women were practised up to the 1970s—in effect, a form of genocide. Ireland's treatment of its Jewish community also compares well with other countries over time. Despite traditional Roman Catholic hostility to Judaism and the prevalence of murderous anti-Semitism in Europe in the first half of the 20th century, the 1937 constitution explicitly recognised the Jewish faith, and members of the community have always played an active and unhindered part in political, commercial and cultural life.

Treatment of the Protestant minority has been much the same, particularly when compared to many other newly founded states, where those associated with colonial rule were left to the mercies of a new order. In countries such as Algeria, Uganda and Zimbabwe, those linked to colonial rule suffered ethnic cleansing and mass property expropriations. In Europe, the successor states of the Austrian-Hungarian empire—Czechoslovakia and Romania—forcibly expelled some of the ethnic Hungarian populations, who were resented for their position of privilege in the old order. Finland provides the closest parallel as a continuously functioning democracy. Despite being recognised as a model in its treatment of its ethnic Scandinavian minority, the proportion of Swedish-speakers fell from 11% of the population in 1920 to 5.5% by 2003. As it happens, this almost precisely mirrors the change in the Protestant population in the Irish Republic. In both cases, the 'pull' factor of a more appealing life in, respectively, Britain and Sweden was the main cause, rather than 'push' factors, such as the curbing of religious freedoms or the right to run businesses.

The relative tolerance of Irish society is to seen today in its reaction to mass immigration. No other European country has adapted as well and as quickly. No violent or thuggish movements have formed. No anti-immigration party has emerged as an electoral force, which can only reflect the absence of bottom-up demand for such a force. And immigrants can be found in every corner of the country doing almost every kind of job. It may be to tempt fate—at time of writing unemployment is rising fast and resentments may yet come to the surface—but even during the bad times to come, there should not be a widespread backlash against foreigners.

## OPPORTUNITY IN CRISIS?

The tolerance and moderation of Irish society will be tested in the difficult times ahead. My hunch is that no matter how bad things get (and they could get very bad), society will roll with the punches and hunker down until the worst is past. If anything, the greater risk is that rather than seeing such a crisis as an opportunity to address the causes of failure, Ireland will slump back into its old ways of accepting under-performance. This would be appalling. It would also be tragic, because the prospect of improvement is better in Ireland than in other countries that suffer serious governance weaknesses. At the risk of reductionism, where bad government exists it is generally a combination of two things: a dysfunctional political culture—those who wield power using it as a means of enriching and entrenching themselves—and dysfunctional institutions, which result in bad policy and bad implementation of policy. Ireland's governance failings are far less the result of a culture of corruption (which is fortunate, because changing culture is a slow and very difficult enterprise) and far more about flawed institutional arrangements.

Any re-evaluation of these institutions must start with the foundations. Ireland's constitutional weaknesses are too great to be ignored any longer. The 1937 constitution has served the country well, but its flaws and rigidities require nothing less than a new beginning, not least because piecemeal change would be messy, protracted and stand a too-great chance of being derailed. A new constitution could be the basis of a vision for a new era. A different electoral system would be among the most necessary changes. The Danish model, which combines multi-seat constituencies, such as those that currently exist in Ireland, and a parallel list system, would allow Irish politics to remain closely connected to communities, but limit the effects of localism and draw in a wider range of talent to political life.

A clearer division between legislature and executive is also essential if the quality of governance is to be improved. Ireland's constitution is near-unique in the manner in which it merges these two branches of government. In many countries, ministers cannot be members of the legislature. In Ireland they must be. Becoming more like the average democracy would be good for both branches. Most importantly it would further widen the talent pool of potential ministers (to suggest, as is frequently done, that this would be in some way 'undemocratic' is to suggest that other countries' democracies are in some way inferior to Ireland's). Ireland has no shortage of people with the knowledge and expertise, the patriotism and drive to govern effectively. If the inadequacies of the existing political class, so clearly demonstrated during the current economic crisis, do not generate a desire to bring such people into government, nothing ever will.

The rigidities of the constitutional superstructure further inhibit effective government. Ireland is unique to my knowledge in having to put all changes to its constitution to a popular vote—a super majority in parliament is the norm almost everywhere. In recent years this has resulted in the need to hold referendums on issues as diverse as bail and adoption, participation in the International Criminal Court and deeper European integration. With turnout frequently as low as one in three voters, it is difficult to see precisely what gain this method of constitutional change offers over the international norm. Its costs, on the other hand, are considerable and can be seem most clearly in relation to the country's position in Europe, with two consecutive treaties being rejected on grounds that are difficult to explain to any rational outsider.

A further rigidity comes from the power of the judicial branch of government and the manner in which judges have chosen to exercise those powers in recent decades. Combined with the weakness and ineffectiveness of the executive branch, power has become unbalanced. The judicial branch is considerably stronger than the other branches when compared with other democracies. The Supreme Court has the power to review legislation both before and after enactment, which is far from the norm. It has not always used these powers wisely and in recent decades has, at the very least, over-used them. The frequency with which judicial review is exercised has jumped since the 1960s, and some decisions have been not only bizarre, but damaging—on sexual abuse of children and health insurance, for instance—and if Ireland exits the EU in the future, the beginnings of that process will be traced back to the crankish Crotty Judgment in the 1980s.

The structure and culture of administrative mechanisms also require urgent reform (this can be done without changing the constitution). Good policy will not be made, and no policy will be well implemented, unless the wider public service is made more efficient and more flexible. An infusion of expertise is needed and depoliticisation of some functions of government is necessary. Management of the public finances and other economic and regulatory functions stand out in this regard (see Chapter II). Collegiality and consensus-building are strengths in the Irish administrative culture, but they can be weaknesses when they inhibit questioning and frank evaluation (see Chapter III). This has too often been the case in Ireland, as is being revealed as the tide of prosperity recedes over the horizon. In a small homogenous country, formalised devil's advocate structures are needed, peopled preferably by foreigners appointed on a one-term-only basis with a mandate to report publicly on executive and administrative decisions and, as important, non-decisions, in order to squeeze out inertia. For whistle-blowers, it is not merely protection that is needed, but incentivisation.

From the wreckage of the current economic crisis, it is to be hoped that the Irish people will hold a mirror up to themselves and attempt to draw some honest conclusions about the failings of their political institutions and culture. If that happens, there is a real possibility of better government to avoid for the future the failings of the present and past. Ireland has the cohesiveness as a society and it has people capable of doing far better. If the country's human resources can be reconfigured, much can be changed for the better. If an attempt is made to muddle through, the future will be a repetition of the awfulness of the 1950s, 1980s and the dark years ahead.

> '*A state without the means of some change is without the means of its conservation.*'
>
> EDMUND BURKE

———

## IRISH POLITICIANS HAVE MANY FAULTS, BUT CORRUPTION IS NOT ONE OF THEM

*11 November 2000*

The affairs of a small number of politicians in the Republic have convulsed public life for half a decade. Outbursts of outrage and calls for retribution are understandable. They are also warranted if they ensure that wrongdoers are brought to book and the tempted deterred. Yet perspective needs to be regained if faith in a flawed but well-functioning political system is not to be irreversibly eroded.

Despite many years of widely circulated rumours that some people in lofty positions were not playing by the rules, opinion surveys over decades have found the Irish to be among the most satisfied in Europe with how they are governed. It is difficult to see how this could have been if abuse of power had been as endemic as is now frequently suggested. Indeed, given the temptations of high office—and when compared to their counterparts in Europe, never mind the rest of the world—Irish politicians have succumbed relatively infrequently.

Start with campaign donations. Though often impossible to distinguish from plain palm-greasing, they are a perennial problem in all democracies. Everywhere even politicians who are not on the make fear being outspent at election time by their rivals. But lest anyone think our lot have a monopoly on the crooked contribution, consider the woes of office-holders, past and present, in Europe's largest countries in recent months.

In the UK, Formula 1's Bernie Eccelstone quietly helped the Labour Party with costly campaigning before the 1997 election. Once in power, Tony Blair's government helped to have Formula 1 exempted from an EU directive banning tobacco advertising which would have left Mr Eccelstone out of pocket. In Germany, former chancellor Helmut Kohl's retirement is little happier than Charles Haughey's. He did some service to state and continent but along the way he channelled cash to party slush funds. Unlike the grey area inhabited by those appearing before Flood and Moriarty, German politicians are explicitly prohibited from taking such contributions. Worse still, Dr Kohl was not compromised by a greengrocer or builder, but by a shady international arms dealer. West of the Rhine, President Jacques Chirac's past regularly returns to haunt him. The latest ghost is a deceased political fixer who appears in a video alleging he witnessed the President pocketing brown envelopes. But Mr Chirac, by virtue of his office, has to do nothing so undignified as to account for himself before an upstart judge.

When straightforward bribery is considered, the Republic looks better yet. The State in most regions is by far the biggest single employer, provider of housing and buyer of goods and services. Such economic power will inevitably attract the unscrupulous. Despite this, it is unheard of for politicians in the Republic to secure Civil Service jobs or local authority homes in return for backhanders or votes. Not so in other countries. In Portugal pockets are sometimes lined when public services recruit. In Austria the housing queue can be jumped if a vote is promised.

As regards the links between government and business, with the exception of the building and beef industries it is hard to find business people in the Republic who complain that kickbacks and connections are needed to obtain government contracts. In France, where politicians glide easily between public office and the pinnacles of the state's business interests, entrepreneurs often need deep pockets and influence if they are to be considered when public contracts are tendered. In Italy, where poor politicians are thin on the ground, most people take it as given that a career in politics is a route to riches. Bettino Craxi, a one-time prime minister, shocked even sleaze-weary Italians. He held court in one of Rome's grandest hotels in the manner of a decadent Renaissance prince— and all on an MP's salary. In the Republic, by contrast, where the lifestyles of TDs are closely observed, there are few fabulously wealthy politicians. Those who are can account for their wealth. Mr Charles Haughey, whose high living raised eyebrows precisely because it was so unusual, is the exception that proves the rule.

But corruption is about far more than elected representatives dishonestly feathering their nests. In Belgium the leader of the Francophone Socialists was assassinated. Alain van der Beist, one of his ministers, is to be tried for the murder. In Spain Jose Barrionuevo, a former interior minister, was jailed for a kidnapping committed while in office. In Scotland one out-of-control local council has been rapped for sectarianism, physical intimidation and nepotism. Little wonder, then, that in many places around the world, and sometimes in Europe, too, the man in the street hopes that unprincipled politicians will keep their snouts in the trough—compared to graft, there are much worse abuses of power. And in this respect the excesses of Irish politicians pale in comparison with some of their counterparts abroad.

Without playing down the unacceptable behaviour of some, our politicians suddenly do not look so bad in this context. With the mechanisms to catch the miscreants among them working well, they look better still. So why such disenchantment? Transparency International, a corruption-monitoring organisation, has an explanation. It says that when erring politicians get their comeuppance, and wrongdoing is aired in all its tawdry detail, bar-room whispers become newspaper headlines. Such prominent reminders reinforce the feeling that politics is rotten.

Although the instinctive reaction may be to reach for one brush to tar all elected representatives, this would be wrong on two counts. First, it is unfair. Take the ongoing economic miracle. Though politicians would like to take more credit than is their due, tough political choices and good policies played no small part. But even if one's heart does not bleed for put-upon politicians with thin skin, there is a second and far more serious effect of dismissing them all as self-servers. If opinion polls are anything to go by, voters will desert political parties in droves at the next election, and the largest collection of independents ever will descend on the Dáil.

The complexity of forming coalitions and, more important, keeping them together increases exponentially the greater the number of parties and independents involved. And as independents look on politics primarily as squeezing what they can out of government for their constituents, their concern for any wider national interest is often limited. If their role is magnified, the short-termism of government survival will predominate. Politicking will take precedence over policy and, ironically, patronage will probably increase. It is no coincidence that Italy, the country in Europe in which this sort of fragmentation is most evident, is also the most poorly governed.

A country can get away with weak and unstable government in times of plenty when hard choices are few. But think back to the dark days of the 1980s. Successive governments were hobbled by their reliance on independents. This was a significant factor in the delayed restoration of economic stability, the price of which was paid in joblessness and emigration. With public and press ever less tolerant of transgression, and rightly demanding better conduct from politicians, and the tribunals rooting out wrongdoing, standards in public life are rising, not falling. Without a recognition of this, the baby may go the way of the bathwater to the detriment of all.

*Originally published in the* Irish Times

————

## BRINGING SENATORS TO CABINET TABLE WOULD INJECT DYNAMISM INTO POLITICS

*10 October 2003*

Parachuting the likes of Bono into the job of minister for, say, development aid might sound strange in Ireland, but it is what most democracies do. Italy's dynamic health minister, Girolamo Sirchia, is an internationally regarded haematologist. France's dashing foreign minister, Dominique de Villepin, is a diplomat by profession. His American counterpart, Colin Powell, was a career soldier before taking high office. They, like many holders of executive office all over the democratic world, have two things in common—each has a lifetime of experience of his brief, and none has ever faced voters in an election.

To some ears that will sound undemocratic. But to see why it is not, consider one of the guiding principles of democracy; that power be divided among the branches of government so it is more difficult for its wielders to abuse it. This separation, most democracies believe, is vital because regular elections alone are not enough to keep manners on those who hold power (think of our own unrehabilitateable Charles Haughey, who faced no fewer than five general elections in a dozen tawdry years as Fianna Fáil leader).

But separating those who make law and those who execute it has never been a priority in the Republic. As a result, those two branches of government have always been essentially one, with negative consequences for both. For TDs, the lure of executive office distracts from their real duties: the scrutiny of legislation and the holding of ministers to account. From a ministerial perspective the ill-effects are worse still. A lifetime spent struggling to win and retain elected office in the cauldron of Irish constituency politics means most elected representatives are career politicians with limited expertise in areas such as health, transport and education. As the current cabinet line-up shows, drawing the executive branch of government from such a tiny pool of career politicians often leads to less than dynamic ministers and a dearth of radicalism when it comes to making policy.

Admittedly, the result of all this over 80 years has been far from disastrous. With only a dozen countries worldwide having enjoyed longer periods of unbroken democratic rule and fewer still our social calm, the Republic, as a political entity, has been an outstanding success. Yet despite this, few would disagree that things could always be made better. So what to do without tearing up the constitution and writing a new one? A start could be made in the Seanad, whose members have just begun a period of self-examination. While there are many good ideas about how to reform that legislative backwater, using to the full an existing rule—whereby two senators at any given time can sit at cabinet—could do many things to invigorate the political system.

First, although bringing senators to cabinet would not in theory make a clearer distinction between the executive and the legislature, in practice it would. A non-career politician appointed to the Seanad by the Taoiseach for the express purpose of coming to cabinet would be more a creature of the executive than the legislature, not having been elected and not having a constituency to cultivate. This has happened twice before, most recently (and successfully) in the 1980s, when Garret FitzGerald appointed Prof. Jim Dooge to the upper house so he could make him foreign minister.

The most obvious advantage of senator-ministers is that they can spend time on policy rather than having to watch their backs in a Dáil constituency where young aspirants are always nibbling at incumbents' heels. This would be a major advantage because there are few democracies in which ministers are less involved in policy formulation than in Ireland (the old jibe of Fianna Fáil being a policy-taker, not policy-maker, holds true to a considerable extent for the other parties too).

A further advantage of clearer separation would be the lessening of the tendency for ministers with Dáil constituencies to provide goodies for constituents—be it decentralised Civil Service jobs or better roads—in order to boost their chances of re-election. Without such pressures, senator-ministers could allocate resources for the wider good without fear or favour.

A second big plus of widening the ministerial talent pool would be to bring those with specific expertise and experience to any given portfolio. Erudite academics, hard-bargaining trade unionists and dynamic business-folk are the sort of upstanding civic-minded types who are drafted to serve their countries in most other democracies, not least because it is felt that politics is far too important to be left exclusively to professional politicians.

And if there are any doubts about the benefits of this, just think of what two such people have done for another once-sleepy institution of the State—the presidency. Without detracting from the professional politicians who filled the role before 1990, it would be hard to contest that Mary McAleese, and her predecessor, Mary Robinson, have brought something to the job that most members of the political class could not.

A final benefit would be for the Seanad itself. Congenitally defective and then hobbled after birth because de Valera never wanted it to constrain government's powers (he felt obliged to establish it only because the Vatican's 1930s third way between liberal capitalism and godless communism advocated such structures), it has always been the neglected child of Irish democratic institutions. But by making its members hold to account one or more of their number sitting at cabinet, they would have a real job to do. They would also have an incentive to shine if they thought the prize of ministerial office was on offer.

So is it conceivable that Bertie Ahern would show uncharacteristic boldness and pension off some of his cabinet under-performers to make way for more able senators? Hardly. But for the languishing opposition parties it might be the sort of proposal to catch voters' imagination. Promising a couple of McAleeses or Robinsons at the cabinet table could hardly be a vote-loser at a time when satisfaction with the same old Dáil faces is low and going lower.

*Originally published in the* Irish Times

————

## DANISH VOTING SYSTEM COULD BE BEST FOR IRELAND

*8 August 1999*

If the current electoral system in Ireland has reached the end of its useful working life, then a look at the arrangements within the member states of the European Union, the core of the world's well-established democracies, is a useful starting point in the debate on reform.

The mixed member proportional system (also known as the additional member system), under which a percentage of MPs are elected in single-seat constituencies and the remainder from top-up lists to ensure proportionality, is employed in Germany, Greece and Italy. The majoritarian first-past-the-post system is in place in France and the UK. With the exception of Ireland all others have settled on the party list system of proportional representation (List-PR).

It is noteworthy that, with the exception of Italy, those countries in the EU that have tinkered with their electoral systems (or contemplated doing so) in recent years are those that do not use the List-PR system—France in the 1980s, Greece frequently since its return to democracy and the UK since the current government gave the Liberal Democrats a commitment to hold a referendum on the issue before the 1997 general election. It is also striking that as the former Soviet-bloc countries joined (or rejoined in some cases) the democratic European mainstream, more have plumped for List-PR than any other system.

As regards Ireland's Single Transferable Vote (STV) system, not a single country in the world that has participated in the democratisation wave of the past two decades has adopted it. These patterns suggest that the electoral system that best balances the sometimes conflicting objectives of legitimacy and proportionality on the one hand with effectiveness and stability of government on the other is List-PR. With only one other example of STV worldwide (the tiny island state of Malta), they also suggest that its deficiencies have been considered to outweigh its advantages.

Chief among these deficiencies is the excessively local orientation of STV. There is arguably no country in the EU in which elected politicians have as little input into shaping strategic policy goals as in Ireland. The underdevelopment of the parliamentary committee system relative to the European average is but one obvious manifestation of this.

The cliché that all politics is local has been repeated so often in Ireland that it has become something of a truism. If all politics ever was local, it is emphatically no longer the case as international economic and political dynamics affect states as never before. The sovereignty implications accompanying Ireland's membership of the EU are the most important manifestation of this.

According to Demos, the UK think tank, 30% of all new legislation in the member states emanates from Brussels. The crucial forum in which this legislation is framed is the Council of Ministers. If Irish parliamentarians, and hence ministers, are prevented by their constituency burdens from driving policy formulation at home, the difficulties at Council are magnified many times where a detailed grasp of the issues is essential in winning over 14 other ministers whose interests are often, if not always, different. Given the type of minister the electoral system produces and the burdens it places on them, it is unsurprising that with a few notable exceptions the performance of Irish ministers at Council has been less than stellar.

With Ireland's recent economic performance the envy of many other EU member states and per capita GDP now above the EU average, the strategy of benefiting by pleading small size, relative poverty and peripherality will no longer pass muster. Instead, ministers will have to convince their peers that what is in Ireland's interests is also right for them.

The second major deficiency of the current system is the leverage it gives to independent TDS elected with a mandate that does not include interests beyond those of their immediate constituents. In the 1997 general election, of the three independent TDS upon whom the current minority government depends, none obtained even half of 1% of national first preference votes. As assertive independents have been a prominent feature of Irish political life for so long, the power they exercise receives scant attention, but from a European perspective this appears as more than a mere quirk; it seems downright undemocratic. No other country in the EU has institutionalised structures that allow individuals representing such a tiny proportion of the electorate to wield so much power.

With regard to alternatives to STV, versions of List-PR have proven effective in the overwhelming majority of small and medium-sized mature democracies in Europe. There is little reason to believe that a tailored version would not function equally well in Ireland. Given the culture of particularly close links between TDS and their constituents that STV has engendered, a system that minimises the trauma of loosening these bonds would best suit Ireland. As such, the Danish variant, with multi-member constituencies and a national list, is worth closer analysis.

Multi-member constituencies with open lists allow voters to choose between individual candidates or the party of their choice. This ensures that the MP-constituent connection is maintained. However, the constituency list becomes relevant as approximately 50% of the electorate in Denmark vote for a party rather than a candidate. This makes the predetermined party list more important, resulting in a lower turnover of MPS than in Ireland and less extreme pressure on representatives to compete, with each to be seen to provide for their constituents. In contrast to some other models, it also ensures that no one party dominates constituency seats. The national list in Denmark tops up the seat allocations of parties, guaranteeing very high levels of proportionality. It also ensures a cross-section of society is represented in parliament, offsetting the bias in multi-seat constituencies that favours those whose professions bring them into frequent contact with the electorate.

Currently, the two most common professions in the Danish parliament—public servants and private-sector white-collar workers—account for 58% of MPs (this compares with teachers and farmers making up 40% of the current Dáil). However, unlike in many other countries, the Danish national list accounts for a mere 23% of MPs, limiting the role of party leaders in determining who will be elected—the main argument against List-PR.

Although the Irish are among the most satisfied with their overall system of governance in the EU (according to region-wide opinion polls), the deficiencies of the current electoral system are increasing in the light of deepening involvement in Europe and Ireland's changing relations therein. As STV is not fundamentally flawed, only more imperfect than some alternatives, root and branch reform is unnecessary. With the slight reduction in access to TDs that the Danish model offers (which would be offset, partially at least, by the planned strengthening of local democracy) the electorate would eventually benefit from improved governance at the national level and better representation at the EU level—a trade-off that merits considered debate.

*Originally published in the* Irish Times

———

# MORE POWER FOR LOCAL GOVERNMENT WOULD MEAN MORE BAD GOVERNMENT

*3 March 2004*

It is often said that political power in Ireland is more centralised than in other developed countries. Dermot Lacey (Opinion, 25 February, 'Time for a real debate on local government') thinks this is lamentable and believes it to be self-evidently true that devolving power from Dublin would make for better overall democracy. Evidence from abroad suggests that this contention is dubious. Experience at home shows it to be plain wrong.

Superficially, the case for giving local councils more say has strengthened because devolution often looks like the modern way. Over the past decade and a half Belgium has become a federation, Spain has, too, in all but name, and Italy looks like following suit. Even the most centralised of

European states—Britain and France—have pushed power downwards. There has usually been a dual motive for this: to make governance more legitimate and its workings more efficient. Neither applies to the Republic.

Legitimacy first. In areas where regional identities are strong or strengthening, from Scotland and Flanders to Catalonia and Lombardy, demands have grown that power be clawed back from unresponsive capitals. Such yearnings are limited in the Republic, which enjoys unusual geographic cohesion. While those outside the Pale may occasionally complain about the goings-on up in Dublin or of capital-living Bord Pleanála officials scuppering their plans for dream homes, there is no significant sense of grievance that the interests of Dublin trump those of people outside it (probably because national politics has a considerably greater local focus than elsewhere).

As regards efficiency, what grounds are there to give Dermot Lacey and his council colleagues more power? An American sociologist once said that because of two trends—globalisation and the increasing complexity of government functions—states have become too small to do the big things and too big to do the small things. While this may be true for sizeable countries, it is not for small ones like Ireland. With a population of four million (less than many regions and some cities in other European countries) Ireland has always been too small to influence the big things, such as the rules of the international economy or the management of the planet's environment. But for the small things—policies on education, tax and attracting investment for instance—the Republic's size is just right. And this is ever more important as nimble government is crucial to success in today's world (it is no coincidence that most of the planet's richest economies and best-functioning societies have populations of less than 10 million).

But even if it did make objective sense to devolve some functions of the State, the uninspiring record of local government over more than a century militates against it. Consider corruption. Everywhere, this tends to be more prevalent at sub-national levels of government. In 2002, 50 former US mayors were behind bars. Closer to home, France's city halls are a byword for jobbery, and last summer Madrid's newly elected regional government collapsed when assembly members took payments to miss a crucial vote. Ireland is unusual only in that the corruption contrast between the local and national is starker than elsewhere. While national politics is relatively clean and not as corrupt as is popularly believed (a study by UCC academics Neil Collins and Mary O'Shea gives excellent context), local politics has a long history of sleaze. The only example of anything approaching systemic political corruption recently has been in planning where, after this power was given them in 1963, local authorities' votes were, on occasion, swayed by moneyed interests.

And the inglorious record of local politicians predates even 1963. When local democracy was introduced in 1898, it was quickly blighted by bribery and influence-peddling. By 1926 the gift of council employment was taken from local politicians after repeated cash-for-jobs scandals (its replacement, the Local Appointments Commission, has been a model of probity). Indeed, so bad was the local government experience in its first quarter-century that when the pre-independence Act was modified in 1925, it wisely allowed central government to suspend erring or inept councils for up to three years and place their responsibilities in the hands of professional administrators.

But despite this, local politicians still did not clean up their act, and both governments in the following 15 years were forced to resort to this punitive sanction frequently. Unexpectedly, if not unsurprisingly, it proved so popular that voters sometimes refused to choose another council so that they could keep their appointed commissioners. Outshone by more honest and efficient bureaucrats, power drifted from councils. In 1940 the County Management Act formalised the system. The balance between appointed and elected representatives, which is skewed towards the former more than in other countries, remains largely unchanged to this day.

And it has not only been in relation to sleaze that sub-national levels of government come out worse than their national counterparts. They are also almost universally more spendthrift, at least partly because they know that they will be bailed out by central government if they overspend. Fiscal indiscipline in California opened the door of the governor's office to Arnold Schwarzenegger last year. In Britain, councils had their spending teeth pulled in the 1980s because so many refused to balance their books. In Italy today regional governments sometimes appear intoxicated by their new expenditure powers and struggle to manage their finances.

At home, the abolition of rates in 1977 went unlamented by rate-payers, and there is no grassroots demand for their reintroduction because it would appear that when it comes to the deathly inevitability of paying taxes, people prefer that theirs go to the Exchequer than into local authority coffers. A long history of budgetary chaos, up to and including Dublin City Council's recent crisis, does little to suggest that municipal profligacy would not result if local politicians ever really got their hands on the public purse strings. Given all this, Dermot Lacey should be careful what he wishes for. If he is successful in starting the debate about local government that he wants, it could become a matter of regret; he might end up with fewer powers, not more.

*Originally published in the* Irish Times

———

## McCREEVY FAILED AS FINANCE MINISTER

*9 September 2004*

As Charlie McCreevy leaves the Department of Finance today, the spurious debate about how 'right-wing' he was as minister has obscured his many real shortcomings. Ideologues and the politically partisan talk endlessly of Charlie McCreevy's tax policy. It will, they agree, be his lasting legacy. This view is perplexing for two reasons. First, since 1987 the social partners have had more influence over the broad thrust of tax policy than finance ministers. Second, there was very little change in the tax burden on his watch. The first point is self-evident; the second requires substantiation because the untruth that Mr McCreevy radically cut taxes has been repeated so often it has come to be commonly believed.

Ignore the spin and consider the facts. When Mr McCreevy moved into Merrion Street in 1997 the Exchequer squeezed taxpayers for €21 billion. By 2003, that figure had almost doubled. As a proportion of national income, the tax burden did fall, but only slightly, from 35.4% of GNP to 34%. In fairness, where he had leeway on taxation, he was at times prepared to be innovative. Among the few big positive changes made during his long tenure was the introduction of tax credits. These reduced inequities and helped integrate the benefits and tax systems, making it easier for those on welfare to escape poverty traps.

But for the real story of Mr McCreevy's time as finance minister, one has to consider his spending record, because this is where he had genuine influence. And here the picture is dismal. Start with the recklessness with which he used taxpayers' money for electoral purposes. While governments everywhere tend to loosen the purse strings to win voters' favour, from 2001 Mr McCreevy simply upended the public purse, allowing spending to run out of control.

The splurge mirrored in many respects the fiasco after the 1977 election. The big difference between the two periods was something over which Mr McCreevy had no control—the world economy. Had it taken a serious downturn, as happened in 1979, the Irish economy, and the public finances, would quickly have followed suit. What made his gamble so reckless was how real the risks of global recession were. For some time serious imbalances have existed internationally. These must inevitably unwind. Had they done so suddenly while spending was so wildly out of control, it could well have been back to a 1980s future of unemployment and stagnation.

But Mr McCreevy not only gambled with national prosperity, he repeatedly failed in his duty to ensure that the money given him in taxes was not squandered: he made no attempt to prevent the benchmarking scandal; he did not fight the decision to offer open-ended indemnification to the religious orders; and only belatedly did he make any effort to curb an unreformed health system's insatiable appetite for cash.

Mr McCreevy conjured up another multi-billion loss-maker all on his own. The SSIA scheme would, he said, cool the economy at a time when it was white-hot. But such measures have been tried elsewhere and failed. He knew this because his civil servants told him so. He ignored their pleadings and ploughed ahead. More bizarrely still, he undermined the stated purpose of his own scheme with the astonishingly imprudent injunction to people to 'party on'.

This was illustrative of Mr McCreevy's unco-ordinated and unsophisticated approach to fiscal policy generally. While some of the 20th century's finest minds devoted their lives to understanding the link between public expenditure and the real economy, Mr McCreevy chose to disregard that sum of human knowledge for the fiscal philistinism of 'If I have it, I'll spend it'.

During seven long years and an unparalleled boom he had the opportunity to do much. Apart from his pensions fund (on balance probably a good thing), he did little. Most obviously there was no significant modernisation of the State's archaic budgeting apparatus which fails to evaluate or plan spending effectively, causing needless waste of taxpayers' money (today in rich Europe only Greece and Italy have poorer arrangements). His lack of interest in much-needed reform caused the OECD to give over most of its biennial report on Ireland in 2003 to suggesting how international best practice in the management of public expenditure could be implemented.

But, alas, there's more. Mr McCreevy did little to make the intellectual case against harmonising corporation tax in Europe; he damaged Ireland by deploying pseudo-patriotic bluster against EU criticism of his 2001 budget; he bent rules to help his horsey pals in Punchestown; and he filleted the Freedom of Information Act. Gravest of all was decentralisation. Far worse than a one-off stroke, the plan is an act of political patronage on a scale unlike anything ever attempted before and will, if implemented, profoundly degrade the capacity for good governance in Ireland.

But for all his failings in office, Charlie McCreevy is a decent man and is certainly not the odiously uncaring mean spirit some of his critics claim. He is principled, too. During his party's dark days under Charles Haughey he, almost alone, stood up against the dangerously authoritarian tendencies of the then leadership. He was bullied and left to languish on the back benches. If history judges him kindly it will be for this, not his time as finance minister.

*Originally published in the* Irish Times

———

# POLITICIANS' BUDGETARY POWERS MUST BE CURBED

*17 October 2008*

Had the public finances been well managed during the years of extraordinary plenty, the government would now be in a position to mitigate the effects of recession by cutting taxes and increasing spending. Such steps would have the additional effect of boosting confidence by providing reassurance that those at the helm are capable of navigating a course back to stability and growth. But the public finances were grossly mismanaged during the boom years. As a result, the government and its finances are now a part of the problem rather than part of the solution. This is as appalling as it is tragic.

The need for radical change in the way the public finances are managed would be moot if the current crisis was the result of unforeseeable events at home or unprecedented developments abroad. But the fiscal crisis can be attributed to neither. The precipitous deterioration in the public finances pre-dates even the beginnings of the international credit crunch. Irrefutable proof of the home-grown nature of the fiscal fiasco is provided by comparison with peer countries that have faced the same international environment.

A majority of euro zone members have registered a narrowing of budget imbalances since 2006. Ireland has not only bucked the trend, but the deterioration in its public finances has been far worse than that recorded in any euro zone country over the past quarter century.

If this extraordinary failure was a one-off event, then one could possibly make the case that the lessons of today will be learned and not repeated. But it is no such thing. It is the second time in a generation that the country has inflicted such harm upon itself. In the 1970s and early 1980s, the world suffered its deepest slump since the 1930s. Countries everywhere faced similar challenges. Some rose to those challenges. Others muddled through. Three rich countries—Belgium, Ireland and Italy—floundered. Prior to 1987, Ireland floundered most. By 1985 it was alone among the Organisation for Economic Co-operation and Development countries to have a public debt greater than its GDP.

Belgium and Italy have dysfunctional political systems. Belgium is corrupt, grossly over-governed and unable to overcome its communal tensions. Italy is inherently ungovernable. Ireland's problems are not nearly of the same order as those of Belgium and Italy, but to fail so cata-strophically to manage the public finances twice in a generation does demonstrate a grave deficiency in the Irish system. The answer would seem to lie in the calibre of elected representatives. School teachers, publicans and small-town accountants are deeply rooted in their local communities and ensure the political system avoids the kind of discon-nection with voters that many other mature democracies suffer. This is the enduring strength of Ireland's system. But it is also its greatest weakness. Such people are rarely even remotely qualified to run a finance ministry.

How to maintain the strengths while curing the ills? The answer is to depoliticise aspects of fiscal policy in much the same way as has been done with monetary policy across the world. This would allow qualified people to have a far greater input into the management of the public finances and curb the sort of 'If I have it, I'll spend it' insanity that has led to the current predicament.

It seems hard to believe now that elected representatives in many countries once controlled interest rates. The result, to a greater or lesser extent, was the abuse of that power. Interest rates were cut before elections to generate artificial booms. They had to be tightened afterwards to squeeze inflation out of the system. It was a recipe for boom and bust cycles. The misuse and abuse of fiscal policy in Ireland over decades has had the same boom-bust effect. Real human misery has been, and is now, the result.

Today, independent but accountable central banks manage monetary policy. They do not always get it right, but nobody argues for a return to old ways. This must now be the direction for fiscal policy. What does a depoliticised fiscal policy look like? First, and as is the case in other countries where moves in this direction have been made, it would be fundamentally different from monetary policy, which is a largely technocratic function.

Deciding on the level of taxation and spending is the central contested issue in stable democracies. There can and should be no constraints on any political party offering either higher spending or lower taxes. There must, however, be constraints on any government attempting to do both unsustainably. Three separate functions can readily be depoliticised without having any effect on voters' right to choose the level of tax and spending.

The first is forecasting. Where governments base their budgets on in-house forecasts for economic growth and tax revenues, the outlook is almost always rosier than that of independent forecasters. By making more optimistic assumptions and ignoring risks, governments can spend more and tax less. Instead of the Department of Finance generating its own economic forecasts and projections, the entire function should be handed to the Economic and Social Research Institute, with additional safeguards to further bolster its independence. The minister and his officials would then base budgets on a given set of assumptions and would not be able to succumb to the temptation to massage the figures for political ends.

The second function ripe for depoliticisation is the evaluation of spending programmes before implementation. Ireland lags far behind the European norm in this regard. Subjecting spending proposals to scrutiny is needed both to ensure that the objective is not political (eg decentralisation) and that it is being achieved at the lowest cost to the taxpayer. Such a function would require a new free-standing institution peopled by auditors and economists. To be effective it would need statutory powers to amend, delay and perhaps even block proposals for which a minister cannot make a coherent and costed case.

The final function that lends itself to depoliticisation is the auditing of spending after it has taken place. The Comptroller and Auditor General in Ireland already does this, but his office is less resourced and has fewer statutory powers than in many other jurisdictions. It should be beefed up and given more and sharper teeth.

The political class has shown that it simply cannot be trusted to manage the public finances responsibly in the current framework. Real checks and balances are needed to constrain future finance ministers from repeating the recklessness of many of their predecessors.

*Originally published in the* Irish Times

## RADICAL STEPS ARE NEEDED TO PREVENT NATIONAL BANKRUPTCY

*20 March 2009*

Ireland is rapidly moving towards the abyss of national bankruptcy. The government's response, with its forthcoming budget and other measures, must be proportionate to the dangers.

It is difficult now to overstate them magnitude of the crisis in Ireland's public finances. One in four euro spent is being borrowed. The gap between revenue and expenditure is widening with each passing month. Public debt is exploding. So are debt servicing costs. In January and February alone, €175 million was spent paying interest, up a staggering 64% on the same period in 2008.

Most of this money left the country. This haemorrhage will not only continue, but will gush with ever greater force unless every possible measure to staunch it is taken with all due haste. Central to achieving this are leadership changes in the financial institutions and the cabinet because the perception of cronyism and government failings have come together to raise the costs of borrowing.

The foreigners who account for almost all the lending that is keeping Ireland afloat are increasingly alarmed about the country's creditworthiness (this can be seen in ballooning interest rates on Irish government bonds). These lenders look at government actions in relation to the banks and see that every decision taken, and every decision that could have been taken but was not taken, suited financiers. If foreign investors believe that a government is less concerned with repaying them than with looking after its friends, they shun its bonds or seek a risk premium for holding them. This is exactly what is happening to Ireland now.

The perception of cronyism is one reason why the Irish government faces the highest borrowing costs of any country in the euro zone. That perception can and must be changed by resolute action. Though it is far too simple to blame bankers for all of the current woes, those who were involved in managing the banks have failed and must go. The interests of individuals who have failed so seriously cannot now be allowed to imperil the solvency of the state.

For the government to demand publicly the resignation of AIB's chief executive and to refuse to accept Bank of Ireland's chief executive designate would be proportionate, appropriate and fully lawful. On behalf of the taxpayer, the government has given lifelines to the banks. Without these lifelines, which come with great cost and risk to taxpayers, these institutions would long ago have gone under. Having taken such enormous responsibilities, the government has every right to determine who runs the banks.

By taking such a proportionate step, the government would trumpet to the world that no one is being protected because of his connections, that there is no cosy clique that runs Ireland in its own interests, and that those who have failed so badly are not rewarded at the expense of everyone else.

The point should be driven home by finding replacements to run the banks from outside the country. The appointment of foreigners with no links to the government would offer a clean break up the past, show that Ireland is serious about the long and difficult task of restructuring and rebuilding its financial system, and that as an open and internationalised economy its seeks the best talent regardless of nationality.

But it is not only among financiers that a clean break is required. New appointments to the two main government economic portfolios—Finance and Enterprise, Trade and Employment—are needed as much as change in the banks.

Brian Lenihan, by his errors and inaction, bears much responsibility for what has become the worst budgetary disaster in the history of the OECD. His credibility is too seriously damaged to be repaired. He has become part of the problem. To set out the inadequacies of Mary Coughlan as Minister for Enterprise, Trade and Employment would be inappropriate and unhelpful. It suffices to say that at a time of national emergency the patently and grossly unable, by their mere presence, should not be allowed to obstruct efforts to prevent outright meltdown.

Where other countries bring the best and the brightest from society to ministerial office, Ireland's constitution states that only Oireachtas members can sit at the cabinet table. For the position of finance minister its adds the stipulation that he/she must be a sitting member of the Dáil. These are serious constraints, but they must be worked within.

As there is nobody on government benches who has economic expertise, the Taoiseach himself should take on the role of finance minister. By so doing, Mr Cowen would signal that he understands the extraordinary gravity of the crisis and that he will bring his full prime ministerial authority directly to bear on attempting to solve it.

For Enterprise, Trade and Employment, a non-political figure of high international standing could be brought into the cabinet via a senate appointment (one of the sitting Taoiseach's appointees could surely be prevailed upon, in the national interest, to stand aside). Peter Sutherland is the most obvious candidate given his stature in international policy-making circles, in the European Union and in the financial and corporate worlds. Knowledge that he has a hand on helm would calm the bond market and reassure our European partners.

Most important in regaining credibility will be the supplementary budget the government has so belatedly conceded to drawing up. There are two separate issues here: the credibility of the strategy it decides upon and the credibility of the arithmetic underpinning that strategy. On the first issue, there have been calls by some normally authoritative figures to focus on raising taxes. Such calls are based on instinct and political preference—not evidence. The literature on fiscal consolidation processes internationally shows clearly that success comes from cutting spending, not trying to raise taxes (higher taxes can work when economies return to growth, but not while they are mired in crisis).

The Swedish experience in the early 1990s has been cited by some advocates of higher taxes. This is more than a little curious. The administration of Carl Bildt, which was in office during the worst of the crisis from October 1991 to October 1994, focused on expenditure containment. Those with a preference for tax increases may have found support for their instinctive position in a recent interview on RTÉ radio by Jens Henriksson, a one-time advisor to former Swedish finance minister Goran Persson. He stated that during Sweden's crisis in the 1990s, the burden of adjustment was placed equally on tax-raising and spending cuts. What was not clear from the interview was that Persson became finance minister in October 1994, when recovery was already well underway (Swedish GDP grew by almost 4% in 1994 and by more than 4% in 1995).

If Nordic-watchers really want to find a parallel for Ireland's current predicament they will look eastwards. Where Sweden endured a recession in the early 1990s, Finland suffered a depression, just as Ireland is suffering now (output by 2010 will be 10% below 2007—the usual definition of a depression). Finland is the only developed country to have experienced such conditions in living memory. Both the centrist administration of Esko Aho from 1991 to 1995 and the social democratic administration of Paavo Lipponen thereafter put their adjustment emphasis on expenditure reduction and containment, not new tax-raising.

But one does not even need to look abroad for guidance on what must be done now. Ireland's own experience before and after 1987 should be sufficient. Before that date the public finances continued to deteriorate because there was too little expenditure containment and too much tax-raising. When the emphasis was reversed after 1987, consolidation happened quickly.

The second dimension for the supplementary budget is that the numbers add up. The government and Department of Finance severely damaged the country's credibility when they published in October and January sets of figures that had, respectively, no and partial connection to the current awful realities.

There is no more room for error. Every data point in the April programme must look credible. In order to ensure this, and convince others that it has been achieved, the government should work with the European Commission in drawing up the numbers. Its non-national stamp of approval would reassure that the government's political weaknesses and Finance's technical inadequacies are no longer factors.

In the coming weeks radical and urgent action is needed. It must be far beyond anything that has hitherto been contemplated. And the government must get it right. The wrong decisions will change the course of Irish history.

*Originally published in the* Irish Times

――――

## THE FF-PD GOVERNMENT LEANS LEFT, NOT RIGHT

*6 June 2003*

How do you judge where a government really stands on the left–right spectrum? Among the best ways is to look at its spending habits. Because the left in government is usually impatient to right social wrongs, it is often accused by the right of irresponsibly throwing taxpayers' money at problems. For all its talk, this government's fiscal record fits perfectly the stereotype of socialist profligacy. Never in the history of the State (or, indeed, any European country) has so much been injected into public services in so short a period for so little gain. The upshot: in just 24 months the public finances deteriorated more rapidly than in any other EU country and a mountainous budget surplus was turned to deficit.

So with no sign of right-wingery on spending, it is worth examining the other side of the ledger—how and where tax revenue is raised—for another perspective. If changes in inequality are used as a proxy for assessing political orientation (admittedly, a crude measure), the government's record shows that it tilts to the right, but only ever so slightly. Brian Nolan of the scrupulously independent ESRI has dug deep to find out who benefited most during the economy's wonder years. His conclusion is, surprisingly, that inequality did not 'uniformly or substantially increase during the boom'. His analysis also shows that government budgetary policy contributed to the (small) widening of the gap in 1998–2000, but the budgets in 2001–02 had the opposite effect. In another study, the think-tank's big brains found that the percentage in persistent poverty, the most comprehensive measure of misery, actually fell from 11% of the population in 1997 to 6% in 2000.

So the Coalition's record shows that it has been slightly right of centre on tax and well to the left on spending. But what about another point of departure for left and right—market intervention? Rightists advocate leav-ing well enough alone because they think that interfering in markets rarely makes things better. Besides, they say, interventionism invites unintended, and usually unwanted, consequence. Leftists have fewer qualms. They believe that markets sometimes fail and even when they don't, their out-comes are all too often iniquitous. They like to use the hand of the state to get the outcomes they want.

And so, too, does this government. Start with the jobs market. The Coalition introduced a minimum wage—a demand of the left which is opposed by economic liberals because they believe that putting a false bottom into the labour market hinders, not helps, the marginalised trying to get into work. What's more, the Coalition has been an unstinting sup-porter of quintessentially continental social partnership—a non-market pay-setting mechanism, and the sort of un-American activity that the Cabinet's heaviest hitters might usually be thought to frown upon.

In another important market—property—the government has been busier still. It paid economic consultant Peter Bacon handsomely to churn out three separate sets of sometimes contradictory measures designed to halt dizzying price increases, exactly the sort of 'meddling' that is anathema to real free-marketeers. But that was not the end of interventionism in the property market. In a move to increase the supply of housing for the needy, the government legislated to oblige property developers (among the fattest of cats, incidentally) to hand over 20% of their land. Such a measure would be considered by real right-wingers to be an arbitrary act of theft by the State and one that even openly socialist parties on the continent have shied away from.

And this is not the only time the capitalist classes have got it in the neck. When Charlie McCreevy's fiscal ineptitude finally starting catching up with him, he looked for soft targets to shake down. To the money men's consternation, he plumped for the banks, slapping a €300 million levy on them. Now contrast the lot of landed tycoons and the banks to the government's most un-Thatcherite readiness to give trade unions what they want. Public-sector unions extracted an astonishingly generous deal from the State in the benchmarking agreement on evidence that was so flimsy it was never published. When Eircom workers said no to privatisation they were paid off with a whopping 15% of the company's shares, an arrangement without precedent in the EU and one that even rebranded communist parties in eastern Europe today would not countenance.

As for privatisation more generally, this government has shown less zeal for disposing of State assets than recent continental governments in France and Italy led, respectively, by socialists and leftists. Take Aer Rianta. For the real right, there is no logic in having civil servants run airports, and even less when they thwart the terminal-building ambitions and thrusting private enterprise of the likes of Michael O'Leary.

Much more serious are grave charges that government policy on immigration has hints of the nasty extreme right. Thankfully, this is not the case. There is no question that the country's commitments under the 1951 UN Convention on Refugees have ever been breached. Nor have any manifestly unjust provisions been introduced. That Ireland's approach remains fairer than that of most rich countries is evinced by the asylum application figures: last year the Republic received the third highest per capita number in the EU. As regards straightforward economic immigration, Ireland is even more welcoming. Last year 40,000 work visas were issued to non-EU nationals, a number far ahead in proportional terms of even the US, the most open of developed countries.

So this government shows no signs of far-right intolerance and, on socio-economic issues, what it does (as opposed to its talk) is left of centre. But does it really matter how we label governments? In truth, not much. The moderate left and right both want what's best for society and share the same democratic values—justice, liberty, solidarity and the like. What has traditionally separated them is that they prioritise these values differently. But even this difference, in practice if not in principle, is narrowing. 'What matters is what works,' said Tony Blair to his shocked party, when still wedded to doctrinaire notions. But in the Republic such pragmatism has always been a virtue; those words could have been spoken by any Taoiseach since the State's founding. It's hard not to sense that our pragmatic political way, once considered quirky for its absence of ideology, is the way of the future.

*Originally published in the* Irish Times

# IRELAND'S OPEN SOCIETY

*29 July 2004*

Ireland is among the most meritocratic of societies. When it comes to those who make it to the top—in wealth, politics and administrative power—what is so striking about Ireland is just how few were born privileged and how many have succeeded on the basis of ability alone.

Start with money. According to the *Sunday Times* Rich List, most of the wealthiest 10 started at the bottom of the money pile, and of those who didn't, none were born into anything approaching the lifestyles to which they have become accustomed. The only one of the 10 who started life with a silver spoon in his mouth is an American citizen resident in the Republic.

This is quite extraordinary. In most countries, super-rich cliques are usually closed golden circles dominated by blue-bloods and moneyed dynasties. Even in zealously egalitarian Scandinavia, the tentacles of inherited privilege spread far and wide. In Sweden, the Wallenberg family empire is worth $100 billion and controls close to half of the value of the entire stock exchange. In Denmark, the Maersk dynasty is almost as dominating, holding preference shareholdings in companies in every significant sector of the economy. In Ireland, there is nothing remotely similar to such an embedded concentration of economic power, and rich patriarchs (think O'Reilly or Smurfit) look like small-time nouveaux by comparison. At the other end of the wealth spectrum, there is also plenty of social mobility. Richard Layte, a sociologist at the ever-authoritative ESRI, believes it is a mistake to consider the poor as a single unchanging group of unfortunates. Although there is a grave problem of an impoverished underclass, he says that 70% of those who endure poverty in Ireland have escaped its privations within three years.

But it's not only Irish wealth that is determined by merit rather than inherited privilege. Consider political power. A majority of the 11 Taoisigh started out in non-fee-paying schools. Compare this to Britain, where eight out of the last 10 prime ministers went to elitist Oxford. And the office of Taoiseach looks set to stay patrician-free. When the next general election comes round the choice will probably be Bertie Ahern or Enda Kenny. Neither is rich, neither is high-born, and both were educated by the Christian Brothers. In the US, for instance (and by contrast), both serious contenders in November's presidential election are Ivy League-educated, fabulously rich and from establishment families. For another perspective, look at the current Cabinet. The line-up of school teachers, small-town solicitors, farmers and accountants—almost all from modest back-grounds—may be mostly undynamic, but it is about as demotic as any government anywhere.

The third big locus of power in any society is its bureaucracy. Frank Litton of the Institute of Public Administration makes the important point that Ireland's civil service was modelled on Britain's—with one important exception. Instead of two entirely separate streams—one recruited from Oxbridge to run the empire, the other from the lower classes to labour forever on more mundane tasks, regardless of ability—the Irish system gave everyone who entered the opportunity to rise to the top. The legacy is to be seen today: Irish mandarins are ordinary Joes, not Sir Humphreys; and nobody would contest that advancement is based on ability, not connections and certainly not bribery, as is so often the case around the world.

None of this is to say Ireland is perfectly fair in opportunities (the pro-fessions remain a largely middle-class preserve), nor that snobbery and elitism do not exist. But when compared to any other country, it's hard to find one in which where you start in life has as little influence on where you end up. This is important for the conduct of politics. One might expect that given such equality of opportunity, there would be little demand for the state to act as a leveller—it is often said, for instance, that the American left has never made inroads because in a land of opportunity those at the bottom believe they are destined for the top and don't want big government in the way as they make their journey. This could explain the failure of explicitly left-leaning parties ever to end the Fianna Fáil-Fine Gael duopoly, particularly now that the traditional explanations—Civil War politics, red-scaremongering and hostility from the Church—no longer stand up.

But something is not quite right here. While self-consciously left-wing parties have never thrived, Ireland looks and feels much more like Europe than the US, where trade unions are weak, social partnership non-existent, working weeks long, holidays short, social welfare benefits meagre and worker protection laws few. This is true for tax too. In 2003, government receipts equalled more than 41% of GNP. This is far above the US level of 31% and much closer to the EU average of 45% (figures based on GDP sug-gest the tax burden is much lower, but serious commentators agree that this is woefully misleading in Ireland's case).

So if Ireland's model is influenced by social democracy, why does the left continue to languish electorally? The answer is in its theory of Irish injustice. The main reason for the convergence of left and right inter-nationally is that each has listened to the other's view on social justice. In the past, the right equated justice with liberty, saying equality didn't matter much. The left, by contrast, spoke only of income equality and was cavalier about freedom. Modern social democracy accounts for both.

Without more explicitly acknowledging the importance of liberty in its vision of a just society, the Irish left will continue to frighten the comfortable majority who need convincing not only that greater redistribution can make society fairer (the record is mixed), but also that the liberties that allow Ireland to be so meritocratic will never be curbed. In Britain, Tony Blair calmed majority fears by symbolically removing his party's hard-left Clause Four. Bill Clinton signalled his intent by promising to reform welfare programmes in the 1992 election. What will the Labour Party do?

*Originally published in the* Irish Times

————

## IRELAND COMES TOP FOR QUALITY OF LIFE

*17 November 2004*

What makes life good, and what causes discontent? The human soul's complexities make it impervious to definitive conclusion, but the growth industry of satisfaction studies offers some enlightenment. Today, libraries of serious work exist which show that at societal level certain factors conclusively influence life satisfaction. The Economist Intelligence Unit has aggregated these to create a new quality-of-life index, published this week. The Republic comes out ahead of the other 110 countries surveyed because it enjoys the economic and political gifts of modernity—wealth, liberty, stability and security—while managing better than others to maintain the best of tradition, the civic virtues that keep communities together and the personal ones that make for strong supportive families.

Modernity first. Ireland is now one of the richest countries in the world by any measure. Though money does not guarantee happiness, it helps, and not only for material reasons. Everywhere, the well-heeled are happier than the down-at-heel because they feel more secure and more in control of their lives. And because tigerish affluence has all but exorcised the twin Irish spectres of insecurity—joblessness and enforced emigration—satisfaction levels have jumped.

Politics matters, too. The awfulness of war, the risk of arbitrary arrest, the terror of human rights abuses and constraints on personal freedoms all make people miserable; one reason why brutish Robert Mugabe's Zimbabwe comes bottom of our index. The Republic is at the other extreme, enjoying social calm combined with civil and political liberties which, surveys show, are not bettered anywhere in the world.

In all wealth, security and freedom factors Ireland scores highly, but it is not these wonders alone that make it the most content of nations. The key to life satisfaction, it seems, is to have the best of both worlds: the good of the modern and the best of tradition, a trick that is notoriously difficult to pull off, because when the old stifling stuff is ditched (think dictatorial clergymen, arranged marriages and excessive deference) many good things seem to get lost as well. Moral obligation, sense of duty and self-denial, the practice of which help to hold families together, all appear to wane as countries develop. Virtues that are society's cement—reciprocity, trust and altruism—also become less fashionable. There are, too, down sides to personal choice and individual liberties. Freedom can loosen the ties that bind, and an abundance of choice makes it harder to put up with inevitably imperfect human arrangements (a spiceless marriage or a grumpy aged relative about the house, for instance).

While the prissy everywhere rail against vulgarity, venality and recreational sex as if they were the first generation to have to endure such horrors, it is true that genuinely bad things—incivility, yobbishness and drunken nihilistic violence—tend to become more prevalent in developed societies (and we notice them more because we don't have old worries, like famines and wars, anymore). It is true, too, that there is more family breakdown, scarring more kids, and that social atomisation swells the ranks of angst-filled, live-alone Bridget Joneses. These woes certainly afflict Ireland, but (and this is crucial) they do so less than in other developed countries. Divorce is on the rise, but is still below the rich-world average. Civic involvement has declined (as measured by trade-union membership and participative religion), but not as precipitously as else-where. The European Social Values surveys support our findings. They show that trust in most public institutions is high compared to other countries and that social solidarity, concern for others and willingness to help them, remain unusually strong, as illustrated, for example, by the phenomenon of the Special Olympics last year.

But the index's findings are not all good news. Health, climate and gender inequality are three factors (of a total of nine) that determine contentment where Ireland falls below the rich-Europe average. The first two will not surprise, as horror stories of a creaking health system abound and short grey winter days cause glumness. More eye-catching, though, given tough equality laws and rigorous enforcement, is that gender inequality remains higher in Ireland than elsewhere (pay differentials between the sexes is our proxy).

What about factors like education and income inequality that are often cited as important in assessing levels of development? These are socially important to be sure, but interestingly, research shows that neither influences life satisfaction. While education broadens horizons, it simultaneously raises expectations. The effects on contentment cancel each other out. Relative income inequality doesn't matter either, as most people don't begrudge the better-off their good fortune. And if this raises eyebrows, think how people vote across the world, Ireland included. Parties who promise to raise taxes for the super-rich and lower them for everyone else rarely make serious electoral headway, however irrational that may be of the majority. Envy politics, universally, it seems, has little appeal.

That Ireland has topped our index will convince neither unworldly parochials who think Ireland is worst for everything nor determined gloomsters who believe that the country is fast going to the bad. But thousands of returning emigrants and arriving immigrants who vote with their feet know that there are few better places in the world to live.

*Originally published in the* Irish Times

———

## IMMIGRATION NEEDS MORE ACTIVE MANAGEMENT

*6 January 2007*

Immigration has been the biggest social and economic change to have taken place since the State's founding. A transformation of the magnitude that has taken place in Ireland in recent years, and in particular since EU enlargement in 2004, rarely happens without public unease. To assuage concerns, frank discussion about the nature and consequences of the phenomenon is essential.

The debate in Ireland has been measured and calm compared to most other countries. It also differs in focus. Elsewhere, alarmism about immigration is usually most loudly voiced by those who fear or dislike diversity. In Ireland, it has come mainly from those who talk of a 'race to the bottom' in worker protection and pay. But despite the alarmists' talk of a slippery slope to Dickensian working conditions, 'worker displacement' and 'wage degradation' have not come to pass.

On worker protection, this was entirely predictable. Claims that immigration is accompanied by an inexorable decline in standards were always bogus. Standards are a political issue, not an economic one. Unlike wages, they are set by government, not the interplay of supply and demand. The more concern exists about their erosion, the more pressure there is on lawmakers to reinforce them.

This is exactly what happened in 2006. The latest social partnership deal raised labour standards and made their enforcement more rigorous. Nor is there a shred of hard evidence to suggest that displacement has taken place. Joblessness has hovered steadily just above 4% since the beginning of the decade. This did not change when 75 million additional Europeans gained access to the Irish labour market in May 2004. Developments in long-term unemployment—probably the best indicator of displacement—have been even more reassuring. It stands at just 1.3% of the labour force, among the lowest in Europe. That it has actually declined since early 2004 gives the lie to claims that people are being pushed on to the scrapheap by the newly arrived.

So far, so rosy. But what about salaries and wages? Those who worry about immigration are on much firmer ground when they fret about its effects on incomes because an increase in the number of workers can put downward pressure on pay rates. The good news is that there has been no 'wage degradation' (falling wages, in plain English). On the contrary, since the EU's 2004 expansion, economy-wide pay has continued to rise. It is true that rates of increase have decelerated marginally, but as this trend's origins preceded enlargement, immigration can only be said to have played some part in change since 2004.

Even when developments in the sectors of the economy in which immigrants have clustered are examined, the picture is largely the same. In the building trade, which has by all accounts attracted an unusually large number of foreign workers, pay patterns show no correlation with those of immigration. Wage growth accelerated after enlargement, slowed sharply in the first half of 2006, then recovered in the autumn.

Only two sectors—manufacturing and the hospitality industry—have seen a discernible slowdown in wage growth since enlargement. In the former, too many factors are in play to attribute lower pay rises to immigration. Only for those waiting tables and pulling pints could it be suggested that immigration has depressed wage growth, and even here caution is needed because limited data make precise evaluation impossible.

When it comes to other benefits and costs of immigration, things become even harder to weigh up. Some upsides of immigration—fresh dynamism, new skills and different ideas—are as unquantified as the downsides: extra congestion, a further inflating of the property bubble and stretching the education system in places.

Also hard to evaluate is the effect diversity has on social cohesion. Robert Putnam, a guru on the subject to so many politicians—the Taoiseach included—published new findings on the phenomenon in 2006. He says that society's glue is eroded by greater diversity: the less people have in common, the less likely they are to hang together in pursuit of common goals. It would be wrong, however, to exaggerate this. A lot of nonsense is spoken about social capital. Everyone cosying together may warm the cockles of collectivists' hearts, but rowing in at community meetings, parish events and the local scout troop is probably less essential for society's wellbeing than voguish social capitalists suggest.

All that said, given the speed and scale of the recent change, the many unknowns about the benefits and costs of immigration, and the risk that problems similar to those in other countries could arise in the future, a more focused, co-ordinated and strategically minded response may be needed.

One way to achieve this could be to appoint a junior minister to take a more holistic approach to the multi-dimensional challenges the phenomenon throws up. This could help ensure the mistakes of other countries are avoided, the lessons of their successes are applied and those who are uneasy about recent changes are reassured. To continue with a hands-off approach would be to tempt fate. If something were to go wrong—an economic downturn, for instance—the experience could yet turn sour.

*Originally published in the* Irish Times

———

## AFFLUENZA AFFLICTS LAZY MINDS

*25 January 2000*

The effects of new-found prosperity have given rise to all manner of concerns. In this and other newspapers commentators and letter writers attempt to gainsay the advances of the past decade and unpick the compelling case for economic growth as a force for good. For some, it seems that having failed to deliver utopia, the ongoing boom rings hollow. The most serious charge of the gloom merchants is that the neediest have been passed over. This is simply wrong. According to the ESRI, whose study is the most authoritative to date, poverty fell from 15% of the population in 1994 to 10% in 1997.

This figure has certainly been further reduced as unemployment, poverty's ever-present attendant, has since been halved. Furthermore, as the cost of emigration fell disproportionately on Ireland's poorest it was never the college-taught bright sparks that ended up in Kilburn's hostels. Its stemming has been of most benefit to the least well off. If the gap between the richest and poorest has not narrowed, that does not detract from the real achievement of moving more people further from real want. Moreover, crude income comparisons often mislead. Consider, for instance, the emergence of a band of young multi-millionaires in the hi-tech sector. Their well-rewarded endeavours will result in the widening of income disparities between the richest and the poorest. But as wealth creation is not a zero-sum game, their gain is nobody's loss. Quite the contrary, in fact. Their businesses lead to the creation of job opportunities for others and tax revenues for further redistribution to the less fortunate.

Another line of attack by the gainsayers of prosperity is that it results in crass materialism. It is one of the great fallacies of our time that economic life is about mere material gain. For those who do not want for basic needs (now the overwhelming majority in Ireland), prosperity is more about choice and the empowerment and fulfillment that comes with it. Economic growth has widened the range of careers to suit all abilities and leanings. It has also provided better jobs—there are no Satanic software mills and few financial services sweat shops. Growth has provided the resources to invest in education: empowering individuals, opening minds and giving access to all those interesting jobs.

To boot, growth has made emigration a matter of choice. Young people still leave, but now for horizon-broadening adventure and career-enhancing experience, safe in the knowledge that they will find ready employment if and when they wish to return. No more the post-Christmas departure-lounge trauma of sobbing parents and red-eyed twentysomethings. Growth has even affected family size. Unlike our fellow European nouveaux riches, the Italians and the Spaniards, we choose to have more babies (a boom of them, even) while the Latins see their populations dwindle. However wearisome a little material exhibitionism, compared to the limitations and hopelessness of the past, it seems a small price to pay.

The argument that relationships become increasingly based on transactions of a calculating economic nature, leading inexorably to selfishness and excessive individualism, is as pervasive as it is wrong. Take giving to and participating in charities. Between 1995 and 1998 public donations to Goal rose by 106%, outstripping incomes growth almost fourfold. For Amnesty International's Ireland section, the prosperous 1990s were a boon. Membership rose fivefold while donations grew ever more rapidly. This happy picture, repeated for most charities, has philanthropes across the voluntary sector cock-a-hoop. The broader point is that only when people are unshackled from the brutalising constraints of material deprivation do they have the freedom to be concerned about others.

The social conservatives have also waded in with their own brand of anti-progressive griping. For them, the erosion of their fixed-in-time notion of Irish culture and tradition is to be bewailed. But this is to forget that culture is neither monolithic nor immutable. It is the decisions of millions of individuals in the aggregate as to how they wish to live. Today, people, both natives and newly arrived, are free to live according to their own preferences. This is not dilution but enrichment, and Ireland is all the better for it.

Besides, the baby has not followed the bathwater. Look, for instance, at the proliferation of Gaelscoileanna in the 1990s, the result of bottom-up action by empowered communities, not top-down dictums of cultural commissars. Long gone are the days (thankfully) when one view of culture was propagated from on high. Politicians have understood this. Those who lament the passing of illusory halcyon times would do well to do the same.

So, given the gains, why the misgivings? It is perhaps that the self-flagellators, to explain our protracted period of under-performance, spent so long playing the role of victim (be it of British colonialism or European peripherality) that they are ill-equipped to enjoy success. Alternatively, it may be the same fatalism that wants always to dwell on the negative. Why else do we see a sprouting of famine memorials, nowhere matched by monuments to the vanquishing of TB?

Whatever the reasons for all the hand-wringing, it augurs ill for focused debate on problems that public policy can genuinely affect. Tackling homelessness, devising a sustainable pension system that provides more generously for the aged and eradicating stubborn pockets of urban deprivation are conundrums that require hard thinking and bold measures. New problems abound, for progress is never costless. These include the working poor, transport gridlock and a dearth of affordable housing, all of which need imaginative solutions, not pop social commentary and fuzzy thinking.

*Originally published in the* Irish Independent

## IS IRELAND EUROPEAN?

*December 2001*

Ireland is transformed. The national question is all but answered. Economic failure, endemic unemployment and enforced emigration are increasingly distant memories. Sound policies, individual commitment and inspiration, changing mindsets and good fortune have all contributed. But credit is not exclusively Irish. America's politicians and businessmen have played no small part.

In the early 1990s, Ireland worked hard to couple the peace process train to Bill Clinton's presidency. us foreign ministry officials worked almost as hard counselling against involvement. They said that from a strictly us viewpoint, Northern Ireland was a strategically insignificant conflict. They knew too that getting involved would infuriate the uk, their most dependable ally. But a greened White House ignored its diplomats' advice and ran the risk. It paid off. The authority of the office of the us president advanced the peace process by years. Corporate America is also owed a debt of gratitude for helping to remedy once seemingly incurable economic ills. us firms have poured investment into Ireland. Today the wages and salaries they pay sustain 100,000 households. But that is only part of the story. Over the years they have handed over billions in taxes and taught Ireland's less than dynamic businessfolk a thing or three about wealth creation.

The world-weary would say that all of this has little to do with the goodness of American hearts. They would be right for the most part. But also important in the choices of Americans to involve themselves in Ireland are history, language, family and strong emotional ties (one need only think of Ireland's reaction to the events of September 11 to see how strong). Contrast all this with Ireland's loosening European bonds. Feelings have never been particularly strong. It is unimaginable that any European leader would ever be feted like a Kennedy or Clinton. A language barrier has made emigration to the continent the exception rather than the rule. As a result, family connections are few.

And as for the European Union, despite its leading role in Ireland's transformation, it is not loved. Indeed, if the rejection of the Nice treaty is a straw in the wind, indifference may be turning to outright hostility. For a slice of the political class it already has. Charlie McCreevy enjoys knocking his fellow finance ministers when he can. He feels they pick on him because they envy his success. The Tánaiste's antipathy is, if anything, stronger still. Behind every desk in Brussels she sees a meddling socialist who lives only to extinguish Ireland's entrepreneurial flame. Mary Harney, who first framed the Boston versus Berlin debate, believes that Ireland is more American than European. Given close ties with the US, few with Europe and spats with the EU it is easy to see how such a conclusion is reached. But scratch Ireland's American surface and what emerges is distinctly European. Though the European and American branches of western society share much, there are differences. In most of these (not inconsequential) things Ireland is, to borrow a phrase, spiritually closer to the continent of which it geographically forms a part.

## God, government and tolerance

Where there is not only difference, but divergence between Europe and the US is the political influence of the conservative-religious right. In Europe it is an unresurrectable irrelevance. In the US its rise seems inexorable. On both continents the 1960s brought a social revolution unlike any before in human history. The state began to remove the last vestiges of legislative inequality and allow individuals to decide for themselves on conduct increasingly considered to be in the realm of private morality. It is perhaps America's greater religiosity, and its evangelical strain in particular, that explains the strength of the backlash against these changes in the US. The forces of American illiberalism may be motley, but their influence is growing. While they cannot make a Republican Party presidential candidate, they can certainly break one. With this power comes influence. Among George W. Bush's first moves on taking power was the appointment of John Ashcroft—a religious fundamentalist to his critics—to the highest legal office in land. A bureau for 'faith-based' initiatives was also established in the White House in contravention, say opponents, of the 200-year-old First Amendment, which separates church and state.

Europe could scarcely be more different. Europe's reactionary right obsesses about immigrants, not Godlessness. Even the continent's moderate Christian Democrats, despite their name, long ago accepted that religion is best kept out of the public sphere. And without a politically powerful religious, the conservative response to the 1960s was weak and short-lived. Ireland is now rapidly approaching convergence with the secular European norm—precisely at a time when the US edges in the other direction. Another divorce referendum, to reverse the result of 1996, is unthinkable. Nobody rants against homosexuals. While Ireland remains an outlier in the western world on abortion, discussion of the subject now generates less heat, in contrast to the US, where the debate is increasingly fevered. As a power to reverse the sea-change wrought by late-to-arrive 1960s liberalism, the Church is a spent counter-revolutionary force. But even though it has undergone great change, religion has not been entirely vanquished in Europe. Divested of ecclesiastical power, Europe's religious have refocused their energies on the poor and the marginalised. Ireland is no different. It could be said that the Christian Church throughout Europe has come full circle.

## Crime and punishment

Another area of public life that is markedly different between the two continents is crime and the state's reaction to it. Compared to Europe, there is roughly twice as much reported violent crime in the US, much of it committed with firearms. In Europe, guns are tightly controlled almost everywhere. The US is awash with them because the bearing of arms is a jealously guarded right. Besides, say American weapons enthusiasts breathlessly, it is not guns that kill people, but other people. Sophistry, retort Europeans, who point to the US murder rate (far higher than in any European country) and ask about the rights of all those shot to death. But while guns are tolerated in the US, crime is not. And woe betide those who get caught. An American man is eight times more likely to find himself in prison than a European male. Moreover, incarceration can seriously damage convicts' health. Murder and rape in prison are more common than in Europe, mainly because American jailers are not liable for any harm that comes to inmates. In Europe, by contrast, it is the state's duty to guarantee the welfare of those it locks up.

Goethe's 200-year-old warning—to be suspicious of those whose desire to punish is strong—is taken to heart in Europe. Particularly when it comes to those who support the death penalty. Capital punishment is not only unpractised in Europe, it is prohibited under the legally binding European Convention on Human Rights. In the US, by contrast, recourse by individual states to the ultimate sanction is on the rise, and this year, for the first time in since 1963, the federal government rejoined those states practicing capital punishment when it executed mass-murderer Timothy McVeigh. Ireland is incontrovertibly European when it comes to crime and punishment. Paramilitaries' (mostly silent) firearms notwithstanding, gun ownership is strictly curtailed. Reported crime rates and the prison population are low even by European standards.

## Tax, spending and faith in government

There are few things that separate Europeans from Americans more than attitude to government and the state. Americans distrust the institutions of government, be they state or federal. For them, the less government the better because in so many cases their forefathers left their countries of origin to escape too-powerful governments and rulers. A libertarian gene thus evolved, giving Americans an inherited predisposition to small and limited government. Another reason for this is that there is more opportunity and social mobility than in Europe, where classism persists and old school ties still count. As a result, government intervention is neither needed nor wanted to give Americans at the bottom a leg-up.

Europeans are different. They have faith in government. When things go wrong, they look to the state. When they want better health, education and transport they expect politicians and civil servants to come up with answers. Today, there is hardly a country in Europe in which elections are not decided on who can most convincingly claim to be best able to provide these services. Ireland lies squarely on the European side of the Atlantic in this respect. Despite years of tribunal revelation, Europe-wide opinion polls show that the Irish trust in their state institutions more than any other EU country. And because the state is not viewed with suspicion (even if politicians are), people have faith in it to solve the big problems.

Attitudes to government, and what it should do, are also reflected in how much tax people are prepared to pay. Reflecting Americans' preference for the private over the public, US government spending is equivalent to a low 30% of national income. In Europe, the figure is half as much again at 45%.

At 37% of GNP (a measure agreed by all economists to be the best for gauging Ireland's true wealth) spending was half way between the US and the EU average in 2000. Strip out the cyclical element—economist-speak for the coffer-swelling effects of boom—and the underlying situation moves Ireland nearer to Europe than the US. The remaining gap is mostly accounted for by Ireland's ungenerous (and unEuropean) state pensions, of which there is curiously little made. But when it comes to other forms of public provision, Ireland is much more European. Take health. Public spending is budgeted to overtake the US and EU average in 2001 as the government's health budget soared to £5.3 billion—equivalent to over 7% of GNP.

But it is not the amount of public money that separates the two sides of the Atlantic (contrary to popular European prejudice, the US spends more public money on health than do EU governments). The big difference is that hospital treatment is free in Europe, but not always in the US. Many Americans go without essential procedures because they fall between two stools—too well off to qualify for the US equivalent of a medical card on the one hand, not in a position to get private insurance on the other.

In Europe, the sick sometimes go untreated. But not because procedures have to be paid for. Europe's problem is that supply is frequently insufficient to meet demand. One result is rationing and waiting. Another, even in countries as zealously egalitarian as Denmark, is that people who do not want to wait, and can afford insurance, queue-hop, enraging those left in line. Cold comfort though it may be for Ireland's waiting listees, but theirs is a tale of woe told, to a greater or lesser extent, in all European countries.

## Multilateralism and the world

September 11 was nightmarish. But in the three months since that day we have seen America at its best. As its leadership in the titanic struggles against 20th-century totalitarianism showed, when the US gears up to take on dark forces it is unequivocally a force for good in the world. It is to be hoped that its careful diplomacy, coalition-building and, when necessary, targeted use of force heralds a US engaged more actively with the world. With its unique power and authority, it can achieve much, to the benefit of Americans and everyone else.

Pre-September 11, the US had often been uncomfortable with rules-based international arrangements (multilateralism in the jargon) and often preferred to go it alone. It rejected the Kyoto Protocol on global warming, opted out of the International Criminal Court, refused to sign up to the Land Mines Convention and failed to ratify the Nuclear Weapons Test Ban Treaty. This preference for unilateralism is mostly to do with power. As the world's undisputed heavyweight, the US can get what it wants most of the time without having to bend to the will of others. Europe is different. Again, mostly because of power, or lack of it, in Europe's case. Its big countries are no longer global players. With a few exceptions its small ones never were. Together they calculate that international fora, treaties and frameworks are the best bet for getting what they want. After all, rules fairly made and enforced are the best protection the weak have against the strong.

But there is more to the difference in approach than *Machtpolitik*. Other things matter too. Compared to Europeans, Americans are, generally speaking, less internationalist by instinct. One reason is geography. Until September 11, vast expanses of ocean had helped protect the US from foreign threat—during its 20th-century wars not a single shot was ever fired in battle on continental US soil. Also important is that Americans can justifiably claim to have less to learn from others than others from them, leading the world as they do in almost every field of human endeavour from science and business to the humanities and popular culture.

For Europeans, history matters. Having chaffed against each other for centuries, they have finally learnt that co-operation works better than conflict. They are now willing to submit to multilateral constraint, however irksome it may be at times. Most spectacularly in this regard they have thrown their lot in together in the EU, ceding sovereignty in historically unprecedented measure. Ireland, in action and instinct, is European. It is a staunch supporter of the UN, has a proud record of participation in peace-keeping and has worked the EU better than any other country. Until recently, at any rate, the only voices against the EU were in the wilderness. But even these naysayers do not call for withdrawal, unlike their more frenzied counterparts in England (Europe's least European nation) and elsewhere.

But history and traditions also influence the way Ireland deals with foreign matters and foreigners. A long-standing presence of religious and lay missionaries in the developing world has created a particular concern for the world's chronically poor. This is reflected in foreign-policy priorities. Aid budgets, to assist underdeveloped countries, have increased sharply in recent years and Ireland is now on target to become one of the biggest per capita donors in the world.

A sad history of emigration may be the reason that Ireland has been better than most European countries at integrating immigrants (though not nearly as good as the US). While too many of the newly arrived have suffered shameful racist abuse, compared to other countries unused to cultural diversity, Ireland has made a good, if sometimes shaky, start. There is no white supremacist movement as in Denmark and Sweden, no thuggish National Front as in France and the UK and no political party in government seeking to make populist hay from immigrants as in Austria and Switzerland. A crankish one-woman show, the National Platform for the Control of Immigration, is the sole public expression of anti-newcomer sentiment.

So Ireland is a distinctly European country. But does it matter to any-one other than the professionally curious—journalists, academics and the like? The answer is an emphatic yes, for two reasons. First, knowing who we are is helpful in deciding on the policies that best suit. Societies decide where they want to go and how to get there on the basis of where they come from. Whether to ditch the quintessentially European social partnership arrangement or cut taxes and spending are questions answered, in part at least, by this understanding. Second, in terms of foreign engagement, greater certainty about our European identity should calm those who are nervous of Ireland's involvement in an integrating

Europe. The country's interests are best served by deepening involvement in the EU (the future of governance in Europe) and nurturing already strong ties with the US (the world's sole super-power until mid-century at least). As a very small niche player on the international scene, Ireland can do both. There is no trade-off. That is why, in foreign policy terms, the Boston versus Berlin debate is irrelevant.

*Originally published in* Magill *magazine*

*Chapter* II ～

# A TIGER COME AND GONE: FROM HUBRIS TO...

*'We have not learned enough yet about how countries grow.'*
ROBERT SOLOW (NOBEL PRIZE-WINNER IN ECONOMICS)

## INTRODUCTION

Why are some countries poor and others rich? What causes economies to spring to life? What is the role of the state in economic success and failure? These questions have long been pondered. But convincing answers are not in abundant supply. The speed and suddenness with which the unpredicted global financial and economic crises have washed over the world are one indication of how little we know about how economies function. Irish economic history provides another example of the gaps in knowledge and understanding. No two economists agree on the precise combination of factors to explain why, after decades of underperformance, the Irish economy took off in the 1990s to record a period of expansion quite unlike that ever seen in an already developed country. There may be more consensus on the cause of the subsequent collapse, but there is little on how deep it will be or how long it will last.

What is clear at time of writing, in May 2009, is the extraordinary nature of the current crash. The world is experiencing a period of declining output as it readjusts to a much changed economic landscape, caused by the caving in of the international financial system. This will cause per capita incomes almost everywhere to fall for a time. They will fall more sharply in Ireland than in most other countries because the magnitude of the collapse has been greater—it has both a domestically generated dimension and an international dimension. But significant slippage down the global league table of rich countries would only happen in the event of an extended period of policy errors or inaction. The right choices can do much to prevent protracted stagnation. Thus, Ireland remains, to a considerable degree, the author of its own destiny.

In times as grim as these, there is a danger that pessimism can turn to defeatism; fear to capitulation; and uncertainty to despondency. Just as hubris during the boom allowed one excessively positive view of Irish economic performance to dominate, now negativity is in the ascendant. Situations are rarely as good as the Panglossians would claim or as bad as the gloom-mongers would have it. Balance is always needed. It is needed now more than ever. Given this, and the rapidity with which the situation is changing, it is difficult to assess the short-term outlook and it would be unwise to try (any assessment could be out of date before this book is published). Instead, the focus here is on Ireland's long term economic and policy-making strengths and weaknesses.

## THE REAL 'FUNDAMENTALS'

It was common during the boom for those who claimed that there was no danger of a property crash to talk of the strong 'fundamentals' underpinning the Irish economy. They were wildly wrong. But that does not mean that Ireland does not have real strengths, of which three stand out: first, a workforce that is one of the most educated in the world toiling in a labour market that functions flexibly; second, a good business environment for international companies and a proven track record in attracting them to locate in the country; and, third, a highly successful internationally traded services sector.

The quality of the labour force and the way it is configured is central. Human capital is one of the bases of prosperity: the more an economy has, the more potential it has. What Ireland and much of the world is facing is appalling, but it is not war or pandemic, both of which destroy output capacity. Human capital survives even the deepest recessions—what is learnt is not unlearnt, expertise does not evaporate and degrees conferred are not taken back by universities. Ireland has a highly skilled workforce, and its quality continues to improve. Of young people entering the Irish jobs market, the proportion with a third-level qualification exceeds four in 10, a level bettered by only four other countries.[1] In the immediate future, the focus on qualifications can, if anything, be expected to become greater with the less ready availability of employment—some young people who may have decided during the boom years to work rather than study will do the latter. Thus, the Irish economy will retain high levels of human capital, even if some will leak out through emigration.[2]

Having good human resources is one thing. Allocating them efficiently is another. Ireland's flexible labour market allowed the economy to grow strongly when demand conditions were good, drawing in an infusion of foreign talent that gave new dimensions, dynamism and skills to the workforce. Although supply does not always create its own demand, the same flexibility should ensure that jobs are created quickly once the recovery takes hold. The importance of flexibility is plain to see when one considers most southern European countries, many of whose graduates endure long periods of unemployment or underemployment, particularly in the early years of their careers. In Ireland in 2007, unemployment among the prime-of-life 25–29 cohort stood at 4.6% according to the OECD, well below the average and far below levels in Greece (14.3%), Italy (10.4%) and France (10.2%).[3]

The quality and flexibility of the workforce provides one of the explanations for Ireland's second real and fundamental strength—its extraordinary success in attracting many of the world's best companies to operate in the country and create employment on a comparatively massive scale. The international explosion of mobile investment in the 1990s came at the perfect time for Ireland, allowing it to become a global success story in the amount and quality of foreign direct investment (FDI) it attracted. There were many reasons for this, including the country's European Union involvement, combined with domestic factors, such as a good business environment, a responsive policy-making community, and those abundant and flexible skills. In my view, the best measure of jobs-rich foreign investment comes from the UN.[4] They measure the number of new foreign investment projects in each country each year. In the 2003–07 period, Ireland averaged 144 annually, the second highest in the EU-27 in per capita terms. Moreover, there was no discernible downward trend over the period,[5] suggesting that whatever competitiveness issues arose, they were not sufficiently serious to choke off the supply of new investment.

Success, therefore, was no fluke. Ireland has been, and remains, a good place to do business relative to most other countries. In addition, the increase in the cost base during the boom years is now being reversed, albeit in the most brutal way possible. Commercial property prices are plummeting and wages are falling. Although, as discussed below, government-influenced aspects of competitiveness have been long neglected, the market is considerably more important in determining overall competitiveness. This should ensure that the sharp, ongoing decline in the cost base helps maintain Ireland's attractiveness as a location for foreign companies.

There are, however, many things that could undermine continued success. Some are external, such as changes to the US tax code, but many are domestically determined, such as poor management of the public finances, any weakening of ties to the EU, the appearance of cronyism in dealing with the financial crisis and complacency in addressing specific cost issues affecting key sectors. Failure quickly to get to grips with these issues risks pushing Ireland off the all-important shortlists that companies draw up when deciding where to locate their foreign operations. Since the 1990s at least, Ireland has been on those lists. Success breeds success—everyone wanted to be associated with a winner. Companies piled in. But failure repels. If Ireland does not deal expeditiously with its domestic weaknesses, companies already in situ will divest—gradually or at a stroke—and new companies will be much harder to attract.

A third real strength of the Irish economy is its development of a world-beating traded services sector. From a virtual standing start 20 years ago, it is now the largest per capita exporter of services in the world. More than $1 of every $40 spent globally on services imports accrues to companies in Ireland. When one considers that only one in every 1,500 inhabitants of the planet resides in Ireland, it is very clear how disproportionate is its world market share. For a high-wage, geographically peripheral island economy this is exactly where it should be. As the absolute and comparative performance of the sector is set out in a number of the articles below, only one additional aspect requires further comment—that of the success of home-grown companies. Over the course of the current decade to 2007, their foreign sales more than doubled, to over €3 billion.[6] Although this is only a fraction of foreign-owned companies' services exports, the rate of growth was more rapid.[7] It is one of the very few examples where Irish companies have been more dynamic than their foreign-owned counterparts based in the country.

But there is no reason for complacency. The sector is dominated by foreign companies. As stated above, maintaining attractiveness is essential, and perhaps even more essential in the case of services companies than those in manufacturing as the former are more footloose than the latter (manufacturers have greater sunk costs, such as factories and machinery, which make them less mobile). In addition, some significant structural shrinking in the financial services and insurance sectors is now all but inevitable given the restructuring and re-regulation of these industries at national, European and international levels. With these sectors together generating exports of some €15 billion in 2008, or 22.5% of total services exports, this change is unlikely to take place without some pain.

## UNDYNAMIC ENTREPRENEURS AND HYPERACTIVE SPECULATORS

The Irish economy has real and enduring strengths. But it also has serious weaknesses, many of which are at least as enduring. The poor performance of indigenous industry is perhaps the most serious. It was certainly the least discussed during the good times. Then, a sense of invulnerability prevailed. One talked only of success. Another reason for the limited focus on weak corporate performance was some real successes—a small but growing number of companies internationalised to become successful multinationals and headline outward FDI data suggested that corporate Ireland was investing heavily abroad (these data may overstate the case: the extent of property investment in these overall numbers is unclear). At the other end of the corporate spectrum, there is little doubt that levels of entrepeneurship have increased and the international successes of the home-grown software sector may be a sign that a new generation of entre-preneurs is more successful than previous generations. But Irish business continues to be less than dynamic. In Chapter 1 it was contended that Ireland is not a society that values ideas and that it remains relatively inward-looking. Both of these traits are reflected in its corporate perform-ance by, respectively, still-low levels of innovation and a lack of export success.

Innovation is central to any rich economy that wants to remain rich. Successful innovation requires ideas and a willingness to invest in them. Irish business lacks both. There is no better measure of an economy's capacity to innovate than the number of patents it generates. In Ireland, the number of patents granted per capita is a mere third of the OECD aver-age.[8] Patent data are not broken down by the nationality of the company, but it is almost certain that the foreign-owned sector accounts for most of these given what we know about business research and development (R&D) spending. More than two thirds of this is done by foreign-owned companies and all Irish-owned companies together spent less than €400 million in 2005[9] (at that time individual property deals of this size were two a penny, which gives some indication of the priorities of Irish risk takers, and those who finance them). And even with the boost from the foreign sector, total business spending on R&D as a percentage of GNP is only two thirds the OECD average.[10] This is not surprising. Irish entrepreneurs and business have a long-established tendency to underinvestment (at risk of generalisation, Irish business folk, once they achieve even modest success, come to be more interested in equine live-stock than corporate capital stock). This did not change in the boom years.

Total spending on machinery stood at 3.3% of GDP in the 1999–2006 period, well below the euro zone average of 5.4%.[11]

The recently ended credit boom suggests that there was not a glut of great innovations that did not make it to market owing to lack of financing. The real reason is an absence of ideas to be invested in. There can be little doubt that the speculative frenzy in the property market diverted resources that might otherwise have been invested in real businesses. But the relatively small number of successful world-class Irish companies is depressing,[12] particularly for an economy with a highly educated, multi-national and young population, a very large science budget and many of the world's most innovative multinational companies (their presence in the country creates huge potential for spillover effects). In the years to come, the highly educated people who lose their jobs may turn to their own capacities and skills. Necessity can be the mother of invention. With fewer employment options at home and abroad, the potential silver lining to the ongoing recession may be that it will end the lemming-like specula-tion in domestic and foreign property and channel energies, ideas and capital into real businesses.

Lack of innovation in products and processes is indisputable. It is also lacking in the exploitation of international markets. Home-grown business is remarkably inward-looking, accounting for less than one tenth of total exports. If all foreign companies disappeared tomorrow, Ireland would be among the most closed economies in the world. The performance has not only been abysmal, it is getting worse. The massive gap between Irish and foreign companies' exports continued to widen over the course of the current decade.[13] Even more disappointing was the sharp decline in world market share. Globally, exports of manufactures from 2000 to 2007 grew by more than 50%. Irish companies managed to increase sales of goods at less than a third of the pace internationally, at just 15%. Again, the very low rates of growth are difficult to explain given strong global demand, the declining costs of international commerce for an island economy thanks to changes in transport and technology, the growing advantage of English as the international language of business and the confidence effects of the boom.

These are the less discussed structural weaknesses of the Irish economy. Some mention is needed of the one that is unceasingly debated—the domestic property price crash. The bursting of the bubble, coinciding with the global crisis, will cause a deeper and longer slump than in other devel-oped countries. There are three seperate, if related, reasons for this. First, the Irish banking system is among the most broken in the world. This will take time and a lot of taxpayers' money (of which there is very little) to fix. In addition, the banking model employed by Irish banks during the boom was dependent on access to easy international funding. This model is now defunct and will be replaced by a more traditional model. The transition period will be lengthy and during that time the supply of credit will be tight, at best. The second reason the downturn will last longer in Ireland is because household balance sheets are in a worse state than most other countries. On the asset side, prices of both property and equities have fallen more sharply than almost any other country. On the liabilities side, Irish household debt is among the highest in the euro area and the burden of this is being made greater by deflation—falling wages and prices mean that the debt in real terms is rising. Repairing balance sheets, by paying down debt, will take many years. Finally, and related to point two, because oversupply of housing is so great, the construction industry will take the best part of a decade to recover.[14] This will act as a drag on growth for years to come.

## THE HAND OF THE STATE

What is the relationship between the state and economic performance? The answer is far from clear, but one thing is certain—good government certainly has some benefit; bad government is detrimental. This asymmetry can be seen everywhere. An extreme case is Zimbabwe, until recently a relatively prosperous African economy. It has in the space of a decade been destroyed by bad government. By contrast, in Botswana, consistently good governance since independence has ensured the county is better off than most in Africa, but it has not come anywhere near achieving income levels enjoyed in developed countries. Closer to home, southern Europeans are poorer than their northern European counterparts. Bad government is, at the very least, part of the explanation. Reunited Germany provides an example of the limits of efficient (and well-funded) government. The formerly communist eastern regions have not closed the prosperity gap with the west over two decades despite massive (and generous) effort. The lesson is thus clear—governments can do far more harm than good by their actions.

None of that means that the role of government is not hugely important. As discussed in Chapter iv, the role of the state is greater today than ever, and as argued in Chapter i, nimble and focused government is more important than ever. But in Ireland the gap between the sort of smart government that could enhance prosperity and the existing quality of government is wide and becoming wider. The weaknesses in Irish political structures (see Chapter 1) apply to economic policy as much as, if not more than, to other areas. And they are getting worse. The increasing tendency in recent decades to use taxpayers' money for political purposes is the most egregious example. In 2001, the decision to grant 'benchmarked' pay increases to public sector workers amounted to the largest transfer of wealth from one group in society to another in the history of the Irish state. It was motivated purely by a desire to buy off an interest group. In 2003, the decision to decentralise the Civil Service brought political patronage to a new level. It was conceived as a means of promising windfalls to rural towns and cities and came at enormous financial cost. It has also caused real damage to the effectiveness of the policy-making system.[15]

As currently structured, the political system for the most part does not produce individuals capable of driving and leading a proactive policy of seizing opportunities, addressing deficiencies and anticipating challenges. More importantly still, politicians have little electoral incentive to do so. In most areas of policy—from energy to waste management, from international trade policy to pensions—change and reform have either been non-existent or glacially slow.

The vacuum created by a weak and disengaged executive branch of government is, to some extent, filled by officials who run departments and policy agencies. The 1994 Strategic Management Initiative to reform the public sector came from within the service itself. But, 15 years on, to say progress in that process has been limited would be a gross understatement. During the boom years the administrative class was almost as complacent as the political class—financial services regulation, and the activities of Anglo Irish Bank stand out in this regard. Much of this is explained by the cautious nature of those attracted to administration and officialdom. It is reinforced by the balance of incentives being strongly tilted towards small and slow change over the sweeping and the radical (the rewards for driving a successful initiative are less than the damage to a career of a failed initiative). Moreover, officials have often been stopped from advancing initiatives by politicians who do not wish to rock the boat and by vested interests that have had enormous sway via social partnership.

A further reason for officials not pushing change is that they sometimes do not recognise it is needed. In many areas, knowledge of policy best practice is thin, both because of a lack of expertise in departments and the limited mechanisms to bring in such expertise when needed. The absence of trained economists across the Civil Service, and in the Department of Finance in particular, has been frequently remarked upon. The failure to seek appropriate human resources to deal with the challenges of modern governance must surely be attributed to the service itself (anecdotally, I have noticed that the fewer economists there are in a civil service, the less likely that service is to bring external economists in to fill gaps. I suspect it is because officials are concerned that they will be shown up by those with deeper expertise).

In many cases there can be no excuse that officials do not know what needs to be done. High quality brain power is available. Externally, bodies such as the OECD frequently provide objective and expert advice. In one of its regular reports on the country in 2003, for example, the OECD prioritised 24 structural reform measures, such as changes to labour laws, taxes and benefits, which would strengthen the long-term functioning of the economy. In a progress checklist two and a half years later it found that: 'no action' had been taken on ten measures; in two cases the opposite to what was recommended had been done; 11 recommendations had been partially implemented; and only one measure had been fully implemented. Domestically, the work of agencies such as Forfás and the National Competitiveness Council provide rigorous comparative analysis and present it clearly and concisely. Their work and a vast number of one-off studies and reports mean that the policy machine frequently knows what needs to be done. Yet knowing what needs to be done is a universe away from implementing the reforms needed to achieve objectives. And with that, we have come full circle to the absence of focused, driven and capable political leadership, the absence of which is the root of most of Ireland's governance problems.

Against this general background of the quality of the policy-making apparatus, it is worth considering the extent to which its weaknesses were the cause of the three major economic management challenges now facing Ireland—the property crash, the collapse of the public finances and the wider range of issues that fall within the general rubric of 'competitiveness' (the appalling rise in joblessness is a result of these developments and until they are resolved there is relatively little government can do to do to help companies restart job creation).

## MANIAS AND THEIR ORIGINS
The bursting of the housing bubble and the resultant undermining of the banking system are among the most serious economic shocks that the Irish economy has ever suffered, or, indeed, that any developed economy has suffered in many decades. Given the extreme nature of the reversal it is understandable that culprits are being sought. But how culpable were

the government and the institutions of the state, and did they do all that was reasonable to prevent disaster? Three clear actions and inactions can be identified. Subsidies and tax breaks indisputably fuelled the property boom, although I am unaware of any studies that have sought to measure the effect. Efforts to cool the market as far back as the late 1990s were effectively abandoned, in part at least owing to pressures from interests who wished to see continued and unhindered growth. A second failing was how banks were regulated. Even without the benefit of hindsight and knowing now what the regulator knew then of practices at Anglo Irish Bank before the crisis, the failure to curb such practices was grave and will have serious costs into the future, both to the taxpayer and in the damage to Ireland's reputation as a place to do business. The clear failures of the regulatory authorities also had a knock-on effect. The hyper-aggressive practices of Anglo Irish Bank drove the other banks to loosen lending practices in order to maintain market share (shareholders deserve their fair share of the blame—they punished any bank that did not keep up by selling its equity). Although a property boom would certainly have taken place even if Anglo Irish had not existed, it is hard to think of any other country where one small, out-of-control institution had such a major systemic effect.[16] A third charge is that the government did not use its moral suasion to warn of the risks and calm the market. Although it is hard to find politicians anywhere who talk down booms, the Irish government ended up believing its own propaganda that the 'fundamentals' were sound. The dangers of excessive indebtedness and the risks individuals would be exposed to in the event of a hard, rather than a soft, landing were dismissed, often with contempt, and the motives of those who did warn of dangers sometimes impugned.

If the government had been less willing to provide the incentives builders and developers sought, if the regulator had reined in the rogue bank and if government politicians had been less dismissive of the dangers, the bubble would not have reached what increasingly appears to be one of the most extreme property busts to have taken place anywhere at any time. But for all that, government deserves only part of the blame. During the boom years, most people got caught up in mania psychology— bankers, builders, property developers, media and almost everyone who bought property. Politicians and officials did, too. The former had every reason to buy into the notion that the good times would roll indefinitely and would not have been rewarded by voters if they had engaged in what became known at the time as 'talking down the economy'. For officials—civil servants, central bankers and regulators—the picture is more complicated. From as early as the late 1990s there were warnings that the extraordinary rates of growth enjoyed from 1995 were unsustainable. Civil servants and officials, in keeping with tradition, counselled caution and highlighted risks. But nobody likes a gloom-monger at the best of times. They *were* the best of times, and as the years passed, those who foretold crash and slump appeared to be proved wrong. There was seemingly ever greater reason for politicians who knew little about economics to discount warnings, and few incentives for officials to advise their political masters to take measures which would not have been popular (one senior civil servant told me that he gave up highlighting risks and downsides because it was damaging his career). This is the psychology of mania. And manias have always happened, even in the best-governed countries—the Nordics are unquestionably the best-governed countries in the world and they have suffered more than their fair share of speculative boom-busts. Given this, it is hard to maintain that politicians and policy-makers were primarily to blame.

And all the more so as the prevailing international orthodoxy also gave more than a little reason to believe that all would end well. During the boom years, it was strongly my view that credit growth in Ireland was far too high and that this was creating very serious risks for the economy,[17] but the international consensus veered towards the view, most famously propounded by Alan Greenspan during his long tenure at the helm of the US Federal Reserve, that officials were in no position to determine when asset price bubbles existed, that intervening risked doing more harm than good and that the only role of government was to step in to clean up the mess if a bubble did burst. An even more widely held view was that the international financial system was managing risk effectively, spreading it in such a manner that, for instance, a housing bust in one country would be easily absorbed by the system as a whole. But this orthodoxy was shattered by the collapse of the international financial system. In many ways, the functioning of that system over recent decades was a giant, slow-burning mania. Having started in the 1980s, it had gone on so long that no serious analyst or commentator believed that it was vulnerable to the sort of collapse that has come to pass. This was of relevance for Ireland in that there existed a misplaced faith in finance generally. More specifically, it was relevant because Irish banks came to rely increasingly on the international financial system to fund their lending, and this was not considered a threat (nobody foresaw funding drying up as spectacularly as it did).

## FISCAL FARCE REPEATED AS TRAGEDY

If government errors and inaction were only one of the causes of the property crash, they were entirely to blame for the second major economic challenge the country now faces.

For sound public finances two things are needed—strong political will to hold the line and solid technical competence. Ireland has had neither.[18] The collapse in Ireland's public finances in the period from 2007 has become the worst, without exception, in the history of the OECD. For this disaster the government deserves excoriation. A serious problem was foreseeable.[19] Despite this, the government continued to lock in massive new spending commitments year after year. Nor did it put in place the modern mechanisms of budgeting that would have resulted in better value for money or set warning lights flashing.[20] This was par for the course. For more than three decades, Ireland's record on managing its public finances has been depressingly awful.

Up until the 1960s, the post-independence generation of politicians favoured Victorian frugality when managing the public finances. Book-balancing was the central objective and few risks were taken (indeed, caution was excessive, resulting in underinvestment). The next generation, in power from the 1970s, abandoned restraint and went to the other extreme. Caution was thrown to the wind and taxpayers' money was increasingly used for political purposes. Elections were now to be bought. Taxpayers were bribed with their own money. The results were soon evident. When the world economy went into recession in the early 1970s, Ireland's relatively small national debt grew quickly. When the second oil crisis struck in the late 1970s, the country was fiscally weaker than many other developed countries. But that did not deter successive governments. Spending growth continued. During the first half of the 1980s, Ireland's public finances position deteriorated more seriously than any other OECD country. While the 1980s were a boom time for most countries, Ireland had a lost decade of economic growth. This was in large part attributable to the protracted failure to consolidate the public finances. A moment of clarity in the late 1980s brought the position back from the brink. But lessons were not learnt. No examination of what happened took place. No structures were created to improve the effectiveness of public spending. No measures were put in place to warn of threats.

The boom of the 1990s provided Ireland with a get-out-of-jail-free card. Unlike the other developed countries who had mismanaged their finances, Ireland's public indebtedness relative to GDP declined sharply (though not because the debt was paid down, but because national income grew so rapidly). Complacency quickly took hold. Even the adoption of the euro did not cause minds to focus—sound fiscal policy became even more important because in the future there would be no easy option of devaluation.[21] Neither ministers nor Department of Finance officials sought the introduction of normal international budgeting practice. Instead, basic book-keeping remained in the Dark Ages: accounts continued to be compiled on a cash rather than accruals basis; no provision for cost of capital was made in spending, making real cost-benefit evaluation impossible; and departments were not required to produce basic balance sheets. Unsustainable revenue flows were spent as fast as they flooded into the Exchequer. The result of such sloth and recklessness has come home to roost. To characterise policy as pro-cyclical would be to gravely understate how it fuelled an unsustainable boom then and is making the most savage contraction in economic activity worse now. Public debt levels are rising even more sharply than in the awful 1980s. National bankruptcy is a real possibility and sharply higher taxes for a generation a certainty.

## THE COMPETITIVENESS IMPERATIVE

The fiscal crisis was entirely of the government's making and it contributed significantly to the property crash. How culpable was it in causing the third major economic challenge facing the country—the competitiveness crisis?

As mentioned above in the discussion on FDI, competitiveness is largely market-determined. Wages, property prices, the exchange rate and the costs of financing are mostly determined by the interplay of supply and demand. Yet there is also a significant role for policy. Governments can remove or lower barriers to market entry—both those that they themselves have erected and those thrown up by incumbents to lock out would-be competitors. More proactively, governments can refine competition laws and strengthen enforcement mechanisms so that competition has free rein to lower prices. In sectors where it may not emerge of its own accord, they can simulate (and stimulate) it by the right regulatory frameworks (networked industries, such as energy and telecoms, are most notable in this regard).

While unnecessary barriers to enterprise have been relatively few in Ireland, willingness to tear down those that exist has been limited and slow, and is one of the reasons for the country's internationally high price level. Energy is perhaps the best example of government failure to confront a public sector vested interest (the Electricity Supply Board). This failure is a key reason for electricity prices in Ireland being almost 50% higher than the EU-15 average and second highest among that group after Italy.[22] Unwillingness to take on private sector vested interests is equally prevalent. Legal costs in Dublin are the highest anywhere, according to the NCC.[23] Maintaining the distinction between barrister and solicitor has become a serious anomaly, among other things, allowing barristers' average earnings to exceed even their highest paid counterparts in the neighbouring common-law jurisdiction. The profession's control of access to training is more typical of a medieval guild than a modern service industry and its form of self-regulation is both inappropriate and inadequate.

At times during the boom years, there seemed to be a political will to push a competitiveness agenda. A government-requested OECD report in 2001 set out a series of changes that would boost competitiveness. Its launch was attended by the then Taoiseach, Tánaiste and Minister for Finance. But if the spirit was willing, the flesh was weak. In an evaluation of progress five years later, the OECD found that 'no action' had been taken on 13 of 20 recommendations and only four had been achieved or were set to be achieved.[24] The impetus to change is chronically weak. Even during the good times, when reform would have been relatively painless politically, it was eschewed.

## WHAT TO CHANGE AND PROSPECTS FOR IMPROVEMENT

There are many underlying strengths in the Irish economy. These should reassert themselves once the world economy returns to solid growth, however long that takes. But whether they are allowed to generate the prosperity that they have the potential to create will depend to a considerable extent on policy choices. Policy choices, in turn, will be determined by the quality of the policy-making mechanism. But because that mechanism functions so poorly, it must be overhauled. Reform of the general constitutional/political order was discussed in Chapter 1. The changes advocated there would provide a basis for improved economic policy-making. But more specific and targeted changes are also needed. The professionalisation of the main ministerial portfolios dealing with economic matters is imperative. Qualified, competent and driven people are needed. They can be brought in to the political system in a number of ways, either via change to the electoral system or by introducing a clearer separation between the executive and the legislature, as is the case in most other democracies.

For the main microeconomic portfolio, currently covering enterprise, trade and employment, a proven track record in managing a large organisation is crucial given the wide remit of the role. It also requires a deep understanding of the dilemmas of business, from the smallest firm to the largest multinational, a capacity to see commercial trends and knowledge of policy design and best practice. For Finance, ministers require, at the very least, a good working knowledge of economics and an understanding of and facility with the European dimension of decision-making in the context of EMU participation and EU membership more widely. But given Ireland's appalling record of managing its public finances, additional measures are required. The depoliticisation of chunks of that function, at least as comprehensive as that implemented in other countries, would help ensure yet another self-inflicted fiscal catastrophe does not take place in the future. There is no shortage of ways that this can be achieved, including by granting greater powers and resources for the office of the Auditor and Comptroller General, creating a new independent body to evaluate spending proposals before they are agreed and to assess whether they have achieved their objectives afterwards, and the outsourcing of macro-economic forecasting to an independent body, such as the ESRI.

As discussed in Chapter 1, unlike in most other countries suffering from poor governance, the potential for improvement in the political system exists in Ireland if the willingness emerges to make real change. The same can also be said of the wider administrative system. Compared to most other European peer countries, corruption levels are low in the Irish public sector, respect for the rule of law and the rights of individuals is strong, and there is a high degree of civic-mindedness. Nor is it 'bloated' by the standards of other similar countries.[25] But it is too costly and rigid, and accountability mechanisms are unusually weak. It is also far from optimally configured. Addressing these problems will not be easy, and resistance to change in the administrative system is likely to be even greater than resistance to reform of the political system. In almost all developed economies, public sector trade unions are among the most powerful interest groups. There are at least as powerful in Ireland given the weakness of the executive and the power of social partnership structures.

But not all efficiency-generating change would result in resistance from public servants and their representatives. In areas where capacity requires beefing up, there would be no reason to oppose the addition of new resources. Central to this is greater economic expertise. Modern governance is primarily about the allocation of resources—from healthcare systems to tax systems to regulation. The study of the allocation of resources is what economics is all about. Introducing greater economic expertise into the policy-making process can be done in many ways. Models abound internationally. In Britain, a separate recruitment stream exists for those with economics expertise; in France civil service training models are highly effective; in Germany a council of wise men gives regular assessments of government economic management; and in most countries ministers have private staffs which can include independent economists to ensure good advice and bolster the minister's arguments if officials resist change. To run modern government without a strong economic input would be akin to running a health system without doctors or a legal system without lawyers. It must change. Pockets of excellence show that it can be done. A highly professional, forward-thinking organisation like IDA Ireland proves that the abilities and capacities to excel exist. If they can be marshalled and run effectively, the potential for a qualitative improvement in economic management can be realised.

> *'Small states have to work consciously at devising mechanisms and procedures to foster strategic thinking. This has not been attempted in Ireland. It is doubtful if it has ever been comprehended.'*
>
> J.J. LEE (1989)

———

# IRELAND'S BRIGHT FOREIGN INVESTMENT FUTURE

*10 October 2006*

The world changed profoundly in the 1990s. Dizzying technological change and falling barriers to cross-border interaction saw greater mobility of people, goods, money and ideas. As a result, science, the arts, education and commerce became more internationalised. One of the central pillars of this globalisation process was an unprecedented surge in mobile investment. In the years between 1990 and 2000, flows of foreign direct investment (FDI) increased globally by a factor of 6.5. This altered radically the structure of the world economy.

The phenomenon affected most parts of the planet, and none more so than Ireland's North Atlantic hinterland. As the European and American economies became more deeply integrated by two-way investment flows, Ireland moved from being on the periphery of Europe to the centre of the new transatlantic economy. It should be acknowledged that if this change had not taken place, there would have been no Celtic Tiger.

Those processes of globalisation and 'transatlanticisation' are among the issues examined in a new report published jointly by the Economist Intelligence Unit in London and the Columbia Program on International Investment in New York. There is much that is relevant to Ireland. Happily, most of it is good news. In 2006, world direct investment will surpass the $1 trillion mark for the first time since 2000. We forecast that FDI will continue to rise over the remainder of the decade, even if the rate of growth will be lower than in the 1990s. We describe the coming period as one of constrained globalisation.

This augurs well for Ireland. The prospect of more foreign-owned companies locating in the country can only add to the existing benefits, of which there are many. Foreign firms employ as many as one in 20 people in the economy. Indirectly, via salaries spent in the local economy and business generated for suppliers, they account for as many jobs again. On average, they pay more and offer greater job security than home-grown companies.

They also invest almost twice as much in staff training, account for nearly three-quarters of all private research and development carried out in the country and annually hand over to the Exchequer more than €2.5 billion in profit taxes. The long list of benefits has silenced even Ireland's diehard anti-globalisers from criticising the multinationals. But could these companies up sticks and move to lower-wage economies further afield? This question has been asked more frequently in recent years as the enlargement of the EU has given eastern European countries many of the same benefits that Ireland has enjoyed for over three decades.

But, argues the report, these concerns are misplaced. The evidence shows that the new EU members continue to attract only a fraction of the foreign investment that flows into western European countries. There has been no step change since accession in May 2004. Nor is one to be expected. We forecast that the new members' share of total EU25 FDI inflows in 2006–10 will be a mere 5%.

There are a number of reasons for this. Doing business in those countries is still difficult. Economic and political instability, serious corruption, organised crime and clapped out infrastructure are just some of the hazards. In addition, the adoption upon accession to the EU of the bloc's stringent environmental and worker safety rules has narrowed the costs gap with western Europe.

Fears about low-wage economies taking all investment are wrong for another reason. There is not a fixed lump of global investment which countries play a zero-sum game to attract. Just as the total amount of investment would shrink if countries implemented bad policies, creating more attractive business environments will generate more overall investment. While there may be some diverting effect in the short term, it is a fallacy to believe that more investment into one country necessarily means less for everyone else.

For Ireland, the greatest threat to keeping investment flowing is complacency at home, not competition from abroad. Making sure more well-paid, knowledge-intensive jobs continue to be created requires a relentless focus on upgrading skills levels, improving infrastructure, easing the regulatory burden and breaking up cosy cartels. Beyond Ireland's immediate interest in its own continued economic wellbeing, the report may also have implications for how the Republic, and other rich countries, aid those less fortunate.

The global economy has been driven in recent years by rapid growth in many parts of the developing world. But some countries have not managed to hitch their wagons to the globalisation locomotive. In his contribution to the report, Jeffrey D. Sachs—a campaigner for development in the planet's poorest countries and one of the world's leading economists— argues that economic growth in the developing world can be accelerated by using more active methods of investment attraction.

He makes a persuasive case, and it is one that could feed into the debate about how Ireland's aid programme should evolve. As the country's aid budget has increased rapidly, few would disagree that there is scope for innovation in its use. A role for IDA Ireland would seem obvious in this regard.Its unrivalled expertise in attracting investment could be drawn on to advise developing countries on building institutional capacity, tailoring policies and targeting foreign businesses.

Making sure all parts of the world benefit from globalisation is a moral imperative, but also a political necessity. The full title of the report—*World Investment Prospects to 2010: Boom or Backlash?*—makes clear that there are risks to our central (benign) outlook. The biggest comes from rich countries, where voices calling for assorted protectionist measures are rising. These voices articulate fears about the pace of economic change and the negative effects globalisation can have. The truth is that participation in the global economy brings large net gains. This is not to deny that there are costs. But extra wealth created by the process allows welfare states to be strengthened, so that hardship for those who lose out is mitigated.

*Originally published in the* Irish Times

# INTERNATIONAL SERVICES SECTOR'S MIRACLE GROWTH

*9 September 2003*

The pattern of economic development across the world and over the centuries never changes. As economies evolve, agriculture is gradually replaced by manufacturing as the mainstay of wealth creation, before it, too, slowly declines in importance as services come to dominate. In rich countries today, things grown and made account for around one third of the value of all output. Providing services—from health to entertainment—generates the rest. And as industrial and agricultural jobs become fewer, owing to technological advance and competition from better-value imports, the importance of services grows. For an economy like Ireland's, services are the future.

It is just as well then that, despite being crowded by an unusually large manufacturing sector, the internationally traded services industry in Ireland has experienced stratospheric growth. The facts are staggering. In just five years there has been a threefold increase in services exports. Last year alone, companies based in Ireland sold €30 billion worth of services to foreigners. Continued rapid growth last year, despite a global slump, made Ireland the planet's biggest per capita exporter for the first time, according to the World Trade Organisation (WTO).

And what makes this boom even more extraordinary is that it has taken place despite the failure of successive governments to support the industry, the latest example of which is the administration's position at trade negotiations now taking place in Mexico. The ranking minister is Agriculture's Joe Walsh, there to do the bidding of the small and shrinking farming sector even when this means sacrificing the interests of the rest of the economy, including services.

So how, in the face of persistent official unwillingness to pursue the State's real economic interests, has the services sector done so well? One reason is the fall in corporation tax to 12.5%. The cut in tax has been a competitive boon for service providers who were handing over as much as a third of their profits to the State as recently as 1998.

Another reason for the success is the changing profile of foreign-owned firms in Ireland, which accounted for three quarters of services exports in 2001 (the latest figures). Where foreign direct investment into Ireland was once associated almost exclusively with manufacturing, inflows are now more likely to be for the setting up of software houses or financial institutions. According to the US commerce department, almost a third of

US investment in Ireland is now in the services industry, from next to nothing just a few years ago.

And it would seem that even foreign firms involved primarily in manufacturing are increasingly getting in on the services act. When once Irish affiliates bought in almost all their services requirements from their parent companies, they now seem to be doing things for themselves, and, when they operate as regional headquarters, for their sister companies on the continent and beyond. This suggests that headway is being made in moving away from screwdriver operations towards higher value-added functions.

The services boom also looks like the coming of Ireland's entrepreneurial age. Home-owned services businesses are growing exports even faster than the foreign-owned sector (in stark contrast to most of their counterparts in the ailing indigenous manufacturing sector). The unleashing of this dynamism is mostly because the traditional handicaps of Irish business—peripherality and small market size—apply hardly at all when it comes to service provision. Nowhere has the 'death of distance' caused by the IT revolution been more keenly felt than in the services industry.

Considering the services phenomenon from an industry viewpoint also helps to understand what is going on. The biggest exporter by far is the computer services sector, which had foreign sales receipts last year of €11 billion—over a third of total. It has been the engine of services growth, and despite the industry's global woes in recent years, it continues to grow. Though a considerable chunk of this growth has been the result of changing delivery methods, there is little doubt that real growth has also occurred, not least by 600 indigenously owned companies.

Illustrative of the magnitude of the changes in the industry is the rise, almost from nowhere, of the internationally traded insurance sector. Its foreign earnings last year, at €3.8 billion, were second only to computer services. Though a good proportion of the insurance sector's huge increase in earnings in 2002 was accounted for by the post-September 11th hike in premia, this does not explain what is going on. That it is difficult to understand exactly what is going on is indicative in many respects of the wider services industry. Despite being far bigger than manufacturing, it has received much less attention in the literature. The statistical data are limited. Policy-makers often fly blind. It would be worth knowing much more, if only to appreciate just how successful the country has been.

*Originally published in the* Irish Times

# THE CELTIC TIGER'S REAL STRENGTHS

*7 October 2007*

Apart from a Dr Pangloss or two in the banking industry, economists are at one in their view that the Irish economy is entering a period of sharply lowered growth. Worse still, even a passing acquaintance with the broad spectrum of key economic indicators shows clearly that the risk of the incipient slowdown tipping into full-blown recession is worryingly real. The near-term outlook becomes even cloudier when the international picture is considered. The us economy, to which Ireland is umbilically tied, is hovering on the brink of recession. The euro, whose appreciation has already eroded competitiveness, is far more likely to go higher than to weaken.

Credit markets, which seized up during the summer, are not yet functioning normally, ultimately raising the cost of financing for businesses and households. In short, there is every reason to worry. But, too often, mood amplifies the economic cycle—raising the peaks as euphoria takes hold and deepening the troughs when despair sets in. At a time of looming downturn, sentiment in Ireland risks becoming excessively pessimistic. It is, therefore, all the more necessary to retain some perspective. While it would be ostrich-like to fail to acknowledge the weaknesses and risks in the near term, it would be equally wrong to ignore the economy's underlying strengths.

Thankfully, the tiger still lurks, unseen by many, in export categories known traditionally as 'invisibles'. Providers of internationally traded services have consistently been the Irish economy's most dynamic wealth creators. For them, business continues to boom. That export growth is accelerating at a time when the wider economy was cooling shows that the sector continues to support economic growth independently of domestic conditions.

Although this snapshot of double-digit growth is impressive, to appreciate fully just how good the Irish performance has been, comparison is necessary with economies which have well-deserved reputations as winners in the knowledge economy. Finland is often rightly held up as a model for others—it is high-tech, open and rich. It is also the economy in the euro zone with which Ireland is most readily comparable in terms of population, size, wealth and geographic peripherality. Yet compare its services sector with Ireland's, and the land of Nokia pales by comparison. Irish services exports in 2006 stood at €55 billion, more than four times the Finns' relatively paltry €13.5 billion. What's more, the goods/services mix in total exports is tilted far more towards the latter: 80% of Finnish exports are still accounted for by merchandise goods, while sales of Irish services to foreigners are moving rapidly towards 50% and will exceed the sale of goods by the beginning of the coming decade on the basis of current trends.

Closer to home, Britain has long been considered the most 'post-industrial' of G7 economies, owing to the early decline of its manufacturing sector and the successes of its vaunted financial, accounting and marketing firms. But despite Britain's traditional lead, the average Irish resident now exports more than four times as many services as his British counterpart. A more exotic comparison can be made with Asia. One hears the words 'India', 'offshoring' and 'outsourcing' in the same sentence with almost clichéd monotony at conferences and business gatherings. It is to be hoped that, for the sake of so many impoverished Indians, their country will one day live up to the talk of it becoming the world's backroom. But that day is some time away yet. Despite a gargantuan population disparity, Ireland's revenues from exported services have exceeded India's for every year bar one during the current decade.

So far, so fascinating. But will this success story continue, discerning readers may ask? Happily, there is every reason to believe that it will. The boom in services is not excessively concentrated in one sector, but spread across many. More positively still, it is happening in all the sub sectors that can be expected to see continued growth in demand globally. Indeed, if one were to ask policy-makers anywhere in the world for the kind of export profile they would wish for, Ireland's is exactly what they would describe. Such people dream of high-value-added industries in which salaries are generous and exposure to competition from infuriatingly competitive easterners is limited. This is exactly what Ireland is fortunate enough to possess. Information technology, finance and business services are the future for any country that wishes the best for its citizens.

Perhaps most positively, indigenous entrepreneurs are having far more success in services than they ever did in manufacturing, and they are far more internationalised. Where 85% of home-grown software firms' revenues today come from abroad, one would be hard-pressed to find any Irish manufacturer which has weaned itself off the domestic market to the same degree. The continued success of the sector, despite wage and non-wage costs rising more rapidly than in similar economies in recent years, shows that services providers are either less affected by competitiveness losses, sufficiently profitable so that they can bear tighter margins, or both. Regardless, it augurs well.

If prosperity in the 21st century turns out to be predicated on winning in the knowledge economy, as most observers believe, then the phenomenon that is the Irish internationally traded services sector suggests that, whatever bumps in the road are ahead in the short term, the country's longer-term outlook is excellent.

*Originally published in the* Sunday Business Post

———

## IRISH BUSINESS GOES GLOBAL

*3 September 2006*

CRH last week acquired APAC, an Atlanta-based road builder. The deal, valued at more than $1 billion, was the business's biggest-ever acquisition and one of a number of major cross-border takeovers by Irish firms recently. Corporate Ireland, it seems, is intent on playing its part in the global boom in mergers and acquisitions (M&A). And that boom has been spectacular. Global M&AS were valued at $2.9 trillion in 2005, a 40% increase over 2004 and close to the all-time high recorded in 2000. A new high-water mark could well be reached in 2006.

This reflects the quickening pace of corporate restructuring after a period of relative calm in the years after the dotcom boom. The shake-up is being facilitated by financing conditions that are about as good as they get: strong profitability, buoyant equity markets, still-low interest rates, and the rise and rise of innovative private equity groups. The M&A machine should continue in overdrive well into next year, and much of this takeover activity will remain international—in 2005 the value of cross-border M&AS reached an estimated US$827 billion, more than a doubling on two years earlier.

Because M&AS are corporate Ireland's main route to foreign expansion, this seems to signal that the internationalisation of the Irish firm will continue apace. Before looking at how fast that has happened in recent years, it's worth asking whether M&AS are a good way for Irish firms to globalise. Observing the almost frenzied global M&A activity over the past two years, one cannot but wonder if the lessons of the past have been unlearnt. The record of success when firms merge or are taken over is far from stellar. Too often, value for the acquiring firm is destroyed, not added to. This, say some, is because managers and shareholders can have different interests. Too often the former may be unwilling to face the slow grind of organic growth.

Acquisitions are the obvious route for impatient execs anxious to achieve rapid expansion (and lots of limelight). Whether exploitable synergies exist between acquirer and acquired is sometimes not given the prioritisation it deserves. There are other reasons many M&As fail. Big managerial egos often cannot be contained in a single business and different corporate cultures all too easily clash.

The history of Irish firms' cross-border M&As, with the (not insignificant) exception of the two big banks, has bucked international trends. The firms targeted for takeover appear in most cases to have delivered the synergies identified. Many attribute this not just to being good at picking winners, but to the manner in which the acquired businesses are brought into the fold.

The 'non-imperial' Irish management style is exemplified by CRH. Though nobody would suggest that the company is anything but a tightly-run ship, its corporate culture appears to value getting buy-in from those it buys over, rather than imposing decisions on managers in the businesses it acquires. But less alpha male behaviour by Irish managers when they go in to run firms they acquire can't explain everything, as the big banks' poor track record shows. The nature of the industries in which Irish multi-nationals predominate—food, building materials and paper—may be another reason for successes to date. Unlocking value by acquisition is likely to be easier in mature low- and medium-tech industries where change is less rapid and challenges not as multi-dimensional.

Moving from the micro to the macro, how globalised is Irish business in general? One way to measure the extent of the internationalisation of the Irish firm is by looking at data on foreign direct investment, or FDI (defined as an outflow of capital used to acquire at least a 10% stake in a foreign business). UN numbers suggest that, as recently as a decade and half ago, Ireland had developing-world levels of outward FDI. The amounts were so small that the Central Statistics Office didn't bother to count them. This changed in 1998, and we now know a lot more.

In the 1998–2005 period, the amount Irish firms invest directly abroad has gone through two distinct phases. In the four years, outward direct investment averaged around €5 billion a year. This was low by the standards of the time and relative to the size of the Irish economy. It's not hard to see why. The late 1990s saw double-digit economic growth. Making money in such conditions was easier than taking sweets from a baby. Going to the bother of entering a new market when opportunities at home abounded seemed senseless.

But when the home market cooled in the early years of the decade, Irish businesses began to eye foreign opportunities with greater interest. Since 2002 there has been a step change, and outward FDI has averaged more than €10 billion annually. Cumulatively, foreign assets directly owned by Irish residents abroad grew more than five-fold in just eight years. By the end of 2005, the total stock of Irish FDI abroad stood at 60% of GDP. This is well above the EU-15 average, if still below the top rankers in the Benelux.

And these figures are likely to understate considerably the extent of Irish firms' foreign expansions. Small countries' businesses tend to tap foreign capital markets when investing abroad. This doesn't show up in the FDI numbers. CRH's billion-euro buy last week is likely to end up being one such transaction. While the successful foreign advance of Irish business has been wonderful for the firms involved, what about the wider economy?

Any really successful multinational will necessarily see its home market sales shrink as a share of its global total. But that need not matter. If businesses keep their headquarter functions in the home base, some of the best-paid and most creative jobs will be retained. But does that happen? CRH's Dublin-based HQ operations have been hollowed out, with a mere 60 staff running the global show. This works out at less than one HQ staffer for every 1,000 people employed across the world.

There has been much talk about the denationalisation of the firm (the flip side of its internationalisation). With the appointment of Tom Hill as the first ever non-Irish head of CRH's overall American operations, could it be that the firm is readying itself to fly the small home nest?

*Originally published in the* Sunday Tribune

————

# GLOBALISATION MEANS GAINS, NOT A RACE TO THE BOTTOM

*10 January 2006*

It is a constant in life that change begets insecurity and, because Ireland is facing new sources of economic change, uncertainties about jobs and livelihoods have grown. The sources of change are well known: immigration; companies relocating to lower-cost sites; outsourcing of jobs; and intensifying competition from eastern Europe, from China and from other developing countries.

These globalising developments, it is frequently claimed, mean that high standards of protection in Ireland and other rich countries will be undercut and that governments are impotent in the face of such forces. Everyone is on a slippery slope, the argument goes, as existing rights are eroded and tax competition reduces revenues needed to fund the welfare state. No matter how plausible these arguments sound, however, the evidence globally, past and present, shows that trends in workers' rights, environmental standards and equality are rising, not heading to the bottom.

The most topical aspect of these changes in Ireland is the impact of immigration. Although the greatest challenge this presents is non-economic—some problems inevitably arise as different cultures get used to rubbing along together—there are economic aspects to the question. The most important are the effects on the rights of those in the workforce, including immigrants already established, and the effects on their wages and incomes.

Rights first. The opening of the Irish labour market in May 2004 to citizens of new EU member states was a major change. The market is still in a period of transition and, as in all such periods, opportunities for the unscrupulous to exploit the vulnerable have increased. The solution to this is straightforward: more rigorous enforcement of existing laws and, if necessary, more onerous penalties for those who flout them. Provided this happens, there is no logical reason whatever to suggest that immigration need erode standards.

The effect of immigration on wages is more mixed, in theory at least. An increase in the supply of labour will put downward pressure on pay levels. This helps maintain competitiveness (to the benefit of everyone), but some see their wages rise by less than they would otherwise have done. Even here, though, the latter effect is usually limited and temporary, and the net economic benefits of immigration are considerable over time.

Acknowledging that immigration can possibly have negative consequences does risk giving ammunition to those who viscerally oppose it, but this is not a good reason not to be fully informed of the facts. Problems rarely go away by ignoring them. In the unlikely event of a real problem arising, it would be easier to face down any bigotry by honestly facing up to the facts and dealing with them.

It is not only labour issues that proponents of the 'race to the bottom' thesis worry about. They fret that other standards will fall too, health and safety and environmental protection most notably, claiming that countries with lower standards will gain competitive advantage, forcing everyone down to their level. While this may sound plausible, worriers are unable to provide evidence that this is happening. Indeed, in Europe at least, the opposite is the case. New national and EU legislation is being enacted all the time and business believes that it is being over-regulated, not given free rein. Employers' organisations across the continent are pleading for a break from more new and ever more stringent laws and it is easy to find small firms at their wits' end struggling to implement them all.

Another claim of the pessimists is that tax competition among states will undermine governments' ability to raise revenue for social spending. Again, however plausible the assertion sounds, it is not supported by the facts. In the developed world taxes rose in the post-1945 era until the mid-1980s. Since then, tax and government spending across the entire rich world (the 30 member countries of the OECD) have remained at about that peak of 40% of GDP. Those countries that chose to tax heavily, such as the Nordics, have not been compelled to change their ways and despite much breathless talk of the supposed dominance of 'neo-liberalism', the welfare state (one of the great social achievements of the past century and more) will not wither for want of tax funding.

What of the effects of ongoing economic changes on inequality? It is asserted frequently that Ireland has become more unequal in recent times. This is bizarre given that the evidence shows the opposite. The most comprehensive, comparative and up-to-date numbers, published by the European Commission, show that between 1995 and 2001 (the most recent available data), relative income inequality in Ireland not only fell sharply, but that the narrowing was by far the greatest of any EU-15 country. The result was that by 2001, Ireland had converged on the EU inequality average. The commonly believed notion that Ireland has become more unequal is simply not supported by any robust data according to the country's leading authority on the subject, the ESRI's Prof. Brian Nolan.

While Ireland may be unusual in the magnitude of its decline in inequality, it is not in the general direction—12 of the EU-15 countries saw a narrowing of relative income inequality between 1995 and 2001. These trends should not surprise. Empirical evidence across the world over decades suggests that when countries begin to develop, relative income inequality tends to rise, but then falls. So frequently is this pattern observed that it has been named; economists call it the Kuznets Curve.

There are a number of reasons to explain this, but one is vital because it also explains why the 'race to the bottom' claim is unfounded. Universally, people seek security. As economies grow and more wealth is created, the scope for protection and welfare increases. Because it is possible and desired that standards rise, that is exactly what happens. Economic history shows that developing countries raise their standards towards rich-country levels as they advance (not vice versa), and fails to provide a single example of any country undergoing a sustained reduction in standards owing to outside economic forces. There is no 'race to the bottom'—for those who believe in progress, the direction the world is going is as heartening as it has ever been.

*Originally published in the* Irish Times

———

## IMMIGRATION'S OPPORTUNITIES AND CHALLENGES

*27 August 2006*

Immigration has been a boon for business. It has kept strong wage growth from going stratospheric, keeping firms competitive and saving those operating at the margin from going to the wall. It has also given recruiters a wider range of skills and cvs to consider when filling vacancies. Less tangibly, say some bosses in a barely audible whisper, it has given relief from demanding Irish youngsters who have absurdly high expectations and too often appear to be planning their next move even before they have put their noses to the company grindstone. This is very different from their newly arrived eastern European counterparts who are keener than mustard to muck in and seem refreshingly grateful for the opportunity to toil.

The story across the water in Britain is similar. Although arrivals of eager European youths have, in proportionate terms, been only a fraction of the influx into Ireland, the benefits for employers in that country have been broadly similar. It would seem curious, then, that IBEC's UK equivalent, the Confederation of British Industry, recently suggested a 'pause' in immigration. Does this make sense and should Irish employers pay heed to the call?

The proximate cause of British business's intervention was the imminent decision on whether to extend to Bulgarians and Romanians the freedom to work in the UK once the two aspiring members of the EU join some time over the next 18 months (governments in the 25 member states are to give the pair a hard accession date in October ). The CBI says that the net economic gains to the British economy of recent immigration are big (something no serious analyst contests), but that the costs in the future may outweigh the gains, particularly if the jobs market doesn't soak up a second big wave.

A careful balance in the discussion is necessary so that the serious consequences and implications can be explored, but without fuelling reactionary sentiment. There are multiple aspects to the immigration question, but space permits discussion of just two today. The first is the impact of inflows of workers on the position of the Irish economy on the value chain. Some straightforward economics is needed to do this.

The three basic inputs to any business are land, labour and capital, which economists call the 'factors of production'. Business people decide what mix of these to use in their operations depending on the price of each relative to the others. An increase in the supply of cheap labour tends to cause a fall in its relative price. This makes businesses more inclined to take on extra workers and less inclined to spend on plant and machinery. If this happens (and, it must be stressed, there is no evidence that it has in Ireland) it would logically make the average Irish company more labour intensive and less capital intensive.

As people's wealth in an economy ultimately depends on the amount of capital each person employed has to work with, any development that causes the stock of capital to grow less strongly is not necessarily a good thing. Indeed, in today's global economy it is probably bad, not least because it would increase exposure to labour intensive economies, like China, which are ultra-competitive.

The second issue worth pondering are the costs associated with immigration. Again, considering the matter from an economist's 'factors of production' perspective is helpful. While the free movement of these factors is generally good, it can have damaging consequences. This was, for example, to be seen in the 1990s when large amounts of capital flooded into many emerging markets, creating unsustainable booms. Crises in Mexico, across Asia and in Russia between 1995 and 1998 caused a major rethink among economists about the downsides of freely moving capital.

In the case of labour movements, there is a theoretical point where the costs of immigration in terms of congestion, strains on social services and higher property price inflation offset the many gains. But because many of these costs are not measured in Ireland, they are impossible to quantify. It would seem prudent to encourage more data collection on these costs because the accession of Bulgaria and Romania has the potential to see considerably more immigration.

What sort of numbers could be involved? Although it is impossible to predict accurately, some basic facts help to illuminate. The combined population of the two countries is 30 million. This compares with 75 million in the 10 member states who joined in 2004. The absolute potential for inflows is, therefore, smaller. However, the attraction of relocating for these 30 million is considerably greater than for their 75 million neighbours already in the EU because income differentials are much greater. GDP per head in Bulgaria in 2004 was US$3,100 and US$3,385 in Romania, but over US$9,000 in the accession 10.

The rapid multi-ethnicisation of Ireland has unsettled many who are change-averse, and politicians of all hues warn privately that passive disgruntlement expressed on doorsteps could become more active and a lot nastier if the spectre of joblessness were to return. But it may not even take such an unpleasant occurrence, as has happened recently in the Netherlands independently of economic developments. Although it would be wrong to extend the parallel too far (Poles are reCatholicising Ireland, while Muslim immigrants to the Netherlands are Islamising parts of that country) it would be unwise to assume that social tensions could not become a reality in Ireland in the future.

Business needs to be mindful of a backlash. If anti-immigration sentiment were to rise and become more focused on individual immigrants, this would be bad for everyone, not least Human Resources departments trying to manage already very mixed workplaces.

*Originally published in the* Sunday Tribune

————

## HOUSEHOLD DEBT EXPOSES ECONOMY TO REAL RISK

*24 December 2006*

For a decade and more, each year-end has seen the Irish economy notch up new records. The regularity is almost monotonous. And yet again, as 2006 draws to a close, there are fresh successes to celebrate and new milestones to mark. This year economic growth will again outpace all other EU-15 countries (for the tenth time in a dozen years). The jobs count surged across the two-million threshold. And new foreign investment continues to flow—more projects with greater high-tech content were secured over the last dozen months than in any recent year, according to the IDA.

But not all developments have been so positive. Export growth rates continued to lag behind European and world averages. As a result,

Ireland's global market share fell further from the high registered at the beginning of the decade. Also, the deficit on the current account of the balance of payments is almost certain to reach a 20-year peak. Perhaps the most worrying trend has been the relentless rise in personal indebtedness, which will be recorded as yet another high-water mark in this year's annual figures. Why has this happened, how does Ireland compare with its peers and what are the risks involved?

The OECD's recently released report on the world economy offers some answers. Surveying the 15 of its member countries for which data are available, it finds that, across the rich world, households almost everywhere have been gearing up—in most cases by very large amounts—since the 1980s. Two factors account for this change: lower interest rates and easier access to financing—and these changes have been self-perpetuating. With too much money chasing too few assets, prices of property, bonds and shares have risen sharply. This has pushed even those who are reluctant to borrow to take on more debt.

In Ireland, over the past decade, these trends have been amplified by the change in interest rate expectations that came with adopting the euro and much greater confidence owing to the protracted boom. But two seemingly contradictory things make Ireland stand out from the OECD crowd. On the one hand, borrowers have exposed themselves to interest rate fluctuations to an extent unmatched by any other country; on the other, they have been exceptionally prudent in taking on debt for purposes other than home-buying.

To see how exposed Ireland is to higher rates one needs to consider total debt levels and the proportion of these borrowings subject to variable rate servicing. On the first, Ireland is among the most indebted nations on Earth. Of the 15 rich countries surveyed by the OECD, debt as a percentage of national income ranged from just 40% in Italy to 120% in the Netherlands and Denmark. Ireland's household debt level is at the high end of that spectrum, standing close to 100% of GNP.

High debt levels always give cause for concern because they increase any economy's vulnerability to adverse changes in economic conditions. Ireland is clearly exposed in this regard. It is made more vulnerable by the persistence of variable rate borrowing, which accounts for around 85% of outstanding loans. This is exceptional. Of the highly indebted countries, only Australia comes close to such exposure, with just over 70% of servicing costs subject to fluctuation. The Danes and Dutch may be more indebted, but they are far less exposed to changes in rates—a mere 15% of their loans are variable.

But this should not distract from the bigger picture. As is the case in almost all developed countries, total debt is high and rising. Among other things, this has led to questions about the direction of change in the financial services industry being asked anew. Liberalisation and greater competition have increased the number, range and sophistication of financing products, making it far easier for more people to access credit. This has been a boon for everyone—most of all for would-be borrowers with dubious credit histories. In stuffier, more risk-averse times, they would quickly have been shown the door by bank managers.

But this process could have made entire financial systems too fragile. All eyes are now on the US, where the economy is turning down. A steady increase in American house prices and construction activity since the beginning of the decade came to an abrupt end in the first half of 2006. The housing market went over a cliff. Prices are now falling and housing starts are collapsing. Rates of mortgage delinquency are rising, particularly among those who would not have had access to credit in the past. Larger numbers are falling behind in their repayments. Mortgage businesses have begun to fail.

How the storm is weathered in 2007 is likely to have a major impact on how changes in the financial services industry in recent decades are assessed. It will also have much relevance for Ireland. Quite apart from US recession being the biggest near term risk for the Irish economy, the collapse of the American property market would suggest that other economies are vulnerable to similar corrections. Thankfully, the interest rate cycle in the euro area is close to its peak. Although rates are set to rise further in the new year, a jump of the magnitude seen in the US in recent years is not on the cards. The era of cheap money appears set to continue for the foreseeable future.

But Irish borrowers will have to service their large debts far beyond the foreseeable future. It may be only if and when rates do rise above the historically low levels of the past decade that the long-term consequences of Ireland's descent into debt will become apparent.

*Originally published in the* Sunday Business Post

———

## FISCAL INEPTITUDE CARRIES COSTS

*13 August 2006*

Staff at the International Monetary Fund called this week for a tightening up of Irish government spending in the near term. This was good economics and an astute judgment of local politics. Think back to the last time voters went to the polls. In the two years running up to the 2002 election, Ireland's fiscal position deteriorated more rapidly than that of any other euro zone country in the past decade; but once the votes were counted, the brakes had to be slammed on to prevent a rapid descent into deficit. Operating fiscal policy in this manner is doubly bad. Jerky spending patterns are inherently inefficient, playing havoc with departmental planning and generating all manner of additional costs. Worse still, economic growth and stability are put at risk. If loss of fiscal control in the run-up to the last election had coincided with an economic slump, as happened in the late 1970s, the result could have been a 1980s-like depression. And there was a real risk of that happening. In the early years of the decade, the world economy suffered a sharp downturn. Had it been tipped into recession by the shocks at the time—the bursting of the dotcom bubble in March 2000 or terrorist attacks in the US 18 months later—the unusually open Irish economy would have been sent reeling.

The risks are, if anything, greater now. Internationally, currency misalignments, large current-account imbalances, asset price bubbles and high oil prices are just some of the causes for concern. At home, near-term risk is centred on the property market and mortgage indebtedness. Given the number and magnitude of economic threats, this is no time to play politics with the public finances. The government got away with it the last time: for everyone's sake, it is to be hoped it does not tempt fate again.

The government should also pay heed to the IMF's umpteenth call for the modernisation of the archaic budgetary process. To do so would kill two birds with one stone: it would make the fiscal framework better able to cushion the economy in the event of a shock, and cut down on the great deal of taxpayers' money that is wasted. Though some efforts are being made to remedy structural failures, the McCreevy Rule—'If I have it, I'll spend it'—remains the government's organising principle for the public finances. Brian Cowen has shown little sign of applying greater rigour to taking care of taxpayers' money.

It's not hard to see why. Moving towards international best practice in managing the public finances means that ministers relinquish some power, either by sharing it with others or placing constraints on their own freedom of manoeuvre, so that the temptation to use taxpayers' money for short-term political gain is circumscribed. Forgoing control is not something any politician does lightly. But, in recent times, governments internationally have moved in this direction because the costs of bad economic management have become too obvious to ignore. Although no country has created a fiscal equivalent of an independent monetary authority, most euro zone countries give an important role to independent institutions outside finance and economics ministries. Academic think tanks have been mandated by law to carry out some of the functions traditionally carried out by finance ministries—usually without transparency. Dull as it sounds, this includes: generating macroeconomic baselines for budgets; providing revenue and expenditure forecasts; analysing and evaluating policy and spending programmes; and making recommendations on the maintenance of fiscal stability in the short, medium and long terms.

In Ireland, the Department of Finance, operating in splendid isolation, is tasked with doing all of these things, despite being under-resourced. Even if its political masters wished, it would not be in a position to carry out the full range of finance ministry functions effectively. Most worryingly for taxpayers, it is far from having the capacity to conduct ongoing and rigorous evaluation of all spending lines, which would save so much money now wasted. Structural changes to how taxpayers' money is managed could be accelerated by adopting international best practice and outsourcing a chunk of the work that Finance cannot do effectively to an independent institution.

The Economic and Social Research Institute (ESRI) is an obvious candidate to do much of that. It is chock-a-block with brainy economists and has a fully fledged economic forecasting capacity. Outsourcing Finance functions would free up department officials to develop greater expertise, introduce greater transparency and add credibility to the entire process—allowing business to be more certain about the fiscal future and, thus, more willing to invest.

Alas, there is no sign of Brian Cowen planning to do as nearly every other European country does. Nor is he showing greater enthusiasm for leading the reform process than his predecessor. Worse still, there are some indications that we're slipping back. One of the few areas where best practice has been the norm—because of external pressure—is the planning and evaluation of capital spending. As Ireland got billions from Brussels, Eurocrats insisted on proper analysis and evaluation before, during and after expenditure. The hope was that these good habits would spread to current spending, but now that Ireland relies far less on EU cash and finger-wagging Eurocrats impose less discipline, bad habits seem to be creeping back in capital spending. Two recent government plans with major capital spending implications, decentralisation and Transport 21, don't appear to have been subject to the sort of scrutiny that would accompany best practice.

Modernising the management of the public finances is urgently needed. Other small countries in Europe facing problems of limited resources have shown the way. Ireland should follow.

*Originally published in the* Sunday Tribune

———

## TANKER-LIKE SHIP OF PUBLIC FINANCES HEADING FOR THE ROCKS

*10 July 2008*

Since it became clear that the property-fuelled boom would not end with a soft landing, the conventional wisdom has been that the government should not curb public spending excessively, even if this means breaking EU budget rules. The conventional wisdom would be correct if the public finances had been managed conventionally before the bubble burst. Unfortunately they were not.

The results of this mismanagement are to be seen in the government's own numbers. Following a massive recent revision, the Department of Finance now expects a general government deficit of nearly 3% of gross domestic product (GDP) this year, having enjoyed a surplus of a similar magnitude as recently as 2006. This six percentage point deterioration amounts to the most rapid two-year decline of any euro area country at any time since the single currency was launched.

Bad and all as the official figures are, they understate the gravity of the position. To achieve the new target, general government revenues in 2008 would have to remain at last year's levels. Given a rapid and accelerating decline in tax revenues in the first half of 2008, this would require a miracle in the next six months. In 2009, even assuming no further reductions in revenues and a curbing of the rate of expenditure growth, the deficit is set to rise towards 6% of GDP or above. Such a scenario is the most likely outcome given the nature and composition of the economy's slowdown;

trends and dynamics in expenditure growth, tax revenues and debt servicing; and the government's repeated commitment to maintain budgeted investment spending come what may.

The two most important pillars of the domestic economy—consumer and investment spending—accounted for three quarters of GDP last year. The latter is now contracting even more rapidly than in any year during the benighted 1980s and forward-looking indicators, such as new housing starts, point to continued collapse. The former is flat-lining as the factors that influence it—employment, wages, asset values (including both homes and equities), inflation and interest rates—all move in the wrong direction. In 2009 private consumption spending is more likely to shrink than to expand. These developments augur awfully for tax revenues.

On the other side of the ledger, the immediate outlook is marginally better, if only because the room for manoeuvre is greater. But even with the belated evasive action now being taken by the government to control expenditure, curbing its rate of growth will be difficult given existing commitments, rising welfare costs and the slow pace of steering the tanker-like ship of state spending.

A further double-headed risk to the public finances comes from the rising cost of servicing a low-but-rising government debt. The recent upward movement in interest rates on most government bonds reflects rising inflation expectations. If fears of higher global inflation come to pass, this trend will accelerate. Making matters worse for Ireland has been a re-pricing of risk by those who invest in government bonds. As recently as last year, investors considered Irish government debt to be as risk-free as any in the euro area. In 2008 investors have been demanding a premium to take on and hold Irish public debt that is closer to the one demanded of Italy, a perennial fiscal basket case, than to rectitudinous Germany. Worse still, if this trend in the bond market continues, a larger Irish deficit will widen premia even further, introducing a self-reinforcing negative dynamic into an already deteriorating fiscal position (having suffered so badly from just such a dynamic within living memory, it is hard to believe that any government has allowed even the possibility of such a scenario to re-emerge).

Given all these factors in combination, the budget deficit is now crashing through the 3% of GDP limit to which the government is officially committed and in 2009 looks set to approximate the largest deficits of any country during the euro era. But the reaction of other EU countries can be expected to be different to Ireland's breach of budget rules. In the cases of Greece and Portugal, new governments inherited these deficits. They blamed their predecessors for past profligacy and were given the benefit of the doubt by their euro area partners.

Brian Lenihan will not be able to pass the buck to a previous administration when Ireland is scrutinised by its partners. Moreover, when the other euro area countries analyse the reasons for Ireland's precipitous move into the red, it will be obvious that its cause was not global economic conditions or some other misfortune, but mismanagement of spending, revenues and the wider budgeting process. The most cursory glance at spending patterns over the past decade shows how big the impact of the electoral cycle is. While most governments loosen the purse strings as elections approach, pre-election spending growth in Ireland before the 2002 and 2007 contests was spectacular. The surge in spending before the last election explains a large part of how an unusually big surplus in 2006 had all but evaporated in just 12 months.

On the revenue side, the government appears to have believed the sophists on property market 'fundementals'. Instead of firewalling windfall revenues from property-related taxes (for instance, by putting them into the national pension fund), it acted as if these revenues would continue to flow into the Exchequer's coffers, and increased spending accordingly. This was imprudent, if not reckless. The government is also culpable for its inaction on reforming basic budgeting processes. Rather than using the policy space provided by the boom years to adopt best practices, successive finance ministers provided little leadership. Existing-level-of-service budgeting is antediluvian, but remains the allocation method of choice in the Department of Finance. Rigorous evaluation of all spending programmes, both before and after implementation, is increasingly the norm in EU countries, but is far from standard practice in Merrion Street.

The one extenuating circumstance Brian Lenihan will be able to plead when the excessive deficit procedure against Ireland is initiated will be the very sharp decline in economic growth. This will earn him breathing space. But as the margin by which Ireland breaks the rules becomes clear, scrutiny of the public finances will increase. As the government is so demonstrably the author of its own fiscal misfortune, forbearance will dwindle fast.

To plead for special treatment for breaching fiscal rules by a wide margin without having another administration to blame will create an unprecedented situation in the euro area. In order to protect the (already-strained) credibility of these rules, the other member countries will feel pressured to subject Ireland to the full rigour of the rules. Given the government's mismanagement of the public finances, they are unlikely to have much sympathy for Lenihan's plight, and those who resent Irish voters' rejection of the Lisbon treaty may be tempted to throw the book at him.

The government has got itself into an appalling position. The choice it is now facing is between worsening the economic downturn by slamming the brakes on public spending, and risking what could be the most serious clash among euro area members since the currency was launched. The awfulness of the former scenario needs no elucidation; the seriousness of the latter is made graver still now that Ireland's very participation in the EU is at risk following the rejection of the Lisbon treaty.

*Originally published in the* Irish Times

———

## BANK GUARANTEE: RADICAL PROBLEM, RIGHT SOLUTION

*5 October 2008*

These are extraordinary times. In such times, extraordinary measures can become necessary. In extremis, they can then become unavoidable. Government action last week to prevent economic catastrophe was one such occasion. The reason for the government's decision to backstop banks' liabilities is simple. The financial system is to the economy what the cardiovascular system is to the human body. When blood ceases to oxygenate cells, vital functions shut down quickly; when money ceases to flow to households and companies, economic activity comes to a halt.

By last Monday evening, it had become clear that the financial system was on the brink of failing. The banks' share prices were in freefall and their deposit bases were being depleted. These developments came on top of extreme difficulties in obtaining short-term market funding, owing to an all-pervasive fear running throughout the international financial system. The result was a chronic liquidity crisis. Radical action had to be taken. Of the available options, the government correctly chose a blanket guarantee of the liabilities of the main credit institutions.

This action has self-evidently achieved its primary objective—saving the financial system from imminent collapse and restoring something approaching normality in that system's functioning. This is far more than other countries' governments have achieved with ad hoc measures on a bank-by-bank basis. It has also dispelled much of the irrational fear that was having detrimental economic effects well beyond the financial system. All this was achieved at no cost to taxpayers (indeed, the proposed charging of banks for such comprehensive underwriting will, in theory, see a net gain to the Exchequer). This is in contrast to the situation in Belgium, Denmark, France, Germany, Iceland, Luxembourg, the Netherlands, Britain and the US, where banks have been nationalised, either de jure or de facto, with taxpayers being handed the tab.

What about the argument that taxpayers will ultimately have to pay via higher debt servicing costs on government borrowing? This argument is wrong, as proved by the reaction of the bond market. Over the course of last week, there were no unusual movements in the yield spread—the difference between Irish government bond yields and those of the German equivalent, which performs a benchmark function owing to its perceived risklessness.

At first glance, this might appear strange. If, at the stroke of a pen, a government exposes itself to the risk of massive additions to its national debt, many of those holding existing debt could be expected to offload it quickly (default risk rises in line with the amount of debt).The result of a large-scale exit from such debt instruments is an immediate widening of the yield spread. The reason that this did not happen last Tuesday was that bond holders had already priced in this risk. As the banking system is too important to fail in any country, it is implicitly understood that a bailout will take place if banks fail. What happened last Tuesday was the making explicit of a guarantee that was already implicitly understood. The reaction of the credit ratings agencies, which reaffirmed Ireland's triple A sovereign debt rating, offers further proof that this is exactly what happened.

What about the other options available to the government? The only alternative was for the nationalisation—in one form or another—of one or more of the banks. Such a step would have been wrong, for three reasons. First, taking control of one institution would not have stopped the rot, given the overall fragility of the Irish system now. The spectacle of one bank after another being nationalised, with all the messiness that such action entails, would have generated far more uncertainty than guaranteeing liabilities. That would have undermined the confidence that remains in the economy.

The second reason is that nationalisation, and subsequent restructuring, would almost certainly have had a strong negative effect on bank lending. It is often overlooked that, despite the credit crisis internationally, lending has held up well. Between August this year and last, Irish banks expanded their aggregate loan book by 12.3%. The last thing the real economy needs now is to have financing conditions tighten for companies and house-holds.

The final, and most important, reason to avoid nationalisation is that it is far from clear that such a step was necessary, given that the immediate crisis was one of liquidity, not solvency. The takeover of a bank, and the real costs involved for taxpayers, is a last resort and only appropriate in the case of insolvency—i.e. when a bank's balance sheet has been so badly impaired that it cannot heal itself. Asset quality is central to solvency. In the case of the Irish banks, their assets are mostly in one basket, that of residential and commercial property. It should be stated clearly that Irish banks are not now insolvent because of their low levels of non-performing loans to date. But it should also be stated, even more emphatically, that the rate of non-performing loans will rise very sharply as more people lose their livelihoods and the price of property falls further. It is easy to envisage systemic insolvency within 12–18 months. If that does happen, the govern-ment would have little choice but to exercise its option of last resort. But by doing what it did last Tuesday, it not only relieved pressure on the banks and calmed fears, but also gave itself time to plan for a worst-case scenario, as well as strengthening its hand in dealing with the banks in the difficult months ahead.

The latter is particularly important. The cognitive failure of bankers to accept approaching insolvency is a recognised phenomenon in banking crises, as is the impeding of regulators during the denial phase. Now the banks are in no position to refuse anything to civil servants. The government needs only to hint at removing the blanket guarantee of liabilities and the money men will quickly acquiesce. Forcing one or two of the most senior of them to stand down immediately would also be an effective way of signalling to the rest the seriousness of the government's intent.

If officials do conclude that one or more of the banks is heading for insolvency, they will surely move quickly to put them out of their misery and avoid the problem of 'zombie banks' that blighted Japan for so long. To do so would be relatively straightforward, if costly. Indeed, so frequently have property busts led to banking crises that there is some-thing akin to a users' manual containing the 'dos' and 'don'ts' of sorting them out. Conveniently, two economists at the IMF updated this manual just last month. Brian Lenihan should ensure that all senior officials keep a copy on their desks for the next year. If the US government can dampen the crisis at its epicentre, if euro zone interest rates come down and if increases in Irish unemployment can be contained, there is a good chance that the banks can survive. Much is at stake and nothing is inevitable.

*Originally published in the* Sunday Business Post

------

# ICELAND'S BANKING COLLAPSE PROVIDES A CHILLING WARNING

*12 October 2008*

'There are decades when nothing happens, and there are weeks when decades happen.' We are now living one of the decades-in-weeks moments that Lenin described almost 100 years ago. And although the end of market capitalism is not nigh, as he envisaged, the economic wellbeing of the world is now at real risk. Many astonishing things happened last week, of which six stand out. The British retail banking system was partly nationalised. Central banks across the world cut interest rates by 50 basis points despite still-high inflation. The European Central Bank abandoned its market mechanism for providing liquidity, guaranteeing open-ended and much cheaper short-term lending to banks. The US central bank moved to bypass the entire private financial system to lend directly to companies. The IMF went into full battle mode. And Iceland's economy sank into the north Atlantic.

Iceland's fate demonstrates just how grave this crisis is. The other developments show the degree to which policy-makers are ratcheting up their response. All have relevance for Ireland. But before looking at our country's situation, it is worth considering briefly how the world got to the awful place it in is today. In August 2007, the world's complex financial market mechanism saw its normal oiling process dry up. This was because of fear and uncertainty about who held US-originated, mortgage-backed assets. These had fallen in value but, because there was no clearing house in which to trade them, they could not be priced. The valuation problem was compounded by a lack of information about who held the assets and in what quantity.

For the real economy, however, these developments had almost no impact because central banks stepped in to keep the mechanism oiled. The credit system thus continued, largely unhindered, to do its main job: channelling money from those who have it but don't need it to those who need it but don't have it. Credit data in Europe and the US show this clearly. But because the mechanism continued to work, complacency set in among financial institutions and market participants, politicians and policy-makers. In hindsight, not nearly enough was done to deal with the underlying problems when conditions were still tolerable.

The 'phony crisis' ended last month and a very real crisis emerged with a vengeance. Again, in hindsight, there is now near universal agreement that allowing the investment bank Lehman Brothers to fail was an enormous error. Institutions with links to it were exposed. Fear surged, spilling out of credit markets and cascading into other parts of the system, including stock markets. As fear levels rose, banks just keeping their heads above water were engulfed. The sight of lifeless institutions caused fear to spread, flooding out of the financial markets into public consciousness. The guy in the street—unsure and afraid—began withdrawing deposits. Although there are few numbers yet, every sign suggests that the real economy is now being hit hard. This is creating a cycle of such viciousness that not even multi-billion-dollar government-backed schemes have been able to halt the slide.

Of these schemes, the most wide-ranging yet put forward is that of the British government. At the time of writing, there remained considerable uncertainty about aspects of the plan, unveiled last Tuesday morning, but at its core is the strengthening of the capital bases of the main retail banks. Why did Britain choose this route, instead of, say, the Irish method of guaranteeing liabilities? One can only speculate on the likely reasons. The first is the immediacy of its banks' bad debt problem. The IMF estimates there are $1.4 trillion in losses associated with the US mortgage market. These are spread far beyond its borders. Although it is not certain who holds what, write-downs to date suggest that the more 'sophisticated' a country's financial system, the more mired it is in the US mess. Given the British financial system is second only to that of the US in its sophistication, exposure is almost certainly greater than in any other large European country. Combined with the darkening picture for the domestic property market, it became clear that the banks were already insolvent, or would be so soon. This favoured recapitalisation. The second reason Britain may have eschewed the Irish approach is the problem of regulation. Given the sophistication of its system, the gap between the regulated and regulators is huge. Systems such as those of Britain and the US are too complex to be regulated effectively in their current form. If market participants were given blanket cover, they could not be stopped from abusing it, and doing so on a massive scale.

But what of the Irish government's decision? With the British move, we have near-laboratory conditions to test the relative efficacy of the two approaches. The broad thrust of the British approach has been advocated for Ireland by a number of academics. UCD's Colm McCarthy made the case for immediate recapitalisation in these pages last week. I made the case for liability guarantees. In revisiting the issue, I have no wish to attempt to score cheap debating points. We are all flying at least partially blind and McCarthy and his associates in Belfield may ultimately be correct. But I believe the move, which was only the end of the beginning of the crisis, still looks like the best available option at this time.

One reason is confidence, or rather its absence, and the prevalence of fear. Opinion polls in Ireland showed support for the government's move. This is likely to reflect a lowering of fear levels. In Britain, by contrast, the public reaction to Alistair Darling's bailout appears muted at best, because it lacks the virtue of (relative) simplicity and entails a multibillion upfront cost to taxpayers. That cost to the taxpayers is the second reason I believe the Irish option was more appropriate. In Britain, billions of pounds will be infused into banks. But even this looks inadequate. The plan's objective is to tempt private capital to follow public capital onto banks' balance sheets. There is no chance of this happening now. It increasingly appears that there is no halfway house under current conditions, and that full nationalisation is the only option if public capital is deemed necessary. In the meantime, Irish taxpayers continue to avoid any costs, as evinced again last week in the bond market, where the yield spread is behaving identically to that in peer countries.

Finally, the British plan does not appear to have made banks more willing to lend to each other, as evidenced by the record-high level of the London Interbank Rate (Libor) up to Friday. In Ireland, short-term funding conditions appeared to ease after 30 September, according to anecdotal evidence (an equivalent measure of conditions in individual euro countries is not available).

An issue on which there is no disagreement is that we are now merely beginning a healing process, and realities must be faced if this process is to succeed. In so doing, Goethe's wise counsel—to beware those whose desire to punish is strong—should be at the forefront of minds. There is a whiff of the mob in incitement against bankers.

Far too many things are in short supply. Blame is not one of them. This crisis is not the fault only of bankers, and the rush to judge and calls for punishment are unhelpful. That said, if any banker attempts to delay or hinder the healing process, he must pay the price—and be seen to pay the price. It does not augur well that the individual in Irish Nationwide who used the liabilities guarantee as advertising copy in an e-mail designed to attract deposits is still in his job.

*Originally published in the* Sunday Business Post

———

# TRADE STANCE IGNORES IRELAND'S NEW ECONOMY

*18 December 2005*

Ireland is one of the greatest trading nations in the world. Last year, goods and services exports were worth €120 billion, more than €30,000 for every man, woman and child in the country. What's more, almost all foreign sales were high-tech manufactures and sophisticated services, the sort of export profile about which policy-makers in most other countries dream. Because Ireland sells so much to the rest of the world, it will benefit disproportionately if ongoing international talks for freer trade succeed, but stands to lose most if they fail.

Despite this clear and vital national interest, the Irish delegation to the biennial ministerial meeting of the World Trade Organisation (WTO) in Hong Kong last week was on a wrecking mission. At the heart of the issue is the EU's Common Agricultural Policy (CAP), which protects Europe's farmers from poor countries' cheaper food. The developing world is demanding that the CAP be made less unfair. If Europe doesn't agree, four years of negotiations will probably collapse. This, it should be noted, is an entirely separate issue from Britain's ham-fisted attempts to change the CAP in its own narrow budgetary interests. Failure of the WTO talks would not be unwelcome in EU countries with big farming sectors and uncompetitive goods producers and service providers.

Ireland was just such an economy two decades ago, but not today. While its modern industries are world-class, farming has been undergoing irreversible long-term decline. It is now become economically insignificant. But listening to Ireland's representatives in Brussels, Geneva (home of the WTO) and at other international forums, you would be forgiven for thinking that the country was still a closed inward-looking agrarian economy for which international trade mattered little, if at all. No other EU country takes a more negative position on making the concessions demanded by poor countries that would allow the talks to succeed. A myopic obsession with holding onto farmers' handouts from Brussels, at the expense of the dynamic export sector upon which everyone's future prosperity depends, heavily influences the government's position.

This gross mis-prioritisation is reflected in the composition of the official delegation to Hong Kong. Micheál Martin—the minister responsible for trade—did not attend, unlike most of his 148 WTO counterparts. The ranking minister at the talks, Mary Coughlan, representing the Department of Agriculture, led the 'no surrender' line on farmers' subsidies, regardless of the consequences. So how does the government justify sacrificing the country's wider economic interests for the sake of a small and shrinking interest group?

Its defence of the indefensible is based on three arguments, each as specious as the other. First, it is said that security of food supply must remain a priority in an uncertain world. This is a valid argument in theory, but not in practice, because Europe and Ireland are more than self-sufficient in food, and can remain self-sufficient, even if they make further concessions on the CAP. Simply put, being fairer to the developing world has no security implications for Europe.

Second, the CAP is supposed to ensure food is safe for consumers. If anything, it does the opposite. National agriculture ministries, instead of focusing on regulating the sector, become its champion in Brussels to maximise subsidies. An unhealthily cosy relationship develops between regulator and regulated. Ireland is no exception (the Department of Agriculture does the IFA's bidding so effectively that it is sometimes jokingly referred to as the IFA's Kildare Street branch). The failure of the CAP to guarantee food safety is evinced by the world's worst food safety fiasco in recent times, namely BSE, or mad cow disease. It originated in Europe. It has been largely confined to that continent. Reflecting this, its human form, vCJD, has killed mainly Europeans and only a handful of non-Europeans have died the appalling death associated with the disease. So much for the CAP guaranteeing safe food.

The third line of defence is that, even if farming itself now accounts for just 3% of Ireland's national income, the food processing sector, which is more important than farming in terms of jobs and wealth creation, will be threatened by CAP reform. The government maintains this fiction even though its own advisory agency has found differently. Forfás prepared a detailed study of the implications of the current trade round for Ireland in 2003. It said that high value-added sub-sectors in the food processing industry (those, incidentally, where Ireland can sustain competitive advantage in the long term) would actually benefit because lower input costs would allow them to compete more effectively outside Europe.

These three arguments are a smoke screen. The reality behind the government's position on CAP reform and the WTO trade round is that it will not show the leadership required to face down a vociferous interest group. This not only damages the economy, it undermines Ireland's position in Europe. It alienates the country's natural allies—Europe's other successful free-traders—and adds to their sense that Ireland is a free rider happy to pocket subsidies but unwilling to stand up and be counted on matters of principle. Although far less justifiably, other countries already feel this about Ireland's ultra-low corporation tax. For a small country with an open economy, free riding is not a sensible long-term strategy. Ireland's stance should reflect its real interests, and complement its half-billion-a-year aid efforts in the developing world. Farmers can and should be helped, but in ways that do not work against the interests of the wider economy. A change in trade policy is long overdue.

*Originally published in the* Sunday Business Post

———

## REGULATION—THE GOOD AND THE BAD

*23 July 2006*

Talk to businessfolk anywhere about their problems and it won't be long before they tell of their frustrations at the seemingly unending barrage of new regulations that rain down on them. Those who tear most hair out are owner-managers of small firms who, because of limited resources, complain of spending as much time untangling themselves from red tape as they do growing their businesses.

There are good reasons for these frustrations. In Europe, and to a lesser extend globally, three big regulatory trends are at play. Two of these add to the burden for businesses; the third partially mitigates the effects of the first two. Perhaps most burdensome has been the increase in environmental protection legislation as concerns about the planet's well-being have moved up the political agenda. No one would argue that these are unnecessary and some ideas are eminently sensible (carbon taxes, which price in the full economic cost of production of goods and services, are one example), but whether green laws are justified or not, they make life more difficult for firms.

Additional health and safety legislation is the second major source of new rules. In a world that is becoming increasingly risk averse it sometimes appears as if there is an effort to legislate away every danger that life throws up. Again, because it is hard to argue against more stringent rules to prevent accidents and the like, business lobbyists are left fighting rearguard actions to prevent the wilder (and costlier) ideas making it into law.

The third big trend in regulation offsets, partially at least, the first two. As concerns have grown about competitiveness in an increasingly economically integrated world, politicians and policy-makers have been compelled to think longer and harder about how their actions can hobble wealth creators. As a result, governments almost everywhere have become more business-friendly and, with the exception of the areas mentioned above, deregulation has helped make life easier and cheaper for companies operating in competitive markets. Against this backdrop, how does Ireland compare with its competitors when it comes to regulation?

The Republic has a reputation for light-touch regulation. But this is far from fully deserved. While it is true that the Irish system does not rush to regulate, it is also very slow to deregulate in the areas where cutting controls is needed. Positively, the Irish system displays neither the meddling instincts of statist Europeans, mostly in the southern part of the continent, nor the excessive officiousness of those who are rules-obsessed, mainly to be found further north. The Irish labour market illustrates the first point well. The biggest political/economic issue facing many countries today is weak job creation and, consequently, high unemployment. This is caused largely by the accumulation of excessive labour regulation that has reduced firms' ability and willingness to take on staff. Ireland has avoided this mistake. The Irish economy has created massive employment and most agree that the balance between the rights of employers and workers is generally fair.

With at least half of all new legislation effecting business enacted at EU level, how governments 'transpose' (in eurojargon) these laws onto national statute books is important. Overzealous bureaucrats in national capitals sometimes go beyond what was envisaged in Brussels to 'gold-plate' EU legislation, making the rules even more burdensome. Irish civil servants have, generally, resisted this temptation. But while Ireland has been cautious in heaping new rules on business, its big weakness remains its failure to clear away existing regulations that have become obviously obsolete (if they were ever a good idea in the first place).

The latest OECD report in Ireland, published last February, showed that progress in the five years since the government committed itself to a programme of deregulation has been pitifully slow. Efforts to remove antediluvian controls in the electricity and gas markets, which would cut costs for all firms, have gone nowhere and walls of rules continue to protect a range of professional services sectors to the detriment of everyone else.

A further weakness in the Irish system, which reflects slow reaction times and not inconsiderable inertia, is how Ireland lags in adopting international best practice. The lack of impetus to screen systematically all new legislation, with a view to cutting out elements that undermine competitiveness, is a case in point. 'Regulatory Impact Assessment' (RIA) is all the rage, and internationally, the Netherlands is recognised as being at the cutting edge. But despite having a good model to work towards, Ireland has moved slowly. The government's 'Better Regulation Forum' is peopled more by those who draw up regulations (civil servants) than by those who are on their sharp end, and only a fraction of new bills are scrutinised for their impact on businesses.

Thankfully, the negative effects of the sluggishness in putting proper RIA structures in place is lessened, to some extent at least, by a unique feature of the Irish system—officials' awareness of just how important foreign investment is for the country's prosperity. The imperative of attracting and keeping foreign firms has soaked deep into every nook and cranny of the apparatus of the state in a way that is not to be observed elsewhere. This has made policy-makers across the system alive to the dangers of making the business environment less attractive. And just in case functionaries forget this for a moment, the IDA hovers omnipresently to let others in the system know if what they propose might make its investment-luring job harder.

In many ways the strengths and weaknesses of the Irish approach to regulation are two sides of the same coin. Caution and conservatism serve to prevent nuttier proposals making it into law, but they also hinder good ideas from being implemented quickly and efficiently. Given this weakness, it is all the more necessary that political leaders provide the impetus for change from the top.

*Originally published in the* Sunday Tribune

## WHY PRIVATISATION OF AER LINGUS IS THE WRONG MOVE

*July 2006*

International experience of privatisation, the failings of employee share ownership plans (ESOPs) and the evolving structure of the aviation industry are just some of the factors that complicate decision-making on Aer Lingus's future. But when all are weighed up, it is hard to avoid the conclusion that keeping the carrier in state hands is the least bad option.

Privatisation makes for more efficient firms, lower prices for consumers and, by taking ownership out of the hands of politicians, less patronage and corruption. When the sale of state-owned assets began in earnest internationally in the 1980s, all these benefits were presented as reasons for lifting the dead hand of the state and freeing management to manage on strictly commercial lines.

After more than two decades, there is an abundance of evidence from across the world to draw solid conclusions about what happens when corporate ownership moves from public to private. On the big picture, there is little disagreement: the net gains have unquestionably been positive, but these have not been as great as originally trumpeted. There are two reasons for the benefits being somewhat less than anticipated. First, a small minority of sell-offs have been failures—mostly in networked industries where natural monopolies can exist. Second, the importance of ownership was over-stated. Firm behaviour is determined more by external market conditions than internal structural arrangements. (It is for this reason, among others, that EU-level liberalisation has focused on prizing open markets, not reducing state ownership.)

Where does the seemingly interminable saga of what to do with Aer Lingus, which continued to drag on this week with unions fighting for further pre-privatisation concessions, fit in to the wider ownership picture? At first glance, the privatisation of the national carrier makes sense because the aviation industry is highly competitive and not prone to monopolisation. But the government's proposal to sell off only a part of the airline muddies the waters. If the state retains a shareholding, potential investors know that they can expect efforts to exert political influence over commercial decisions in the future. This will result in the discounting of the share price at time of sale, meaning less cash raised to reinvest in the company. Also likely to reduce the attractiveness of the offer to investors is the extent to which existing work practices are being locked in as ongoing talks with trade unions see many concessions being granted. Leaving even less to plough back in to modernise the carrier' s fleet will be the allocation of a chunk of the receipts from the sale to fill the hole in the airline's shot-up pension fund. In short, the proposed sell-off will do little to achieve its stated aim of allowing for significantly greater investment.

But the flaws in the current plan don't end there. The government is determined to gift the staff 15% of the firm though an Employee Share Ownership Plan (ESOP). Whenever publicly owned assets are handed over to private interests free of charge the reasons need to be compelling. They are far from compelling in this case. Internationally, ESOPs are designed to bring the interests of management and staff into closer alignment, usually in the hope of getting employee buy-in for restructuring when firms are ailing. But in the case of Aer Lingus, painful change has already been implemented. Willie Walsh trimmed the fat and the carrier is now profitable. Advocates of windfalling the staff such a big stake could argue that over the longer term it will make managers and managed closer in their views, thus making tough decisions easier to take. This is unlikely. International evidence shows that ESOPs have only limited effects on curbing adversarialism. Closer to home, the case of eircom merely adds to that body of evidence—few would argue that bosses and staff are closer to seeing eye to eye since the eircom ESOP was launched.

The current proposal is flawed on a number of levels. So of the alternatives—full privatisation or retaining the status quo—which is best? Though advocates of the status quo include those who are prejudiced against free enterprise and ideologically committed to statist solutions, one of the points made about the strategic risks of full privatisation is valid. There is a danger that direct connections to the US could conceivably be reduced, or worse still, ended altogether. To see how it could happen, consider how the aviation industry is evolving.

The effects of liberalisation on the European industry are still working their way through the sector. Eventually, the structure of the industry will look as it does in the only other comparable market— the US. This can be expected to result in four to six large carriers becoming dominant by swallowing up the smaller fry and replacing existing routing structures with the hub-and-spoke model. Because this model cuts the number of point to point flights, routing most trips through a central hub, it could happen that travelling to the US from Ireland would mean a first leg to London, Amsterdam or Paris before crossing the Atlantic.

Given Ireland's dependence on US investment, such an outcome would be seriously damaging. And all the more so at a time when US firms are warning that Ireland is losing some of the advantages that made it so attractive in the past and when other locations are becoming increasingly attractive.

Full privatisation is the best and most straightforward option, but it carries risk. Although the probability is small, the cost of losing direct transatlantic links would be great. Such risks are usually worth insuring against. The cost of keeping Aer Lingus in state hands is a premium worth paying.

*Originally published in the* Sunday Tribune

___

# THE EURO REMAINS IN IRELAND'S BEST INTERESTS

*5 May 2000*

The euro's seemingly inexorable decline since shortly after its introduction has preoccupied policy-makers in the euro zone and beyond. The decline has been eyed with particular concern in Ireland. Owing to its very high proportion of trade with non-euro countries, the Irish economy's exposure to exchange-rate fluctuations is unequalled among EMU participants.

As most now agree, price stability in Ireland is largely a function of international inflationary pressures and the exchange rate. As the euro slumps, prices of goods from the UK and US have soared. This could hardly have come at a worse time, adding as it does to still-relevant domestically generated price pressures in the services and non-traded goods sectors, the labour and property markets.

Such bad news requires a revisiting of the reasons for signing up to monetary union. With a free float advocated by none, the alternative was to peg the pound to the currency of a major trading partner. As sterling and the dollar ruled themselves out, not least for political reasons, a link to the euro was the only choice. However, in a world where the volume and velocity of mobile capital is ever-growing, exchange rate régimes other than a free float at one extreme and currency union at the other are at increasing risk of being sundered by speculators.

Since the 1992–93 ERM (Exchange Rate Mechanism) debacle, flows of hot money have grown ceaselessly, heightening further the risk of currency crises. And not only in emerging markets. Look at little Denmark, an EU member state that rejected EMU but pegged its currency to the euro. In the brief bout of turmoil on international financial markets following the devaluation of the Russian rouble in September 1998, base rates were pushed up to defend the krone from speculative assault, yield spreads widened and foreign currency reserves depleted.

Had squall turned to storm, the consequences would have been dire. This spectre still haunts the Danes. Little wonder almost all interest groups are advocating a yes vote in September when the issue is put to plebiscite. Such pressures may even render untenable managed float arrangements, like Ireland's régime in the 1993–98 period, particularly as there are now fewer currencies with such régimes, a fact which makes those that do have them more vulnerable to being picked off.

But even if this were not the case, the introduction of the euro has changed the cost/benefit calculus of such an arrangement. For foreign direct investors, exchange-rate stability with major EU markets is a key consideration. In the UK, for example, hardly a week now passes without the chief executive of a foreign manufacturer publicly groaning under sterling's unbearable strength.

With greater exchange rate risk for EMU 'outs' and less for 'ins', Ireland's attractiveness has increased relative to non-participants. Given the importance of foreign direct investment to the Irish economy, in particular as a source of intellectual and fixed capital formation—corner-stones of sustained wealth creation—what is good for foreign direct investors is good for Ireland. In sum, while EMU participation is far from perfect, it may only be the least bad solution. Once the project went ahead Ireland had little choice but to join. This is still true today and will remain so for the foreseeable future.

But there is also good news. Without in any way downplaying the negative impact of current levels of price instability (inflation is touching 5%), the surprise is that it is not higher given the euro depreciation. Although likely to feed through when firms' forex reserves are depleted and the replenishing of inventories can be postponed no longer, there may be a more optimistic explanation.

According to the ESRI, a growing number of Irish firms are now able to demand of their UK suppliers the invoicing of goods in euro. By so doing, they pass on the exchange rate risk, doing much to insulate the economy from imported inflation. Few would claim that such an exorbitant privilege would have been available had we retained the puny pound.

A further, and less talked-of, benefit is the lifting of the balance-of-payments constraint. In times past, politicians and bureaucrats carefully considered their words and deeds lest they induce a rush to the exit by investors. As the recent Committee of Public Accounts into non-payment of DIRT heard, the law was not enforced for fear that flight of capital would precipitate a currency crisis. Such crises caused real pain, as mortgage holders remember from the futile attempt to protect the pound in 1992–93. Thanks to the euro, they can never happen again.

As for calls for withdrawal, not only would such a course lead to unprecedented economic uncertainty, the political consequences would be incalculable. With the euro as weak as it is now, the announcement by a participating state that it intended pulling out would, at the very least, cause a further sharp depreciation of the fledgling currency. Such an act would never be forgiven.

But before such apocalyptic vistas are even pondered, perspective in the debate needs to be regained. When the currency was introduced, analysts everywhere expected a gradual appreciation as it took on the mantle of an alternative reserve currency to the dollar. It is only with weakness that commentators cast round for explanations. In France, some normally sensible newspapers suggest a British plot.

Cross the Channel and 'Anglo-Saxon model good, Rhine model bad' summarises much of the simplistic talk about euro depreciation. Despite the predilection of anglophone commentators to disparage supposedly sclerotic European economies, the euro area outlook is bright, with fore-casts of higher growth, lower unemployment and corporate restructuring boosting profits across the zone. In contrast, and without gainsaying the phenomenal performance of the US over the past decade, that country's prospects are now finely balanced. Should the willingness of foreigners to hold over-valued US assets evaporate suddenly, a sharp reversal in foreign exchange markets is in store.

The reality is that few prices are as prone to wild and groundless fluctuations as those of currencies, and the euro's weakness is as clear a case of an undershooting exchange rate as one is likely to find. Sooner than some might expect, this will be reversed and the euro's real value will be reflected in its price.

*Originally published in the* Irish Times

*Chapter* III ～

# ENGAGEMENT OR ISOLATION: THE CHOICE FOR AN ATLANTIC ISLAND

*'An té nach bhfuil láidir, ní foláir dó bheith glic.'*
*(He who is not strong must be smart.)*

ANON

## INTRODUCTION

It is often said the small countries do not have foreign policies. There is much truth in this. Being largely powerless, they can do little to shape the world. They exercise what limited influence they have by allying themselves with others, by the quality of their ideas and the presentation of themselves as models for others. They focus their energies on seeking out opportunities and niches, and doing what they can to prevent the outside world causing damage at home.

In the past, small countries suffered for their powerlessness, often being invaded and subjugated by larger powers. But the world has become less violent and more ordered.[1] The weak and powerless have benefited disproportionately. At the same time, the benefits of smallness have increased. Smaller countries adapt and manage change more easily and more quickly because they have fewer interests to mediate. This nimbleness is now a real advantage in a world of rapid economic and technological change, as is to be seen from the league table of the world's richest countries. The top ten in per capita terms in 2007 were, in ascending order: Luxembourg, Norway, Iceland, Ireland, Denmark, Switzerland, Qatar, Sweden, the Netherlands and Finland.[2] With an average population of 4.5 million, their fortunes contrast with the 10 most populous states—China, India, the US, Indonesia, Brazil, Pakistan, Russia, Nigeria, Japan and Mexico—of which only two are rich and stable.

## FRIENDS LIKE THESE

Not only has the world changed to Ireland's great benefit, but the country is also fortunate to inhabit the most secure region of the planet. The stable Atlantic zone of democracies is unique in its peacefulness and levels of co-operation among its states. This is to be seen in how Ireland interacts with its neighbours. Relations with Britain, so long made difficult by history and partition, have normalised. The passing of time, a more balanced economic relationship and the changing European political context have all helped drive the normalisation process. So too have changes within both countries, not least in the abandonment of their respective forms of jingoistic nationalism. This created an environment in which their positions on Northern Ireland—the most serious cause of poor relations for so long—became less about who governed the place and more about the quality of its governance. All of these developments have created a self-reinforcing cycle of improving relations.

The benefits of the special relationship with the US, seemingly permanently durable, are barely calculable. What may be a weakness for the US itself—the openness of its political system to lobbying by well organised interest groups, both domestic and foreign—has been a boon for Ireland. Most notably this allowed the overcoming of traditional British resistance to US involvement in Northern Ireland.[3] It is difficult to imagine any other country having become involved in the internal affairs of another state in a way that offered so little gain and risked so much. Most astonishing about Ireland-US relations, despite the level of support the US offers Ireland and its immense absolute and relative power, is that it demands so little in return. It has, to date, not pressured Ireland to change its tax laws, which allow US companies to avoid paying billions of dollars to the US treasury. Politically, it makes no attempts to seek payback for its friendship and support in the form of toeing its line: Ireland did not join the 'coalition of the willing' before the Iraq invasion and it takes a position on the Israel-Palestine conflict that is diametrically opposite to that of the US. Given how benignly the US exercises its power over the country, it is curious that so many Irish people are prepared to see only ulterior or wicked motives in how the US acts in the rest of the world.

But more important for Ireland than any bilateral relationship has been the emergence and evolution of the European integration project (this is the subject of Chapter v). Ireland's net gains from membership since joining have exceeded those of all other countries and even the most ardent and persistent opponents now accept it was right to join and would be wrong to leave. Nobody disputes its benefits in terms of dynamising the

economy, helping to attract foreign investment and providing cash transfers. But there is far more to membership than money. Most basically, the
EU provides security in a way that is now so taken for granted it is barely
remarked upon. For small countries, international law is the only way to
achieve real and durable security without depending on others because the
rule of law protects the weak from the arbitrary actions of the strong.
This is precisely what the EU allows small countries to achieve because it is
the only example in history of sovereign states accepting the rule of
non-national law in any meaningful way. In short, Europe's highly
effective multilateral system levels the playing field, limiting the scope
for big countries to push small ones around (this is under-appreciated
for the good reason that what could happen, but does not, usually goes
unnoticed).

One good example of this levelling effect is the protection of the Irish
corporation tax régime. In 2004 the Cadbury Schweppes case was taken by
Britain against Ireland on the grounds that the former's tax base was being
undermined by what it claimed were the latter's unfair tax structures and
incentives. The European Court of Justice threw out the case, finding that
it was legitimate for member countries to set their tax rates as they wished.
Many opponents of the EU and the Lisbon treaty claim that Europe threatens Irish tax freedom. The truth is that rule of European law protects it.

Two very recent examples of how big countries can treat their small
non-EU neighbours further illustrate the security offered by the rule of
European law. Germany has long believed that the international financial
services industries of smaller countries, such as Ireland, Luxembourg and
Liechtenstein, undercut its tax base. But it has always been constrained
from acting against EU members—including Ireland and Luxembourg—
because they are in a position to haul Germany before the EU's Court of
Justice. Liechtenstein has no such protection.[4] It paid the price in 2007
when the German secret service bribed a Liechtenstein national to break
his own country's laws by passing on information he had stolen while
working at one of the country's banks. The stance of the UK government
towards Iceland when its banks collapsed in September 2008 is another
example of big country bullying that would probably not have happened
in an EU context. Britain invoked anti-terrorist legislation to freeze
Icelandic assets in its jurisdiction. Because Iceland cannot resort to the
European Court of Justice, it was powerless to respond. It is worth noting
that at the same time, Britain reacted very strongly to Ireland's decision to
guarantee the liabilities of its main banks—and spun the line that Ireland
was threatening others by so doing—but it confined its actions to spin. If

Ireland had not been protected by European law, the British action would have almost certainly been more substantive, and potentially more damaging.

## THE EUROPEAN RESCUE OF THE IRISH STATE

As if these benefits were not enough to have an overwhelming majority of Irish people voting enthusiastically for more Europe at every opportunity, the gains of membership do not end there. Not only has the EU prevented other countries from acting in a way that could harm Ireland, but its mechanisms and structures have limited self-harm. By improving the quality of policy-making and implementation and, very importantly, placing some external constraint on bad policy choices, the EU saves governments from themselves. This has been particularly important for Ireland. As outlined in Chapter 1, the effects of political parochialism have been rising in recent decades. Fortunately, this coincided with deepening European integration. Examples of the EU's restraining effect range from compelling governments to abide by the environmental rules that they themselves collectively set, to requiring capital spending programmes to be properly evaluated, to preventing the giving of taxpayers' money to multinationals who threaten to move jobs elsewhere. Without EU membership the effects of localism in Irish politics would be felt even more acutely than they are.

But participation in the EU not only limits bad government, it has a positive effect on the quality of thinking by policy-makers, a benefit that is particularly important for a small, non-ideas-orientated country such as Ireland. Civil servants from many, if not most departments, and from a relatively low grade, travel to Brussels to participate in meetings relevant to their departments. They see how their counterparts from other countries operate and are exposed to policy ideas. Although it would be wrong to exaggerate the effect, the broadening of horizons for civil servants has been a further gain from membership.

## CHANCES TAKEN?

How well has Ireland exploited this (until recently) extraordinarily benign external environment: to guarantee its physical and economic security; to pursue its interests; to leverage its influence; and to maximise the goodwill that makes achieving its goals easier? The answer is mixed, at best. Just as in domestic affairs, the policy failings that were submerged under the high tide of prosperity are now re-emerging into view, to add to others of longer standing. On security, Ireland has maintained, over more than half a century, its non-involvement in NATO, the region's most important security structure. NATO is also the institutional embodiment of Euro-American relations. Despite Ireland's eternal interest in good relations with both sides of the Atlantic and good relations *between* both sides of the Atlantic, it never joined this alliance. Its voluntary rejection of membership, while at the same time doing nothing to guarantee its own security, was unique in Europe (of the other neutrals, Austria and Finland were prevented by the Soviets from joining the alliance during the cold war, while Sweden and Switzerland paid for their neutrality by supporting large independent armed forces). Ireland's position over six decades has been to free-ride. It is not one any Irish person should be proud of.

Nor has Ireland's position on multilateral trade liberalisation covered it in glory. A small open economy should, by any rational economic and political calculation, support open international trade and its attendant political structures. Any country genuinely concerned with the advancement of the developing world would have a further reason to support multilateral liberalisation. But instead of acting as its interests and values dictate, Ireland continues to be among the most vocal opponents in Europe of freeing of international trade. This position is seen abroad, by those who care to look, for what it is—the handing over of policy-making to a vested interest (in this case farmers). Such cronyism, which has been evident in other spheres more recently, is not how a modern, open, successful country should be run. There are other costs, too. In an EU context, Ireland's positioning of itself in the obstructionist camp on trade weakens relations with the small, northern European, free-trading countries with which its shares many interests.

Ireland's wider participation in the EU, by contrast, has been much more successful, with the opportunities of membership having been taken advantage of in many ways. At a most basic, quantifiable and comparative level, Ireland was alone among the countries eligible for large cash transfers to take up its full allocation of funds (this reflected the stronger capacity of the administrative system relative to those of the other, mostly Mediterranean countries, who also qualified for EU largesse). More widely and much more importantly, Ireland has been mostly successful over the years in ensuring that EU-level rule-making is as well suited to Ireland as possible, from milk quotas, to structural funds, to corporation tax, to a hundred other issues. The country has also earned goodwill and respect as a result of the efficient and unself-interested manner in which it ran successive six-month rotating presidencies of the bloc.

Perhaps the most important factor in raising Ireland's stature was its economic success. The country's rapid development from the mid-1990s owed a great deal to its membership of the EU. And Europe made much of its transformative powers, taking for itself at least its fair share of credit for the emergence of a tiger on its western fringe. None of this was lost on aspiring members to the east who found the prospect of emulating Ireland mouth-watering. Their ardour to join the bloc was heightened and this contributed to hastening the pace of pre-accession reform. In effect, the example of Ireland strengthened the hand of existing members during often difficult negotiations and contributed to accelerating the entire transition process in former communist Europe.

But Ireland's economic success brought with it new challenges vis-à-vis other member countries. Inevitably, an element of envy emerged, and many in Europe convinced themselves that Ireland's success was solely or mostly the result of their cash transfers. Others took a more hostile view: Ireland pocketed EU cash and then slashed its corporation tax to lure jobs and investment away from those who had been so generous to it. Little was done to address calmly and systematically these charges by, for instance, making the (strong) intellectual case for low corporation tax. When Ireland was challenged directly on its economic policies—by the European Commission over its budgetary stance in 2001—the reaction, counter-productively, went to the other extreme. There was brainless talk of 'pulling on the green jersey' and contempt was made plain for supposedly economically inept continentals and their European model (shorthand: Berlin) compared to Ireland's super-dynamic way (shorthand: Boston). This aggression and hubris did real damage. Little wonder that now there is more than a hint of *Schadenfreude* as Ireland rejoins the bloc's economic underperformers. As the country's public finances spiral out of control, the risk that it will have to dust down the begging bowl is frighteningly real. If others have to engineer a bailout, there will be a high price to pay.

Beyond Europe, on the wider international stage, the country has continued to carve a niche for itself in pushing issues on the human rights and disarmament agendas. Its ongoing and central role in drawing up an international treaty to ban land mines builds on a long tradition of such work, dating back to shortly after Ireland's accession to the UN in the 1950s, when it made the running on the drafting of most important arms limitation accord that has ever existed—the nuclear Non-Proliferation Treaty. A similar niche has been hewn on development aid, and by 2008 Ireland was among the most generous per capita givers. This was not only good for those who received the aid, but it also assisted in ensuring that, having put its money where its mouth is, the country's voice was listened to and respected on development issues, and other global issues more generally.

But here again, domestic political failings have undermined foreign policy objectives. After the 2002 election, when excessive pre-poll spending necessitated significant cutbacks, the commitment the then Taoiseach had personally given the UN, of reaching that organisation's aid target of 0.7% of national income, was postponed. The unfolding economic meltdown in 2009 ensures that the UN target will not be reached for at least a decade, if not longer. The mismanagement of the public finances during the boom years means that many programmes will be radically cut and much of the institutional capacity built up to allocate and administer aid will disappear or atrophy. This will gravely undermine Ireland's reputation as a reliable partner on development issues.

In terms of tactical diplomatic manoeuvering, one central objective for a small country is to avoid taking positions that cause unnecessary conflict with others. This often involves the difficult process for a democracy of reconciling values with interests. Here, Ireland's record has been good, with the invasion of Iraq a case in point. Domestically, there were calls for Ireland to oppose the war and refuse the US landing rights at Shannon airport. Had Ireland done so, it would not have delayed the firing of a single bullet or dropping of a single bomb. It would, however, have damaged the country's relations with the US, potentially seriously. In the event, a careful balance was struck which ensured that relations with none of the key players—the US, the major European powers or the Muslim world—were damaged. There are few countries which managed to navigate that period of turmoil as successfully.

## INTROSPECTION AND ISOLATIONISM
In analysing and explaining how any country conducts itself in the world, one must examine the three points of the foreign-policy triangle: public opinion, political leadership and diplomatic machinery. The first is foundational and in many ways the most important aspect. Any discussion of a country's posture in the world must start with its people's values and orientations, as these must ultimately be reflected in that posture if it is to be sustainable. Tony Blair's attempt to bring Britain to the heart of Europe failed because it did not chime with his people's Eurosceptic orientation. Attempts by Spain's former premier, José María Aznar, to take a strongly pro-US position in international affairs failed because the Spanish people— on left and right—do not have a strong affinity for America.

As argued in previous chapters, the Irish mindset remains comparatively inward-looking. This introspection manifests in thought and discussion, or lack thereof, on where and how the country should position itself in the world. International relations departments in universities have only appeared in the past decade, there is limited media coverage of foreign matters and even less analysis of the way Ireland conducts its relations with the world, and many opponents of deeper European integration appear oblivious to the limited options small countries have. Moverover, much of the comment on what happens abroad has a black-and-white, moralising tone (the shrillness of both pro-Palestinian and pro-Israeli voices is an example) and hostility to the US, which is marked even by European standards, is quite amazing given Ireland's strong links with that country. On globalisation, opinion polls show that attitudes are less favourable than the EU-27 average despite no country gaining more from that process—in early 2008 40% of Irish respondents viewed globalisation as a threat, compared to 34% who saw it as an opportunity.[5]

The view of the outside world as a threat may explain why some people appear to believe even the most implausible scaremongering about the EU, about what it does and about what it could do in the future. Despite the enormous benefits of EU membership and the absence to date of anything approaching any real cost of membership, Irish voters have rejected two consecutive treaties designed to take small steps toward deeper integration. This rejectionism is also likely to reflect a limited interest in the world beyond Ireland. In Chapter 1, opinion poll data were cited on Irish voters' comparatively limited knowledge of the bloc's functioning. But ignorance is one thing. Being unprepared to overcome one's ignorance is another. Following the 2008 Lisbon treaty referendum, 42% of those who voted against the treaty told surveyors that they had rejected the document because they lacked information on its content.[6] In other words, these respondents took time out of their day to make a negative statement at the ballot box, but they would not take the time to improve their understanding of an issue that every source of informed opinion, both pro-Lisbon and anti, believed to be vitally important. That such a significant percentage of the population could adopt such a stance raises a question about whether membership of Europe's political and economic union sits comfortably with Irish values and orientations. A second rejection of the Lisbon treaty would answer that question definitively.

## THE NEGLECT OF POLITICIANS
In December 2003, on the eve of Ireland taking the rotating presidency of the EU for six months, the then Taoiseach, Bertie Ahern, conceded in a newspaper interview that Ireland was perceived as having drifted to the periphery of Europe.[7] He offered no explanation of how this had been

allowed to happen and suggested nothing in the way of a plan to reverse it. Quite how the man at the helm for the previous six years could observe drift, in the manner of a casual bystander, says much about the importance the political class attaches to foreign matters (this was a particular shame in the case of Ahern, who was a world-class statesman-diplomat when he put his mind to it).

After a people's values and orientations, the second point of analysis of the underpinnings of any country's foreign policy is the political system that prioritises, formulates, articulates, and pursues international goals and objectives. The example above reflects the Irish political class's non-engagement in foreign policy in a way that is without parallel in Europe, but is hardly surprising given the backgrounds of the average elected representative (see Chapter 1). This neglect of foreign affairs has a long tradition—in the 1930s resistance even to establishing a foreign ministry was considerable and the setting up of a parliamentary committee on foreign affairs only happened in the mid-1990s. The consequences of this neglect are manifold and are to be seen currently, and most urgently, in the threat to Ireland's position in Europe—at least part of the reason for defeats of the Nice and Lisbon treaties, in 2001 and 2008 respectively, was the complacency of the political class in general and of the government of the day in particular.

But the failure to pursue Ireland's interests reaches into most areas. On the most basic issue, security, only a handful of politicians down the years have been prepared to advocate NATO membership. Most others, if they ever gave the matter a thought, were content to free-ride. Most amazingly, for a good number, the position came to be explained not by its less-than-noble motive, but by an apparent morally upright desire to remain aloof from security structures. Such juvenile posturing—of failing to take responsibility for one's country's security, but criticising those who do—not only undermined Ireland in the eyes of its allies, it infantilised domestic debate on all security matters. The consequences come home to roost each time deeper European integration is discussed. Paranoid fantasies about the EU becoming a war-monger are trotted out repeatedly. Most emotively, the conscription card is played, often by those who appear genuinely to believe that Irish youth could be press-ganged into some Euro-imperial army. The political class is either unwilling or unable to set out some basic facts on the evolution of military affairs to demonstrate how ludicrous this fantasy is—no military alliance in history has ever required its participants to implement conscription, many European countries have abandoned the practice since the end of the Cold War and not a single one has introduced it.

Energy security has been another victim of neglect. As one of the most import-dependent countries in Europe (90% comes from abroad compared to around half in the rest of western Europe), security of supplies should be one of the central issues in a wider security policy. Despite the need to find new sources of energy (Britain, Ireland's main source of supply, is rapidly running out of North Sea oil and gas) as global competition for resources increases, the issue receives only limited prioritisation. One of the few real options, nuclear power, has been shied away from by successive governments since the 1970s and in 2007 an energy white paper explicitly ruled it out. The most even the bravest politician is prepared to do is to call for 'debate' on the subject. Nor have renewable sources of energy been prioritised. In the energy mix, they account for just over 3% of the total, just one third of the EU average. If the world's supplies of energy ever crunch (as its supply of credit has done recently), the lights will quickly go out in Ireland. The political class's failure to lead has been much in evidence, not only in hard security and energy security, but in economic security too. Being relatively powerless and, at the same time, heavily dependent on foreign markets, Ireland has a greater interest than most countries in supporting and advancing the rules-based multilateral trading system centred around the World Trade Organisation. Bizarrely, Ireland is the most hostile of the EU-27 to the freeing of trade, and the country's position has not changed an inch from the time the economy was relatively closed and dependent on agriculture. This demonstrates not only the degree of inertia within the system, but the incapacity of the system even to recognise how interests can change and the need for policy to change accordingly.

## THE MACHINERY OF DIPLOMACY

The third component in assessing the effectiveness of any foreign policy is the quality of the diplomatic corps which implements it. In this aspect Ireland is fortunate. The foreign service is operationally strong: high levels of professionalism and a good *esprit de corps* result in effective teamwork and a capacity to pull together to rise to challenges. This reflects the generally strong levels of civic-mindedness across the Irish public sector. It is also likely that the non-party political tradition of the Civil Service is important (I have known diplomats from other countries who have worked actively against their own governments because their parties were not in power). Well known examples of this capacity for focus and teamwork include the negotiations leading to the Good Friday Agreement and the running of EU presidencies. A less well known, but perhaps even better, illustration of the

Department of Foreign Affairs' single-minded focus came in 2000 when Irish diplomats went head to head with the Italian foreign service to win a rotating seat on the UN security council. The two western European seats for the 2001–02 period had been earmarked for Ireland and Norway, but Italy, to further its ambition for UN reform, broke with tradition and challenged for a seat (western Europeans have a gentlemen's agreement not to compete with each other for the seats, and only two countries usually present themselves for election to the UN's General Assembly). I observed the race from both Irish and Italian sides, spending considerable time in Rome covering Italy in the early 2000s (a piece on Italy's conduct of its international affairs can be found in Chapter IV). Given Italy's G7 status, its much wider diplomatic network and its foreign ministry's much bigger budget, it was in a position to offer many more carrots to General Assembly members to win their votes. This should have allowed Italy to romp home in the race for the seat. But where the Italian foreign service was disorganised and unfocused, Irish diplomats took to the challenge with relish, easily outplaying their Italian counterparts. Ireland topped the poll.

But despite these real strengths, the foreign service is not what it should be. The aforementioned neglect by the political class is one reason. The corps is small even by the standards of other developed countries of similar size and the recruitment process is stuck in the old British mould of hiring generalists who are given little scope during their careers to develop expertise which they could apply consistently. Where additional resources have been committed in recent years, they have been mostly to open more embassies. Though these can make a real contribution to fostering trade and investment links, they have less added value in an age of instant telecommunications and widely available information (the days when the ambassadorial telegram was the only means of obtaining immediate, relevant and reliable information are long gone). Scarce resources have not been allocated where they could yield greater returns: strategic thinking capacity in the form of specialised units with a brief to analyse and understand global and regional trends so that opportunities and threats can be identified. Nor is there the sort of well-financed international affairs think tank with close links to the Department of Foreign Affairs, academia and the wider foreign policy community as exist in other small, open countries, such as Austria, Denmark and Sweden. The absence of structures to foster horizon-scanning and blue-sky thinking, and mechanisms to encourage constructive challenging of consensus, have hindered the Department from filling the vacuum created by neglect at political level. Their absence has also contributed to a groupthink problem in the service. This is reflected in a lack of engagement with outside entities, such as think tanks and journalists. The posture of officials I have interviewed formally, talked to informally at conference events or chatted to in social situations has generally ranged from lack of interest through observable suspicion to bristling hostility. Of the 50-odd business cards of Irish diplomats in my Rolodex, there are only a handful who will engage in frank, off-the-record discussion. No other European foreign service I have had any dealings with is as closed.

## THE NEOCONSERVATISM OF THE GOOD FRIDAY AGREEMENT

Groupthink in the Department was most obvious in the case of policy on Northern Ireland, particularly in the years after the agreement was signed when the extremes were gaining ground at the expense of the moderates and the IRA remained fully operational and engaged in violence. The aggressive and dismissive manner in which some Irish diplomats reacted to questioning of their tactics and strategy on the peace process often brought to mind American advocates of the invasion of Iraq: they held the same fervent and unlimited belief in the capacity of democratic institutions to conjure harmony from discord and the same disdain for those who dared even raise questions about the efficacy of such an approach.

Over the years, Northern Ireland, its problems and its future have been the focus of the country's most sustained single diplomatic effort. From the 1970s, a steady and determined push was made to support moderate nationalist opinion in Northern Ireland and to pressure Britain to address underlying causes of nationalist insecurity and alienation. If diplomacy is about patience, doggedness and a willingness to chip away at problems (and it almost certainly is), then these efforts were second to none.

But what of the strategy underpinning policy that ultimately led to the Good Friday Agreement? 'Politics works' is a view frequently expressed and almost universally shared in the Republic. It summed up the strategic approach to tackling Northern Ireland's problems and reflects a deeply held belief, itself a reflection of historical experience, in democratic politics as a means of overcoming differences and generating peaceful and prosperous co-existence. But the belief that creating democratic institutions engenders democratic behaviour is hard to sustain looking at evidence from around the world and, in particular, at evidence on how divided societies move away from conflict. Northern Ireland is but one example.

Whereas the architects of the Northern strategy believed that power sharing would lead to a 'withering on the vine' of the extremes, it was the moderates who withered, and rapidly. Relatively early on, the DUP and Sinn Féin eclipsed their respective rivals and are now permanently entrenched in their respective communities. Today, Peter Robinson (the rudest and most unpleasant politician I have ever interviewed, incidentally), appears incapable of fulfilling any kind of unifying role, Sinn Féin remains consumed by its irredentist fantasies and the two communities are as divided as ever. It frequently appears forgotten that the strategy never envisaged such an outcome.

It could be argued in response to this that all strategies produce unintended consequences. There is some truth in this. But equally, there is a need to revisit the fundamentals of strategy and the detail of tactics if they are not delivering. In the case of policy on Northern Ireland, strategy has never been reviewed and failing tactics remained unchanged for a full seven years after the deal was signed, both because of the groupthink problem among officials and the habit of the then Taoiseach, Bertie Ahern, to put process before outcome at all times (he later admitted that a blind eye had been turned to criminal activity, which included murder). As the process lurched from one crisis to the next after 1998 and during the first half of the current decade, the IRA changed little, engaging in continued criminality, thuggery and killing. It took the Northern Bank robbery in late 2004 and the appalling murder of Robert McCartney (and its aftermath) in early 2005 to shake the government out of its stupor. Tactics finally changed. Some stick was added to carrot in dealing with the Provisional movement, bringing in almost immediate results—decommissioning took place within months and criminal activity by the IRA declined dramatically. It is hard to avoid the conclusion that many of those killed in the 1998–2005 period would be alive today if the government had been less chronically inflexible in its tactics.

## CHARTING A NEW COURSE
Ireland's place in the world is rapidly changing as the country and the world undergo wrenching upheaval. The international environment will not be nearly as benign in the future as it has been in recent decades. In the immediate future, global economic recession will lead to a reduction in foreign investment and trade, and generate all manner of political tensions and strains. At the very least some increase in protectionism is to be expected. Under that general rubric, changes to the US corporation tax régime are to be feared. Any such changes could undermine US investment in Ireland, which is still the economy's greatest single source of dynamism. Then there is Europe. Even if the Lisbon treaty is accepted by the Irish people, the first rejection, combined with the earlier rejection of the Nice treaty, makes Ireland a semi-permanent problem in the evolution of

European governance structures. A small country simply cannot afford to make such a nuisance of itself. Relations with Britain can also be expected to be more challenging in the years to come. The Conservative Party, which has little natural affinity for Ireland, appears all but certain to return to power in the near future. On Northern Ireland, a party that has such difficulties accepting the multilateral constraints of EU membership will always be less amenable to taking Dublin's views and concerns into account. A Tory government would pose other challenges, too. Regardless of whether Irish voters choose to remain with Europe when they vote on the Lisbon treaty, Britain could well become a barrier to the continent if it implements the positions on the EU that it has committed to in opposition.

With such an environment abroad and economic collapse at home, repositioning will not be easy. The enormous prestige that comes with being a model for others has evaporated. It is not coming back. A foreign aid budget, which grew very rapidly to become one of the largest in the world relative to the country's size, is being slashed. It was important for what it was, but also for how others saw us, and how we saw ourselves. So too are scandals emerging from the banking system and the ineptitude of government economic management. Going from boom to basket case, from benefactor to mendicant in a single year has already done much to erode international prestige. And whatever political energy exists in normal times for foreign matters is likely to disappear as the political system focuses on domestic economic woes and their destabilising effects.

Chapter 1 concluded on a relatively optimistic note. With honest reflection, effort and imagination, Ireland can redesign its institutions of government to improve their performance. It can still be a successful and prosperous country. If the current crisis produces the sort of changes to the constitutional architecture discussed earlier, it would also certainly improve the conduct of foreign policy. A political system designed to deliver more efficient outcomes would almost by definition give a higher priority to foreign affairs, in part by being less locally oriented. It would also be likely to beef up the institutional capacity needed to conduct a coherent, strategically-minded foreign policy, with a better resourced Department of Foreign Affairs and a much greater focus on analytical functions.

Beyond the institutions of government, autonomous capacities, such as those that exist in other small open countries, could enrich thinking on opportunities and challenges. An independent institution devoted to international affairs and Ireland's place in the world, modeled on the Economic and Social Research Institute,[8] would both widen perspectives and raise the quality of available analysis. Just as the ESRI provides authoritative, policy-relevant material on socio-economic issues, such an institution could give input into the foreign-policy formulation process and offer constructive critiques on policy positions, and their implementation and execution. Again, as is the case with the ESRI, foreign talent could be attracted to such an institution, thereby enriching perspectives and helping to break the tendency towards groupthink. But even if all these changes were to be implemented, a question remains about Irish people's values and orientations. The most sophisticated structures in the world cannot lead a people to a place they do not want to be led to. Isolationism may be preferred to realistic engagement with the world. The price would be high.

> 'A movement to political confederation in some form
> is indeed a natural and logical development of eco-
> nomic integration. Henceforth our national aims
> must conform to that emergence, in a political as well
> as in an economic sense, of a union of Western
> European States, not as a vague prospect of the distant
> future but as a living reality of our own times.'
>
> SEÁN LEMASS

_____

## IRELAND'S EUROPEAN IMPERATIVE

*4 April 2004*

Never since the emergence of the modern state system 3½ centuries ago has a small country enjoyed an international environment as benign as the Republic has over recent decades. Apart from freedom from external military threat—thanks to geography and a de-facto American security guarantee—this has mostly been because of EU membership. Ireland has permanent access to the largest market in the world guaranteed by the rule of European law. Relatedly, tidal waves of jobs-rich foreign capital have dynamised its once-sclerotic economy. And we have been the recipients of some of the largest cash transfers any sovereign state has ever been gifted. For all these gains one would expect, at the very least, some rules and regulations imposing constraints on freedom of policy manoeuvre. That, after all, is the definition of multilateralism, and the EU is the world's multilateral organisation par excellence. Amazingly there have been hardly any ill-suited to Ireland.

Heretofore, where European integration has been deepest—subsidies and economics—it has been almost tailor-made to Ireland's advantage. Where integration would have imposed unwelcome constraint—taxation, judicial matters and foreign policy, for instance—it has been less advanced. In short, we have enjoyed all the gains of multilateralism, but few of the costs. This happy circumstance was always too good to last, and the best-of-both-worlds era is now drawing to a close. Though tomorrow's enlargement is generally good for Europe, and therefore for Ireland too, it will not be without its downside.

Looking narrowly, competition for foreign investment will intensify as the central Europeans, thanks to membership, become more attractive to globalising firms. Happily, this effect is likely to be limited, not least because Ireland's environment for doing business is still better. Widening the focus, greater opportunities for Irish firms in the bigger EU will offset this negative, partially at least.

Although it is almost vulgar to mention it after 35 years of receiving Brussels' largesse, Ireland will start paying for membership in 2007, and the bill will be all the bigger because the new countries' needs are great. Though this is hardly cause for taxpayer joy, only the most myopic would grumble. And even if they do, there is the consolation of knowing that as a paymaster, the country's clout will be increased.

Enlargement will affect Ireland's influence in other ways, too. Instead of 14 other countries trying to have their say, there will be 24. A small country's voice could be lost in the cacophony. But in Europe, as anywhere else, whether people listen to you is less about how loud your voice is and more about what they have to learn from you and whether they think you are worth a hearing.

Because the new members are so impressed by how Ireland has exploited its EU membership and are transfixed by its tigerish economy, they tend to hold the country in high esteem. This will actually increase influence, particularly important now because some members of long standing resent what they see as Ireland's free-riding (low profits tax is a particular bugbear).

Enlargement will also affect relations between Europe and the US, which show no sign of returning to happier pre-Iraq days. Widening differences in interests (and how these are perceived and pursued) make continued strains a near-certainty. This is profoundly worrying for Ireland because its relations with the US are so important. Politically, the US continues to be an even-handed influence in the North, and economically about one in eight jobs depends directly or indirectly on US companies. If the continents draw further apart and a chasm opens up in mid-Atlantic, Ireland will be closest to its edge.

In the EU of 15, France's sometimes unnecessarily confrontational approach towards the US is now dominant, and of the big member countries only Britain cleaves closely to the US. The pro-American new members (and Poland in particular) will shift the centre of gravity back towards greater balance between the two positions, hopefully lessening the risk of continental drift.

Compared to the last enlargement (a decade ago three rich, small and neutral countries joined), this one will have its downsides, even if the pros outweigh the cons. But combined with the soon-to-be-agreed constitutional treaty, will EU membership remain in Ireland's interests? The answer is Yes, emphatically. To see why, consider Ireland's defining characteristic as a player in the international system: small size and relative powerlessness. The over-riding strategic objective of the weak is to constrain the powerful because when interests collide the former will always come off worse (the Irish understand this better than anyone, having endured the unwanted attentions of a powerful country for most of the last millennium).

For small countries, international law is the only way to achieve this. And because the EU is the only example in history of sovereign states accepting the rule of non-national law in any meaningful way, being fully engaged in Europe's highly effective multilateral system not only brings with it good things, it prevents bad things from happening.

And if this sounds a little academic then look at history from independence to EU accession. In the 1930s and again in the 1960s Britain unilaterally slapped taxes on Irish exports. The results for Ireland were, respectively, disastrous (the Economic War) and damaging. Because European law forbids such unilateralism, never again can any other EU state threaten our prosperity or use its economic clout to get what it wants politically.

All too often in international affairs, choices facing countries are between the awful and the unpalatable. Fortunately, the EU, post-enlargement and with a constitution, will be neither for Ireland. While it will not be as good as it has been, staying deeply embedded in the European multilateral system will remain the strategic imperative for the protection and pursuit of Ireland's interests as far into the future as one can see.

*Originally published in the* Irish Times

## SAYING NO DOES NOT MAKE FOR AN EFFECTIVE FOREIGN POLICY

*2 February 2003*

The State's historic neglect of foreign affairs did not matter much when what happened abroad had limited impact at home. But with the increasing globalisation of the economy and the Europeanisation of politics, the cost of neglect is rising ever faster.

Having an electoral system that produces the least cosmopolitan political class in western Europe is not without pros, but the big downside is that few TDs have an interest in foreign matters and those that do have little time to do much about it because of the demands of constituency work. The resulting lack of political push, combined with the under-resourcing of the excellent diplomatic corps, presents a growing threat to the country's interests both economically and politically.

Consider prosperity first. Some 30 years ago, farming was all-important. But today agriculture accounts for only 3% of the wealth created in the economy. In terms of the livelihoods of the overwhelming majority, it is irrelevant. While agriculture has shrunk to insignificance, Ireland has become the greatest trading nation on earth, exporting more per capita than any other country. Everyone now depends, to a greater or lesser extent, on how exporters do.

Given the importance of exports and the insignificance of agriculture, the State should back the latter over the former when trade-offs have to be made. But this does not happen because although economic interests have changed beyond all recognition, the institutions of the State have been slow to acknowledge this and act accordingly.

The result is seen most clearly in global talks about making international trade freer. Given that Irish exporters are the best in the world, Ireland would benefit disproportionately if these negotiations were to succeed. But instead of working to this end, we are one of those rich countries blocking a deal by refusing to listen to poor countries' pleadings that we change the way our farmers are protected and subsidised.

Until such time as we stop dumping food on the world market, under-cutting poor countries' farmers and pushing many out of business, they will agree no deal. The State, by opposing change, is not only acquiescing in the IFA's defence of the indefensible, it is failing to promote the country's real economic interests. And this is not to say that farmers should not be supported. They should. But not so much that it costs every family in the

EU €1,500 a year and certainly not in ways that help to keep the Third World in poverty.

But it is not only international economic matters that are being neglected. Politically, Ireland's most important vehicle for the pursuit of its interests in the world—EU membership—has been allowed to fall into disrepair. Ask diplomats from other EU countries their opinion of Ireland these days and they'll mutter through their canapés about Eurosceptic ingrates. So why have we become so unpopular? Some of the bad feeling is because of the country's very low rate of profits tax for American multi-nationals and the continued receipt of big subsidies despite becoming rich. But these things are not the main reason for all the ill-will, because after all, what Ireland does has next to no real effect on anyone else owing to the country's small size.

The real problem is one of attitude and presentation. Negativity does most damage. Ireland says no to tax harmonisation. Ireland says no to more co-operation on foreign policy. Ireland says no to co-operation on defence and criminal justice. (These days it is sometimes hard to avoid parallels with unreconstructed unionism.) While it is of course right and proper to say no when necessary, there are often better ways than blunt rejection. Not only does such rejectionism frustrate and annoy those on the receiving end, it rarely gets you what you want (unionism again comes to mind).

Visceral anti-EU opinions expressed occasionally by politicians, including people in the Cabinet who should know better, don't help either. These outbursts have tended to relate mostly to how economies are run. Since Ireland awed the world with its economic miracle, a hint of we-know-best arrogance has slipped into some ministers' utterances on Europe. Continentals are infuriated to be lectured that tax cuts solve everything by people they have subsidised so generously for so long.

Another reason for falling stock is that all too often the pragmatism of many Irish EU insiders comes across as scepticism to the many Teutonic bores and Latin wind-bags who drone on endlessly about pie-in-the-sky proposals. To them, Irish eyes cast heavenwards are proof of apostasy, and this matters because showing you are a true believer is essential in a club where hostility to more co-operation is considered akin to barbarism.

The failure to put a positive spin on issues in Europe is all the more astonishing given the proven ability of our diplomats to influence developments abroad. Think of what happened in the US when the peace process was in its infancy. Although the British embassy in Washington was 500 strong, a handful of Irish diplomats ran rings around them, winning the argument in the White House, in Congress and in the media. With the national question all but answered, it is past time these skills were applied to European matters.

Nowhere could these skills be better employed than in winning the tax harmonisation debate. They could also be applied to sharing the lessons of the Nice referendums. Having campaigned twice on the Nice treaty, our politicians know better than anyone about bringing the Union closer to voters. Spreading the word would be in everyone's interests. But to date this has not happened; there have been no government contributions to the multitude of EU-focused think tanks that influence key players, no speeches to the never-ending round of EU-related conferences and no articles in the international media.

But of all places the machinery of influence could be used, the best is the constitution-drafting Convention on the Future of Europe. Although criticism of the government has been exaggerated—many other countries haven't got their Convention acts together and ground lost to date can still be made up—the slow response was all too typical.

Although Brian Cowen's speech on the Convention last month proved that the government is out of the blocks, it was short on constructive suggestions and again betrayed a siege mentality—he did not speak of pursuing Irish interests but of 'defending' them, as if other countries were ganging together to do Ireland down. The Tánaiste intervened too, and although constructive, she just can't help hectoring when it comes to Europe—Europeans were told what they 'must' do no fewer than 18 times.

Without greater efforts to win friends and sharpen the political focus on foreign affairs, the country will find itself increasingly marginalised and exposed. In a world where all politics is now global, failure to right the greatest systemic failure of Irish governance will become ever more costly.

*Originally published in the* Irish Times

————

# IRELAND'S DRIFT FROM EUROPE COULD BREAK THE NICE TREATY

*4 April 2001*

In the past when Europe's electorates have had a chance to express their opinion on plans for ever-closer union they have shown themselves to be far less enthusiastic than their politicians. Almost a decade ago the Danes voted against the Maastricht Treaty. They changed their minds only after securing a series of opt-outs. The French said yes to Maastricht, but only by a wafer-thin margin.

With support for membership across the EU falling from more than 70% in 1990 to 50% in 2000, governments have since steered clear of referendums—with one exception. Owing to a constitutional quirk, Ireland's voters will be alone among the Union's 15 member states' electorates in giving their opinion on the latest changes to the EU's founding treaties. Without their approval in the poll, the treaty cannot come into force.

For proponents of a yes vote, Nice has the advantage of having a clearly defined and easily understood big idea: allowing countries in central and eastern Europe to join the Union. But for the pro-Europeans, the good news ends there. Enlargement may be simple to understand, but fellow-feeling for their cousins in former communist countries will not have the inhabitants of the EU's westernmost member state flocking to the ballot boxes.

Moreover, if long-established trends are anything to go by, the result of the referendum will be closer than any of Ireland's previous polls on Europe. Since holding a referendum on accession in 1972, the proportion supporting further integration has fallen in each successive vote, from more than 83% to below 62% in May 1998. Since then, the Irish have become cooler still, with support for EU membership down five percentage points in two years, according to the European Commission's biannual 'Eurobarometer' poll. The decline in enthusiasm reflects rapidly changing interests, orientation and outlook as Ireland's dash for economic growth has seen the country go from European laggard to leader in less than a decade.

As a result of its new-found wealth, Ireland will go from being the largest beneficiary of EU funding to a net contributor within five years. Having consistently pointed to large cash transfers as the best reason to vote yes in previous referendums, the mainstream political parties— all advocates of a yes vote—will find it more difficult to convince the electorate to vote for further (fundless) integration.

In terms of economic interests, Ireland's deepening integration with the US has been startling. In 1998, the year of the Amsterdam referendum, Germany was a more important market for Irish exports than the US. In 2000, the US is likely to have accounted for a share equivalent to Germany, France and Italy combined—the euro area's three largest economies. The deepening trade links with the US are mostly the result of Ireland's success in attracting export-orientated US multinationals. The presence of these firms, which offer well-paid jobs and spread know-how to Irish companies, has had an Americanising effect, not least on the business community and politicians—traditionally the strongest advocates of closer ties to Europe.

The most dynamic indigenous entrepreneurs now look across the Atlantic when they want to raise capital and policy-makers increasingly attribute economic success to US-style policies. Little wonder then that disparaging comment on the 'European social model' in the British and US media is given greater credence. And while they warm to America, business people feel unease at continental pressure to abandon low rates of corporation tax. Commission attempts to dictate how the macroeconomy is managed have caused wider disquiet. The high-profile censure of Ireland over finance minister Charlie McCreevy's 'give-away' budget in February has left a sour taste in the mouths of politicians and public alike.

Even if these developments do not make the government less than whole-hearted in its advocacy of the treaty, there will be other difficulties to overcome. Chief among these will be the financing of an information campaign. The government is prohibited from spending public money to support its position other than the equal sums it is bound to give to both sides in all referendum campaigns. The political parties can be expected to chip in, but with an election in the offing they will be reluctant to commit much from their campaign war chests.

Another situation likely to reduce the yes vote is the declining importance of agriculture, weakening a strong pro-EU constituency dependent on generous Common Agriculture Policy funding. The numbers employed in agriculture have been shrinking as farmers are lured to better-paying jobs. Moreover, for some, including agrarian Poland, enlargement will merely hasten the dismantling of price floors and result in income support payments being spread ever thinner.

Finally, although the Nice treaty does not involve any advance on existing security and defence plans, small but vocal groupings who oppose any form of military co-operation have linked the two. These noisy few advocate a rejection of the treaty, saying that it is an opportunity to stop the 'militarisation' of the EU in its tracks and prevent what they believe is an attempt surreptitiously to involve Ireland in the creation of an armed superpower. This has always struck a chord with some where neutrality is still cherished. Isolationists believe it will ring truer now that they can point to the government's back-tracking on its promise to hold a referendum on participation in NATO's Partnership for Peace framework.

Although the ranks of the rejectionists will swell, past majorities should not be overturned in a country where support for Union membership is second only to Luxembourg. Those who believe that Ireland's future is inextricably linked to the continent of which it is a part are likely to win the day. But it is more finely balanced than most think. If it goes the other way, there should be no surprise.

*Originally published in the* European Voice

———

## IRELAND WILL NOT BE A PRIORITY FOR GORDON BROWN

*6 June 2007*

For most of Ireland's post-independence history relations with Britain were blighted by poisonous historical legacies, reactionary nationalism, imperial condescension and profoundly different worldviews. Happily, these causes of discord have waned owing to deep and fundamental change in both the Republic and Britain.

For Ireland, the passing of time has lessened historical resentments and, in common with the rest of western Europe, drum-beating nationalism has become an embarrassing anachronism. Integration into the European polity has widened perspectives, and because the EU is a union of laws, it has had a levelling effect on the relationships among its participant states regardless of their relative size. A more balanced economic relationship has also evolved. Britain has declined in relative importance for Ireland, while the rapidly growing Irish economy has become more important for Britain (Ireland is now the UK's fourth largest export market, and the UK Ireland's second, recently pushed from top spot by the US).

Changes in Britain have been as significant in the bettering of relations. Those generations imbued with the mindset of empire have largely passed on and a new consensus has emerged that the subjugation of other nations in the past is a blot on Britain's history, not a source of pride. A changing ethnic and cultural profile—although not without its own problems—has generated a genuine cosmopolitanism in domestic and international affairs. These changing values and perceptions of interests in the Republic and in Britain were crucial in dealing with the North's troubles. In our 'post-nationalist' times, the central and shared interest has become the quality of the North's governance, not who governs it.

Relations between modern democratic states in which power is widely diffused are determined far more by their context—the dense webs of economic, social and political connections that exist—and far less by individual agency. But leaders still make a difference. As such, the passing of the British premiership from Tony Blair to Gordon Brown today can be expected to have implications for Ireland–Britain relations.

As always, the North will loom large. Despite the restoration of devolved legislative and executive institutions, further crises are all but inevitable. The DUP's erratic fundamentalism and Sinn Féin's obsessive irredentism should see to that. Brown, even if he chooses to deploy his prime ministerial authority as liberally as did Blair, is unlikely to be as calming. He has neither the outgoing leader's patience nor his gentler powers of persuasion.

Although Blair was willing to expend his energies on major global issues, he did not see smaller matters as being beneath him. This was unusual in such a powerful figure. Brown is far more typical. He brushes aside those issues he considers trifling. Given that he cannot always hide his irritation at what he sees as petty parochialism among his co-nationals in Edinburgh's parliament, he will not concern himself excessively with squabbles in Stormont.

Nor is he likely to be as well disposed to Dublin. Leaders of larger countries prefer photo opportunities in the White House rose garden and imparting their wisdom to the UN's general assembly to the tedium of summits with small countries. This dynamic, which bedevils relations between big and small states, was absent during Blair's premiership. It should reassert itself under Brown's. This would be less than helpful if any crisis in the North were to lead to the collapse of devolved government. The 'Plan B' option envisages an intensification of engagement between the governments. But Brown by inclination would be tempted to revert to a more traditional unilateralist approach, less willing to consult Dublin before he acts, and less willing to pay heed to Dublin's input when he does choose to consult.

The handover of power to Brown will have implications not only for Ireland's bilateral relationship with Britain, but also for relations in our shared European multilateral space. Britain's size and proximity exert an inescapable gravitational pull on this island. Should it drift away from the continent, Ireland would inevitably be disturbed in its European orbit.

There is reason to believe that such a drift could take place on Brown's watch. British public opinion is as sceptical as ever of EU membership and there are dwindling numbers of prominent figures and organisations willing to make the case for engagement. This is unsurprising. No country can easily transcend its history. From the end of the Hundred Years' War more than half a millennium ago, our neighbouring island has sought to limit its continental entanglements. Centuries of semi-detachment have left their mark. More recent history explains the further waning of the enthusiasm for engagement. The case for participation in the European project in the 1960s and 1970s was founded first and foremost on the clearly superior performance of the major continental economies. Much has changed since. From a position in the 1970s of decades of relative decline, Britain has outpaced France, Germany and Italy on most economic measures since the 1990s. No one personifies Britain's new-found belief in the superiority of its economic performance than the man who claims most credit for it—Gordon Brown.

How will Britain's stance in Europe change under him? This remains something of a mystery owing to the care he has taken to avoid setting out his stall on foreign matters. But there are straws in the wind. As Chancellor for 10 years he has rarely given the impression that he considers meeting his fellow EU finance ministers anything other than a chore. He also tends to be dismissive towards their ways and looks to the US for policy ideas. More recently, the debate over how to reform the union's ground rules suggested, at the very least, that he sees no case for deeper integration. The original constitutional text, which was rejected by French and Dutch voters in 2005, was agreed by Britain three years ago. Blair said then that it was a good deal for his country. Last week he fought to prevent many of its most significant elements being included in a new draft. It is hard not to see Brown's hand at work. Economic, political and social trends in Britain suggest that, if anything, it will become more detached from Europe. Blair, who had a genuine desire to bring Britain closer to the EU's heart, worked against those trends. Brown is unlikely to do the same.

Strong relations with Britain and full engagement with Europe are both vital national interests for Ireland. If Britain and Europe draw apart, Ireland may be forced to choose between them. If this comes to pass, or if co-operation on the North becomes more difficult, nostalgia for the New Labour era will quickly take hold. It may be that with Blair's passing, the best of times in Ireland–Britain relations have passed too.

*Originally published in the* Irish Times

# THESE ISLANDS' PERPETUAL PEACE

*April 2006*

Relations between Ireland and Britain have never been better. Changes in society, politics and economics in both countries explain the improvement, and most of the dynamics affecting relations between the countries give reason to believe that they should continue to improve.

For many who think deeply about relations between and among states, relative power has always been, and will always remain, the principle determinant in how they interact. But while it is true that power remains crucial in international relations, the 20th century saw many other factors come to the fore. As a result, the way states deal with each other has changed far more in the 84 years since the Irish state's founding than in the previous 300. The reasons are manifold: the waning of belligerent nationalism and the waxing of self-constraining multilateralism; the multiplying of identities and increasingly pacifistic publics; and changes in the type, amount and geographic spread of economic activity. All of these forces, and others besides, have been at work in both Ireland and Britain, and have had a profound effects on relations in what Patrick Keatinge, the doyen of the Irish international relations discipline, called the 'British Isles sub-system'.

## From war-war to jaw-jaw

The emergence of the modern state in Europe in the 17th century, when combined with the rise of nationalism in the 19th, saw an ever more unrestrained exercise of national sovereignty, culminating in the wars of 1914–45. Ultra-nationalism did not bypass these islands. The cathartic effect of blood-letting was, for example, a shared theme of two contemporary poets—Pádraig Pearse and Rupert Brooke. But by the standards of most other nations in Europe at the time, the Irish and British strains of extreme nationalism were far less virulent, as demonstrated by the War of Independence—a relatively brief, unbloody and restrained affair when compared to the period's other wars and subsequent struggles for statehood elsewhere.

By 1945 belligerent nationalism was discredited almost everywhere. Inter-state conflict became increasingly rare as a result. While might remained an arbiter in international affairs, rules-based mechanisms to manage relations among states became increasingly common, from the UN to a panoply of issue-specific international organisations. Where ultra-nationalism had wreaked most destruction in free Europe, the willingness to submit to multilateral constraint on the exercise of sovereignty went further than anywhere else. The six democracies most devastated by war pooled sovereignty, first in the European Coal and Steel Community, and later in the far more functionally wide-ranging European Economic Community.

The periphery of democratic Europe was less willing to constrain itself to such an extent and stood aloof from the integration project, in part at least because they had suffered less devastation. This, and a lingering desire to maintain great-power status, among other factors, led Britain to eschew involvement in the project. Ireland, largely untouched by the war and isolated from much of new thinking elsewhere, saw little need for change, never mind pool some of its so newly acquired sovereignty. The less changed mindset was reflected in still cool Ireland–Britain relations in the 1950s.

By the 1960s, de Valera and Churchill—statesmen of the first half of the 20th century in every sense—had been replaced by Lemass and Wilson, men much more of their times. Both countries moved towards EEC membership. Throwing their lot in with the continentals was not only a manifestation of change, but a harbinger of it. The countries now dealt not only within the traditional bilateral framework, but in the multilateral European context, with countless meetings of countless committees talking endlessly about their problems and disagreements (the EU is the most effective dispute resolution mechanism Europeans have ever devised). The frequency of meetings and the resulting familiarisation of Irish and British ministers and civil servants undoubtedly aided *rapprochement*. Even more important, for Ireland at least, was the effect of operating as an equal member state with Britain, thus creating a significant levelling of the playing field.

Northern Ireland has always been the elephant in the room of Anglo-Irish relations, and when it turned rogue at the end of the 1960s the effects were as profound then as they are well known now. It is therefore not necessary here to recount the sequence of events, but it is helpful to sketch the changing attitudes of both sides to the issue of sovereignty. At the onset of the Troubles Britain brooked no interference in its internal affairs. Today the Irish government's close involvement in most major decisions involving Northern Ireland looks like something akin to de facto joint sovereignty and Britain long ago stated that it does not have a 'selfish strategic interest' in Northern Ireland. Ireland's position at the start of the Troubles was equally sovereignty-centred, with its constitutionally-enshrined claim to Northern Ireland inhibiting better relations. Today the articles have been deleted and it is explicitly accepted that unionism has a veto on ending partition. The Good Friday Agreement, with its intricate stranded architecture and multiple fora, is designed to keep everyone talking all the time. It is, in many ways, the EU writ small.

## The public clamour for perpetual peace

The practitioners of statecraft—politicians and diplomats—are products of the societies from which they come. And change in domestic politics and society alters not only the manner in which states pursue their interests, but even more fundamentally in how they perceive them. In Europe this has created what Robert Cooper, a British diplomat who now works for the EU's foreign policy chief, calls a zone of 'post-modern' states whose peoples have become increasingly cosmopolitan, accepting of outsiders and, relatedly, pacifistic.

Though it may seem odd to suggest that xenophobia is in decline at a time of concern in both countries about the effects of immigration, a wider view allows a better evaluation. The multi-ethnicisation of urban Europe has taken place over a short period and has wrought great change. To be sure, it has not happened without difficulty and even occasional violence, but given the scale of the phenomenon, what is remarkable is how little upheaval it has caused. Moreover, the focus is on minimising the social frictions and maximising the economic and cultural benefits. Diversity is celebrated, discrimination outlawed and tolerance the cardinal virtue.

Not only is there less xenophobia than in the past, and its articulation less virulent, but there has also been a widening of the sense of solidarity from the merely national, as non-national identities are embraced— European, western, global or whatever one chooses. This can be seen by the rise of non-governmental organisations dedicated to aiding those whom donors will never meet in places they will never visit. This more open vision is also less exclusivist and less prone to make historically inaccurate claims to unique virtue and national exceptionalism.

In Ireland and Britain greater understanding of the other is seen at popular level in surveys which show how perceptions of each other have become more positive, and at an intellectual level in how we see the past: the emergence of the revisionist school in Ireland, debunking the crude ahistoricism of Britain being the 'unending source of all our ills'; and an end in Britain to the chauvinistic extolling of empire and recognition of its many wrongs. It even seems that for some at least the pendulum has swung from national self-aggrandisement to national self-loathing. Irish revisionists often appear to believe that the answer to every difficulty between the islands and their peoples can be attributed to the Irish state and that the onus is on it only to reform, while the British left, with its Manichean world view of a wicked west oppressing the rest, has a habit of seeing Britain's historical role as an exporter solely of misery.

## The moderating mechanism of the market

Changes in how states' interests are perceived and pursued explain more peaceful international relations, but so do changes in interests themselves, and none have changed more profoundly than economic interests. Most important is the manner in which wealth is generated. In the past, land and its resources determined the wealth of nations. Accumulation was about extraction, coercively if necessary. Today, economies are knowledge-based. Wealth is created, not extracted. Coercing creativity doesn't work. Countries become prosperous not by invading each other but by trading with each other. The lessening of territorial expansionism is explained to a considerable extent by this, and Britain's statement in the early 1990s that it had no economic interest in Northern Ireland reflected this changed calculus.

One of the most damaging expressions of extreme nationalism in the early part of the 20th century was the curbing of free trade and rise of autarkicism, not only because it caused impoverishment, but because it reduced countries' dependence on each other, thereby lowering the costs of going to war. Britain, once the champion of international free trade, retreated from that position gradually from the second half of the 19th century and by the 1930s was interested primarily in intra-empire trade. After independence, Ireland enthusiastically went down the self-sufficiency route, seeing autarky as an economic expression of independence from an erstwhile oppressor (most fledgling states in the early to mid 20th century did the same). The lunacy of the times was made manifest in the utterly pointless and, for Ireland at least, damaging and destabilising Economic War of the 1930s.

While the post-war era did not see a return to the economic liberalism of an earlier era in many areas, the democratic world agreed on the importance of reducing barriers to trade, and much of the most successful rules-based multilateral architecture of the post-war period was designed to achieve this. Ireland was the only democracy in Europe to remain autarkic. The consequences were disastrous. But economic failure, and the compelling logic of free trade, meant that no country could remain immune from the liberalisation bug. The Anglo-Irish Free Trade Agreement of 1965 was the first step, followed quickly be EEC accession.

Today, Britain is Ireland's second largest export market and Ireland Britain's fourth, and each is among the largest international investor in the other. This has increased prosperity for both countries, and made them more interdependent than ever.

## The future's risks

Wider forces do not explain everything. Every country is unique and has unique problems. Northern Ireland remains the most serious problem on these islands. Its society is anomalous, remaining only semi-permeable to the forces of moderation. It is by no means certain that the Good Friday Agreement, even if it can be made to work, will deradicalise the extremes of Provisionalism and Paisleyism and foster reconciliation between the two sides.

The future could also bring new problems. The wild-eyed euroscepticism of the Tory party, now untempered by its increasingly sidelined pro-European wing, could conceivably seek to secede from the EU if it returns to power. If Sinn Féin were to get a hand on the levers of executive power in the Republic, it would almost certainly cause serious instability.

There are, too, some niggles that will never go away. The limited knowledge of Ireland even among the most intelligent and worldly Britons never ceases to surprise. For them there will always be bigger fish to fry. By contrast, inhabitants of all small countries, Ireland included, can't help thinking a lot about their giant neighbours, and often feel frustrated and even belittled when that the interest is not reciprocated. The unchangeable asymmetry will also continue to cause concerns in Ireland about cultural domination, just as it does in other small countries existing cheek by jowl with larger countries with which they share so much, such as Canada, Portugal and Austria. But while risks always exist and nothing is irreversible, it is hard to envisage recent gains being lost and it is more likely that, as old grievances fade, relations will continue to improve.

*Originally published on* www.britainandireland.org

-----

# THE TRUE NATURE OF THE PROVISIONAL MINDSET

*21 January 2005*

Northern Ireland's peace process has brought gains, but it has not lived up to expectations. The assumptions that underpin the process are a good place to start in any re-evaluation of current policy, not least because two of these have proved faulty and need urgent revision. The first flawed assumption is that, given the opportunity, mainstream militant Republicans would take to democracy as did gunmen-turned-constitutionalists in the early years of the Irish State. This assumption is wrong because the Provisional movement today differs in profound respects from the parties which emerged after independence. Most important is the depth to which a culture of violence and militarism has permeated that movement.

Most of the current Provisional leadership were involved, directly or indirectly, in the taking of human life from youth into middle age, and lived in constant fear of being killed. Involvement in such a protracted conflict deeply embedded a culture inimical to the practice of democracy. Among others, its characteristics include: a reliance on summary justice; contempt for the law (rather than an understanding of the centrality of the rule of law); unquestioning and unbending beliefs (rather than flexibility and restraint); and sect-like secrecy and paranoia.

Owing to the short duration of the wars of 1919–23, there was no similar embedding of such a culture in the early years of the Irish State. This is best evinced by how anti-Treaty forces behaved after the cessation of Civil War hostilities. Despite the humiliation of defeat in 1923 and a backdrop of ascendant anti-democratic ideologies internationally, within three years the democratically minded split from the fundamentalists, and their move to becoming fully constitutional was completed in less than 10 years. The evolution of Provisionalism since its ceasefire has seen no such transformation.

The peace process's second flawed assumption relates to how a change in political culture can be engineered. Here, again, a misreading of history has resulted in overoptimism. Since the collapse of communism, peace processes and democratic transitions around the world have been underpinned by a belief that, because there is no alternative to democracy as a form of government, it is an inevitability. The policy and scholarly communities internationally came to believe that the habits of democracy would develop automatically provided the right institutional architecture was put in place (the frequently used but flawed analogy of the peace process as a train on track to a single final democratic destination reflects this inevitabilist thinking).

But even before Iraq, evidence had begun to pile up that there is no automaticity. There is also a growing recognition, not only that democratic institutions do not automatically generate democratic values, but that undemocratic values can subvert democratic institutions. And nowhere has optimism been dashed more than in relation to peace processes in divided societies. With the exception of South Africa, processes have either failed outright or failed to bring about the transformations envisaged. Examples of both situations include Sri Lanka, Israel-Palestine, Kosovo and Bosnia. The latter is particularly relevant to the North. Since its Dayton peace accords were implemented a decade ago, the most extreme parties have come to dominate. By promising to protect their respective communities aggressively, they have been able to carve up power and institutionalise a system of government based on predation of their communities. This is not dissimilar from the North today.

Almost seven years after the signing of the Belfast Agreement it is clear that the culture of militant Republicanism (and intransigent unionism) has not deradicalised and democratised as envisaged, and if this happens at all, it will take at least a generation. This has serious implications for the Republic. For the foreseeable future, a movement that does not share the democratic values of the State will continue to use the electoral system to increase its influence. In order to prevent degradation of the quality of the Republic's democracy, the government has a duty to put in place mechanisms to prevent contamination.

As a signal of its intent to end tolerance of any and all paramilitary activity, the government should establish a body of respected, independent citizens to monitor and report on Provisional illegality, as the International Monitoring Committee does on all paramilitaries in the North. And, in recognition of the threat posed, greater resources in money and manpower should be allocated to combating Provisional wrongdoing by, for instance, establishing a specially dedicated branch of the Criminal Assets Bureau.

Moreover, making it progressively harder for Provisionals to break the law in the Republic will help, not hinder, the process in the North. Among the structural weaknesses of the process is the absence of mechanisms to incentivise compliance and punish transgression. Because the Northern state does not have sufficient legitimacy among Catholics to clamp down without risking a backlash, it is even more urgent that the government signal to Provisionals that the State will use all its powers to end activities incompatible with democracy.

There should be a place in the process for concessions, but their sequencing should be changed. Heretofore, concessions have been granted upfront, forgoing the leverage that backloading them would bring. Take the proposed release of the killers of Garda Jerry McCabe. Though it is un-clear what Provisionals had done to deserve this concession, it is entirely inexplicable why it was envisaged that the killers would be released imme-diately, rather than after a period of proven compliance.

The peace process has brought important gains, but the argument for staying the same identical course is wrong for two reasons. First, the constant repetition that there is only one show in town signals to the extremists that they can act with impunity because the process will continue regardless. Second, it suggests that sovereign governments are in some way impotent to address failings and inadequacies in a process they themselves underwrote and helped to construct. Even if there is only one show, the governments are the actors and they have scope to interpret the script.

It has become impossible to avoid the conclusion that Provisionalism as we know it today will not go away any time soon, even if the North's institutions of devolved government can be restored. If the quality of the Republic's democracy is to be safeguarded, and if peace in the North is to be more than the absence of war, an understanding of the true nature and durability of the Provisional mindset must be central to the conduct of the process going forward.

*Originally published in the* Irish Times

––––

## POLICY ON NORTHERN IRELAND NEEDS HONEST EVALUATION

*July 2005*

The seven-year-old Belfast Agreement was based on the belief that a fair deal in the North would cause the culture of paramilitarism to wither on the vine. Well designed democratic institutions would normalise its dysfunctional politics and moderate the extremes. An unfragmented Provisional movement, it was hoped and envisaged, would abandon violence and adopt exclusively democratic ways. Lamentably, the faith invested in this historically ambitious strategy has proved ill-founded.

This has been demonstrated all too clearly recent months by the slaying of Robert McCartney, the systematic and ongoing use of threats and intimidation by the Provisional movement to protect itself from the consequences of the murder, the Northern Bank robbery and the uncovering of extensive money-laundering operations in the Republic. Such blatant wrong-doing on top of so much other evidence so long after the deal was signed has caused government exasperation. The Taoiseach has said that a blind eye will no longer be turned to such actions and a harsher tone is now taken with Provisionals.

But this belies an unchanged basic posture. Most fundamental is the government's mantra-like repetition that it will not consider any change to the Belfast Agreement, despite its demonstrable failure to achieve the objectives set out seven years ago. In every public utterance, the Taoiseach insists, unbendingly and uncreatively, that there is only route forward for the North. The placing of all the government's eggs in the basket of the Belfast Agreement is an elementary error. Statecraft is about working to maximise one's room for manoeuvre so that the chance of achieving desired outcomes is increased. It is also about reducing the freedom of action of one's adversaries by creating for them a calculation of risks and rewards that makes their undesirable outcomes more difficult to achieve.

The government has done exactly the opposite. It has tied its own hands by refusing to consider alternatives, even though there is simply no down-side to letting it be known that it is ready to move on from the Belfast Agreement if it cannot be made to work. A willingness to consider alternatives, moreover, offers only up-side for the government. By abandoning its open-ended commitment to the Agreement, the government would create uncertainty for Provisionals (an alternative might be far less appealing to them than what is on offer now). Uncertainty for Provisionals gives leverage to the government, the absence of which is among the most serious structural weaknesses of the Agreement. In a seeming paradox, the government has a greater chance of implementing the Belfast Agreement if appears willing to consider alternatives to it.

If policies, frameworks or agreements are simply means to ends, to be dispensed with unsentimentally if they fail, or adjusted if their inadequacies become evident, why has the government refused to do this, eschewing all strategic flexibility in the process? The answer lies in a failure of political leadership.

In any policy area there is a division of labour between politicians and officials, with the former setting objectives, laying down the parameters and providing a jolt if processes get stuck in a rut, while the latter focus on the detail of execution and implementation. But bureaucratic inertia can all too easily result if the balance tips too strongly towards civil servants or politicians don't do their counterbalancing job.

In general, the Irish administrative system is more vulnerable to this than most. The Civil Service's strongly collegiate culture and emphasis on building and maintaining consensus is fostered by the personal familiarity

of a small service and its unusually apolitical nature. While these characteristics mean that the service is very strong on teamwork, it is weak on
critical evaluation because questioning the consensus can too easily be
seen as rocking the boat.

Strong political leadership is therefore all the more important as a
counterbalance. Politicians need to ask the tough questions and play the
devil's advocate to ensure that assumptions are challenged, flaws in policy
formulation corrected and process-focused officials do not allow means to
become more important than ends. The Taoiseach, whose temperament
and executive style are more similar to those of a civil servant than a politician—risk-averse, consensus-seeking and non-confrontational—has done
none of these things on Northern policy.

How the Taoiseach has led talks with the Provisional movement also
warrants criticism. Because of his patient sincerity, unimpulsive manner
and seeming absence of ego, which make it almost impossible for those
with whom he deals to dislike him, Mr Ahern has deservedly earned a
reputation as a world-class negotiator (his unacrimonious brokering last
year of agreement on an EU constitution, for instance, was among the great
European diplomatic achievements of recent times).

But splitting differences with democratic heads of state or the social
partners is profoundly different from dealing with those who believe that
justice is dispensed from the barrel of a gun. When basic democratic principles are at stake, the give and take of normal negotiations is inappropriate.
Because Mr Ahern has been as unwilling to threaten sanction as he has
been willing to offer concession, he has left himself vulnerable to accusations
of appeasement. Even after publicly accusing his Provisional interlocutors
of having foreknowledge of the Northern Bank robbery, he refused to
resort to sanction and opposed anyone else doing so either (he was against
the International Monitoring Committee and US government sanctioning
the movement for its transgressions). In his Arbour Hill speech in April,
he gave further reassurance to Provisionals, saying that he would 'not play
the politics of exclusion' (effectively offering them open-ended blanket
political impunity for future wrongdoing) and 'would always seek to persuade and convince elements of Nationalist Ireland' (thereby signalling a
permanent rejection of methods other then gentle coaxing to move them
towards democratic norms).

His Minister for Foreign Affairs, Dermot Ahern, has followed this lead.
In a newspaper article in early April he called on Provisionals to end their
boycott of the North's new policing arrangements so that the rule of law
could operate effectively in the jurisdiction. But rather than making this a

demand, the minister used the conditional, saying that such a move 'would' be a welcome step 'if it happens', and then weakened his hand further by failing to warn of consequence in the event of inaction. It is unsurprising that the Provisional movement did not deem the Minister's exhortation to merit response. Because Provisionals hold in sneering disregard the political class from which he and his Taoiseach come, precisely because they believe it to be weak and effete, the exclusive reliance on concession by the government serves only to reinforce their prejudice.

While the government has been right always to leave the democratic door open to Provisionals, its exclusive reliance on persuasion to bring them through it has, at best, contributed to delaying the political development of the movement and, at worst, invited further transgression. Instead, a judicious mix of carrot and stick is required, with concessions on offer (but only after a proven period of compliance), and the use of credible threat in the form of a graduated, measured and determined political and security response to illegal activities. A recognition is also needed that it may simply not be possible to engineer a change in Provisionalism's anti-democratic culture. The consequences of this are extremely serious, making it all the more important that these are faced up to. It is to be hoped that here, more than anywhere else, the Taoiseach will show strong and resolute leadership.

Underpinning the failures of statesmanship and statecraft has been a third major failure of government policy: a failure of analysis, both of Provisionalism's intentions and how its anti-democratic culture can be changed. Conceptually, analysing the intentions of any entity can be done in two ways: by examining its internal workings and by considering its actions. While governments usually use both methods, emphasis is always placed on adversaries' actions because of the inherent unreliability of intelligence.

The government's analysis of Provisionalism has been exactly the reverse, with endless consideration given to the balance of forces with the movement and a blind eye turned to what its actions say about whether its anti-democratic culture is changing. This has played into Provisionalism's hands. Because it has spent more than three decades preventing infiltration no one can know its real intentions with any certainty. This has allowed it more leeway than it deserves, and the chance to exploit wishful thinking about its intentions. This has occurred even though the movement's more politically-minded elements, such as they are, have stated repeatedly and explicitly that they value the unity of their movement over all else, which implicitly includes democracy and its values.

Politically, speculation about Provisionalism's internal dynamics has helped perpetuate the notion that there are doveish elements within the Provisional movement fighting bravely for peace against darker forces. This has allow the movement's public faces to pose as Mandela-like figures, helping them gain stature internationally and electoral success at home.

A second major failure of analysis relates to the understanding of how political culture is transformed. The government's emphasis has been on the restoration of the Northern assembly and executive because it believes in the power of democratic institutions to transform political culture. There is much to the argument that by giving those unfamiliar with democracy an opportunity to operate in democratic institutions they will gradually adopt the habits and ways of democracy. But this rosy view ignores the countless examples of history—past and present—which show those uncommitted to democracy using democratic institutions for non-democratic ends.

By focusing so much on restoring the institution the government is in danger of placing the bar far too low. In each round of talks it has spun the 'historic' nature of potential developments and talked of 'end-games', as if a declaration or single act would suddenly allow breakthrough to a promised land that is claimed to be so tantalisingly close. This risks allowing a grand gesture by Provisionals—decommissioning or a declaration that its military machine has been disbanded—to be taken as proof of an end to the culture of paramilitarism when it could mean nothing of the sort. Actions can suggest that culture is evolving, but cannot be taken as proof that it is because both kinds of actions—democratic and non-democratic—can be perpetrated simultaneously. Only an extended period of compliance with the letter and spirit of the Agreement can do that.

Nothing in this critique is to say that the Belfast Agreement should be summarily ditched or that the State should suddenly revert to the sort of stance it took against militants in the 1920s or 1940s. But with a curious absence of scrutiny of a vital area of public policy (unthinkable in, say, health or transport), drift has taken place over seven years. When the stakes are so high—real peace in the North and the democratic integrity of the Republic—surely it is time to revisit assumptions, honestly evaluate failures and change policy accordingly.

*Originally published in* Magill *magazine*

## GOVERNMENT FOCUS ON IRISH ILLEGALS IN US IS MISTAKEN

*29 November 2007*

The plight of illegal, undocumented Irish immigrants in the United States strikes a chord in a country with such a long and painful history of emigration. This backdrop has benefited those who lobby the Irish government to make representations on their behalf to the US. Currently, when the issue is aired in Ireland, Cabinet members are only too eager to emphasise how they raise the issue at every opportunity with their US counterparts.

This amounts to a failure of foreign policy on a number of levels. It is inappropriate for the breaking of one country's law by citizens of another to become the subject of a diplomatic offensive. The most appropriate way to deal with the issue of illegal/undocumented immigrants is not at state-to-state level, but for civil society organisations in the US to push for change. And all the more so in this case given the openness of the US system to such lobbying and the strength, vibrancy and clout of Irish-American organisations.

The provision of assistance to such organisations by the Irish government is a more delicate and appropriate means of achieving the goal of regularising those who have made their lives in the US without following the letter of that country's law. Unsubtle pestering and appearing to interfere in the domestic affairs of another sovereign state is decidedly not the correct approach.

The constant raising of the issue of illegal/undocumented Irish immigrants by members of the Cabinet, up to and including the Taoiseach, with US counterparts means that other more important interests do not receive the attention that they would otherwise get. Influence over the US—the sole superpower—is necessarily finite for any country. Ireland's influence is marginal, given its relative powerlessness and hence its limited ability to assist the US in the pursuit of its interests. As such, whatever influence Ireland has in Washington needs to be wielded with great care and consideration to ensure that the maximum benefit accrues.

The government's ongoing campaign at the behest of the undocumented lobby also erodes goodwill among members of the US executive and legislature. To be exhorted by a foreign country to ignore one's own laws causes irritation at the very least. To be harangued on the subject of illegal immigration at a time when hostility to immigration is widening and deepening among voters is particularly inopportune and unlikely to endear Ireland to US officials and lawmakers.

Lest there be any doubt about the importance of wielding influence in Washington, let us remember the range of vital interests tied up in the Ireland–US relationship. First, up to a quarter of a million jobs in the Republic are dependent on US investment—over 100,000 directly, and at least as many indirectly. There are a multitude of issues that require constant attention at government level to protect and nurture these links, not least the need to mitigate growing US congressional hostility to the corporation tax régime that keeps many US companies in Ireland.

Second, in an EU and international context, there are many signs that economic protectionism is on the rise. Ireland is uniquely vulnerable given its position as a hub in the Atlantic economy. Among the many areas in this regard where influence in Washington is invaluable is EU–US trade disputes. In the past these have resulted in both sides being allowed by the World Trade Organisation to impose punitive sanctions on the other. The decision on the geographic and sectoral spread of such sanctions is open to considerable discretion by the imposing country. To be blunt, quiet lobbying in Washington can help ensure that the effect on Irish jobs is as limited as possible.

Finally, there is the political context. It is a long-term strategic priority to ensure that the US remains engaged with Northern Ireland. Although relations with Britain are excellent, and it is to be hoped that this happy situation continues, Dublin and London do not always see eye-to-eye on how that troubled place should be dealt with. As American involvement tends to level the playing field between Ireland and Britain when differences arise, it would be imprudent not to maintain reserves of goodwill. If Americans believe they will receive a browbeating on illegal/undocumented immigrants each time an Irish politician enters their offices, doors are less likely to be open if favours are needed on other issues.

One is loath not to offer support to those who seek to better themselves and their families by dint of hard work, and all the more so when they make the sort of sacrifices Irish citizens in the US have made. But the conduct of foreign policy is designed to maximise the security, prosperity and wellbeing of all citizens. The focus of Irish diplomacy should be on the best interests of Ireland and its four-million-plus citizens, not on a few thousand who have broken the laws of the most important nation in the world.

*Originally published in the* Irish Times

## THE RISKS FOR IRELAND OF AN OBAMA PRESIDENCY

*2 November 2008*

Barack Obama is an extraordinary politician. His orchestration of pro-tracted campaigns against two formidable opponents has been impressive, doing much to allay concerns about his dearth of leadership experience. He has also demonstrated sound judgment, made good appointments to his very large team, delegated effectively, taken advice well and wobbled rarely. Underpinning these achievements is a fine mind, an unusually calm temperament and a profound self-confidence. These characteristics, his life story and his charisma will do much to restore a great country's moral authority in the world.

Although John McCain is also a very fine candidate—there are few more resolutely principled politicians, and fewer still who are more knowledgable about world affairs—he could not offer the sort of fresh start for his country that Obama can. Combined with McCain's uneven temperament and the risk of his unqualified running mate becoming president, Obama is the better choice to lead the US and the world in the difficult and uncertain years ahead.

That is the big picture, but what about the smaller Irish picture? Ireland's interests in the world and vis-à-vis the US are necessarily narrow. As a very small country that has the luxury of being located in the most peaceful and politically stable part of the world, Ireland's bilateral relations with the US centre on trade and investment links between the two countries on which we are so dependent. For Ireland, decisions in the US that could weaken those links are to be feared. Obama's promises and statements, the balance of forces in the Democratic Party and trends in American public opinion all suggest that America under Obama will veer towards protectionism.

Consider first public opinion. A Pew research poll last year found a lower proportion of American respondents were supportive of free trade than in any of the other 50-odd countries surveyed worldwide. Combine this with rising hostility to off-shoring, which was already at fever pitch when joblessness was nonexistent, and it is hard to avoid the conclusion that the US is more hostile to globalisation than any other nation. This hostility can be expected only to deepen and broaden as unemployment rises and economic uncertainty grows.

Anti-globalisation sentiment is widespread in the Democratic Party, which has traditionally been less supportive of economic openness than the Republicans. The Democratic-controlled Congress has opposed free trade agreements and, since 2007, has refused the extension of presidential powers to negotiate trade deals without having for itself line-by-line veto power. This is one of the reasons why the Doha round of multilateral trade talks continues to languish.

As for Obama himself, he has not shied away from protectionist rhetoric during the campaign. But, in fairness, his bite is unlikely to match his bark. His economic advisers are mostly solid internationalists, and one of them, Austan Goolsbee, let slip earlier in the year that Obama would not act on his threats of economic nationalism if elected.

How could these factors come together and play out in relation to Ireland? By far the greatest threat is a change to the US corporation tax code. Many voices are now calling for US companies to be taxed on world-wide earnings in their home country. If American companies located in Ireland were obliged to pay the US rate of 35%, it would mean that, on top of the 12.5% of their profits booked in Ireland, which go to the Department of Finance, an additional 22.5% would go to the treasury in Washington DC.

US companies, which directly and indirectly employ one in 10 people at work in Ireland, operate here for many reasons, but tax is undoubtedly of key importance. Data on output per worker in the sectors in which US companies dominate show that Irish workers produce more (often far more) than their counterparts elsewhere. There can be little doubt that this is attributable far less to the heroic toiling of Irish workers and far more to transfer pricing, which, put simply, is a method of inter-jurisdictional tax avoidance.

Obama has made noises about closing what many Americans consider to be a loophole. US businesses will lobby hard against this, arguing that it would put them at a competitive disadvantage. But as the US fiscal position weakens and as anti-business sentiment becomes shriller, making companies pay more tax in the US may be both necessary and popular. If the US revamped its tax régime along those lines, it would fundamentally change the way American companies view their international operations in general, and their Irish operations in particular. Companies already in Ireland would be more likely to divest, and attracting new ones would be far more difficult. Under a McCain presidency, the existing tax code would be safe, because he believes it is good for American companies and good for America. Reassuringly for Ireland, he even cited approvingly the country's low corporation tax rate in a TV debate with Obama.

On trade, the differences between the candidates are narrower. Philip Gordon, who was director for Europe at the national security council during the Clinton administration, is among the hot favourites to take responsibility for Europe at the state department under Obama. At a conference in Barcelona in June he stressed Obama's commitment to bilateral trade links with Europe, and the importance of the multilateral trading system centred around the World Trade Organisation.

Pragmatic Republicans don't doubt the Obama commitments to avoid roll-back on trade. At a think-in of policy wonks and journalists in Slovakia two weeks ago, John Hulsman of the German Council on Foreign Relations, a hard-headed and worldly Republican, stated that, while Obama would not push for trade liberalisation, he was unlikely to go in the opposite direction. But whether, against his better judgment, Obama will be able to resist moving in a protectionist direction is moot.

Europeans rarely realise that their prime ministers are far more powerful domestically than American presidents are in the US. Where European parliaments have limited powers over the executive branch of government, the US Congress can make life impossible for presidents. In order to get anything done, Obama will have to horse-trade with Congress. If demands for protectionism in the US rise, Congress will pander and even inflame. Legislators could call the president on his campaign promises, such as the renegotiation of the North American Free Trade Agreement. Obama may not be able to resist. McCain would be less likely to cave in. He has consistently taken on protectionists, reaffirming repeatedly that free trade was good for America and good for the world. Having stood up to populists all his political life, he could be depended on to do the same on trade as president.

There can be little doubt that Ireland's investment and trade relations with the US would continue as before under McCain. That can not at all be taken for granted under Obama administration. Most Irish people today wish for an Obama victory. Let's hope that, in time, they do not come to rue such an outcome.

*Originally published in the* Sunday Business Post

# NATO LINK IS GOOD FOR IRELAND

*10 October 1999*

Ireland has been successful in carving out a niche for itself in an increasingly interconnected world. This has been achieved, in large part, by becoming actively involved in the dense web of international organisations and frameworks for co-operation in many fields. However, in one important field—defence co-operation—Ireland has remained curiously isolationist. With the Cold War long over, a rethinking of Ireland's position is required in order to make a contribution to dealing with threats—of a lower order, but more complex—to European security that exist in today's changed circumstances.

If Ireland is to be listened to on security matters, and if it is to allow its armed forces to play a part in meaningfully implementing its laudable humanitarian foreign policy goals, an end to rigid isolationism in defence matters is necessary. That is why the government's decision to approve the terms on which Ireland will join the PfP (Partnership for Peace) is so welcome. In the Balkans, the alphabet soup of multilateral organisations involved in maintaining peace—the UN, EU, OSCE, Sfor, Kfor, NATO along with the PfP—is testament to the complexity of multi-dimensional security challenges. While Ireland has played its part in many of these organisations while remaining aloof from the PfP framework, membership of the PfP allows this State to make a more substantial contribution. Put bluntly, the PfP is where it is at when it comes to military co-ordination in humanitarian crises in Europe.

Membership of the PfP means that the Defence Forces will no longer be hindered in co-operating with others, because everything from spare parts to communications systems compatibility is PfP-standardised. In addition, the opportunities for acquiring the skills that a modern force requires will become available. Although our army is widely respected for its professionalism, there are few countries in Europe with an armed force as small and under-resourced as Ireland's. With bilateral training opportunities now limited, the importance of the PfP becomes even more evident. Membership of the PfP also allows Ireland to demonstrate that it is not shirking its international responsibilities.

At a time when Ireland's economic miracle has attracted green-eyed glances and amid mutterings that it would have remained an economic laggard without ultra-low company tax rates and EU cash transfers, participation in the PfP will send a signal that Ireland is as prepared to contribute to collective security as it is to reap the rewards of co-operation in other fields.

In supporting Ireland's participation, it is as necessary, possibly more necessary, to debunk the myths about defence co-operation (in particular the very existence of NATO) as it is to stress the benefits of the PfP, for many of the arguments against participation in the PfP rest on flawed assumptions about NATO. With the demise of the Soviet Union, the greatest threat to western Europe disappeared. So, say some, why not NATO too? While threats to European security have rarely been so few, war has been a constant throughout human history. To take the current peace in Europe (the Balkans excluded) for granted would be reckless folly.

The most obvious and immediate (but not only) potential threat to European security is Russian recidivism. Falling living standards, endemic corruption and, more recently, terrorism have led to growing support for anti-progressive forces in Russia. The clamouring by former Soviet satellites for the embrace of NATO membership underlines the continuing Russian threat.

A further suspicion of isolationists is that as long as NATO exists there will be a temptation to use its military capacity offensively. Not only does this ignore the fact that NATO has only ever fired shots in anger to prevent ethnic cleansing, it also fails to appreciate the changing way democratic states think about their interests. Today, in the mature and thoroughly democratic NATO countries, policy—both domestic and foreign—is formulated with the good of the greatest number in mind. That number, educated, assertive and far from unquestioning, would have little truck at election time with any party threatening ill-advised foreign adventures, putting lives, or those of family members, at risk. The domestic political repercussions of even limited casualties, as seen in the Gulf War in the early 1990s, for example, has severely curtailed the projection of military power.

But the waning belligerence of democracies owes as much to a sense of injustice as it does to an unwillingness of individuals to die for cause or country. Concern for the welfare of non-nationals is growing—witness the proliferation of groups in rich countries working to relieve debt, speed development and protect the human rights of individuals with whom they share little in common other than that they are fellow human beings. The pressure for intervention in Kosovo and East Timor, where the west's security or economic interests are largely unthreatened, can only be explained in this context.

Apart from doubts in the minds of some about NATO itself, there are concerns that forging any links with NATO will make Ireland complicit in the acts of its member-countries, such as exporting arms to repressive régimes. It is hard to see how Ireland, unilaterally choosing from a menu of humanitarian intervention options, can suddenly be considered complicit in arms sales when it already shares a currency with France, participates in the EU's foreign policy with the UK and enjoys enormous inflows of capital from the US. These three countries are among the world's largest arms exporters.

A further objection to the PfP is that by participating Ireland must, *ipso facto*, distance itself from those uninvolved, thereby undermining the country's relations with the developing world and others. This is to ignore the experiences of other states, most notably the Nordic NATO countries— among the greatest contributors to conflict-resolution internationally. The Norwegians played a pivotal role in the Middle East peace process—their NATO membership inconsequential to the Palestinians. The Danes were actively involved in the peaceful transition to democracy in Nicaragua— their NATO link an irrelevance for the Sandinistas. Moreover, the Finns, not NATO members but participants in the PfP from the outset, were instrumental in ending the west's most serious spat with post-Soviet Russia during NATO's intervention in Kosovo. It is to be hoped that these arguments will allay the concerns of those who are prepared to take a more measured and objective view of what is a minimalist form of defence co-operation.

*Originally published in the* Irish Times

---

# IRELAND'S GIFT TO THE UN: BERTIE AHERN

*11 November 2005*

Because the UN is as imperfect as it is indispensable, questions abound about its future. Important in determining this will be who succeeds Kofi Annan as secretary general. He or she will have two main challenges: first, to persuade members to implement reforms of its failing institutions; second, to be an effective crisis manager. Bertie Ahern fits the bill because these challenges play to his leadership strengths and expose none of his weaknesses.

When trouble flares in the world, the UN is almost always drafted in to fight the fire. But its involvement is not straightforward because there are, in effect, two UNs—the inter-governmental forum centred around the security council and the much less significant international organisation over which the secretary general presides. The big security decisions are taken by huddles of member-country diplomats in the warren of rooms around the security council chamber in New York. The secretary general is, at best, a supporting actor. He does as he is mandated by the members and risks incurring their wrath if he attempts to involve himself without invitation.

Secretaries general, therefore, must be content to work within the constraints of the job and resist the temptation to push tightly circumscribed boundaries. In times of crisis they can persuade and cajole, and deploy their (considerable) moral authority, but cannot bang heads together. They listen, identify where compromise is possible, split differences, facilitate agreement, and then, if requested, co-ordinate implementation. Mr Ahern ticks all these boxes. Most relevant is his stint as EU president in 2004 because that role is so similar to that of UN secretary general, both in its responsibilities and limitations. The manner in which he brokered agreement without acrimony on the now defunct EU constitution was a case study in effective chairmanship, consensus building and dispute resolution.

Mr Ahern's character is well suited to such roles. He is highly self-controlled, only losing his temper when he chooses—in Dáil debates, for example, but never in private negotiations. He does not get entangled in clashes of pride because, unlike most successful politicians, he does not have the over-developed ego that causes the self-important to be ultra-sensitive. He is also patient and willing to soak up criticism if he believes it will help achieve his goal.

The Taoiseach's one (very serious) weakness as a negotiator is his excessive willingness to give in to demands when put under pressure, most notably by concession-hungry Provisionals and grasping social partners. But because it is the members who gift concessions at the UN, not the secretary general, Mr Ahern's weakness in this regard would be of as little relevance as it was when he was EU president.

As important as what Mr Ahern would do in the job is what he would not do. He could be trusted not to attempt to muscle in on members' sphere of responsibilities because of his innate caution and dislike of bold initiatives. Although his reluctance to exercise his prime ministerial power (a defining feature of his time as Taoiseach) may have resulted in many missed opportunities, that limited ambition and cautious restraint are just what a UN secretary general needs if he is to avoid being slapped down by the members.

The second major task for the next secretary general will be to advance institutional reform. Because a blueprint already exists, vision will not be required, just persuasion, tenacity and unceasing effort to ensure effective implementation. Here again, Mr Ahern would be the right man for the job. His diligence and capacity for hard work are not questioned even by his sternest opponents, while his (limited) capacity for creative vision would not be unduly taxed. Mr Ahern could also hasten change by introducing some true Drumcondra grit to the Manhattan bubble which UN staffers and the diplomats in the organisation's orbit inhabit. After Mr Annan (the ultimate UN insider) the leadership style of a down-to-earth political heavyweight from the real world would do far more for the organisation than another urbane polyglot from the diplomatic cocktail-party circuit.

Just as Mr Ahern's appointment would be good for the UN, it would also be good for Ireland. Over the past decade, the country has come to be seen internationally as a model for others. But Ireland's coming of age has yet to be fully expressed politically and diplomatically. Mr Ahern's elevation to the pinnacle of global diplomacy would send a signal that Ireland has arrived not only as an economy, but as a state too. It would also have the happy byproduct of raising the country's profile, adding to prestige, generating goodwill and increasing influence.

Mr Ahern is unquestionably the right man for the job, but there would be obstacles to overcome. The most significant is the feeling among Asians that it is their turn to lead—not since Burma's U Thant stood down in 1972 has the world's most populous continent held the role. But it is a convention—not a rule—that the secretary general job be rotated geographically, and besides, with tensions and suspicions in abundant supply in the region, Asians may be unable to agree among themselves on a candidate. If a suitable easterner does not emerge, the world will inevitably look Europe's way—three of the UN's seven secretaries general have come from small successful European countries. Not only is Ireland unthreatening and small, it is a country whose commitment to the UN system is unquestioned and against whom nobody bears a grudge. This can be seen in who would be likely to support the Taoiseach's candidature (or at least not oppose it).

Most important are the five veto-wielding permanent members of the security council. First among equals is the US, the UN's biggest bankroller. Excellent relations mean that Mr Ahern would be regarded approvingly in Washington. He would also get the nod from Paris, thanks, among other things, to his good relations with the French president. Add an enthusiastic Tony Blair to the axis and only the Russians and Chinese would need buttering up. Beyond the bigs, Mr Ahern would win support from other

EU members and the developing world. With no foreseeable opposition and plenty of support, he would stand an excellent chance.

By the time the UN job comes up Mr Ahern will have spent almost a decade as Taoiseach, longer than anyone since de Valera. This, surely, is more than enough, not least because there is little he is likely to achieve in his second decade that he has not in his first. Mr Ahern should consider the job. He could do more service to country, and the world, in New York than in Dublin.

*Originally published in the* Irish Times

*Chapter* IV  ∾

# REFLECTIONS ON AN OLD CONTINENT

*'Europe is the conscience of the world; the best and the worst have happened here.'*

SIMONE WEIL

## INTRODUCTION

The modern world was invented in Europe: from constitutionalism to the rule of law; from the scientific method to the industrial economy; from banking to the joint-stock corporation; from the steam engine to the car; from vaccination to penicillin; from the radio telegraph to the World Wide Web; from the university degree to the museum; from the newspaper to the encyclopedia; from cinema to soccer. It is only a slight exaggeration to say that the lion's share of the ideas, institutions, and inventions that shape the lives of every human being on the planet are European. But the continent has far more than past achievements to its credit. Europeans have inhabited in recent decades a uniquely peaceful, prosperous and calm corner of the world and in no other region of the globe is so much diversity crammed into so small a geographical space. Though there is much that separates and divides Europeans, they have managed despite their difference to create a uniquely successful mechanism for managing their relations in their European Union (the next chapter is devoted entirely to that entity).

Modesty prevents Europeans from talking up their achievements today. So, too, does awareness and acknowledgment of past wrongs. By the turn of the 19th century, the world was run from London, Paris and a handful of other European capitals. The subjugation of others is now a cause of shame, as are the notions of superiority that so many Europeans acquired at the time. Today, the continent's inhabitants prefer to view themselves as respectful of others and their ways, as generous givers to the developing world via aid budgets and charities, and as stalwart multilateralists.

Simone Weil's words, quoted above, capture well the modern European consciousness, containing as they do conceit, pride and contrition respectively.

## THE STATE OF THE STATE

None of Europe's inventions has shaped the modern world more than the sovereign state. The planet's peoples interface constantly with their respective states and in ways that are barely noticed. State sovereignty and its inviolability remain the organising principle of the international system. And, despite advances in international law, what happens within the borders of states is still very much determined by national leaders, as tyrants from Burma to Zimbabwe demonstrate with depressing regularity. Nor has the state been eroded by the market and the multinational corporation, as has so often been predicted and claimed in recent decades.While there can be little doubt that after the economic crises of the 1970s, market-based solutions became more common, there was no rolling back of the state. In the countries of the OECD, the average state's tax take has barely deviated from 35% of GDP (I know of no other economic data series that has remained so stable over such a long period), while the role of the state as regulator has expanded enormously. Over time, everything from labour standards to health and safety rules to environmental protection laws has been on an upward trend across the world, proving that if the market spurs a race to the bottom, the state is more than powerful enough to check it. And if any reminder of the centrality of the state was ever needed, the reaction to the economic crisis that erupted in 2008 has provided it, as governments bail out, nationalise, stimulate and lend as last and, increasingly, first resort.

In Europe, talk about the withering of the state has been the most intense. Not only did European states have to contend with the globalisation of market forces, but, it was frequently contended, their essence would be sapped by the sucking of powers upwards to Brussels, their draining downwards to regional governments and their diffusion in every direction by the widening of European law. But this has not come to pass: national taxes remain the highest in the world by a distance (averaging 45% of GDP), government provision of services is the most comprehensive and Europeans are still inclined to see the state as offering a helping hand, not waving an iron first that threatens their liberty, as, for instance, Americans often view it. Europe differs from the US on regulation, too. Where the US prefers allowing individuals recourse to litigation, Europeans prefer their law-makers to regulate as a means of protecting the individual. It is true that European states have decided to do much of this regulation collectively in their Union, but so great has been the increase in regulation that there has been more than enough for all levels of government.

The durability of the European state can also be seen in the relative strength of the great powers over centuries. From the Congress of Vienna to the Treaty of Versailles to the present day, the same powers continue to count—Britain, France, Germany and Russia. As detailed in Chapter vi, the decline in interstate conflict, and the reasons for this decline, have changed the dynamic and the stakes of the game, yet these same countries still vie for influence and jockey for position. Watching that game is gripping.

## FRANCE IN FLUX

None of the big four European powers has suffered so many reversals and so few periods on top as France over the past two centuries. Since Napoleonic times it has been constantly eclipsed by its neighbours. In the 19th century, the emergence of a unified Germany changed everything forever. In the race for empire and industrialisation it continuously lagged Britain in the former, and matched neither Britain nor Germany in the latter. The 20th century proved more traumatic still. France suffered the human catastrophe of two world wars on its soil and the national humiliation of invasion and occupation in the 1940s. Its resistance to the mid-century wave of decolonisation led to long and bloody wars in Indochina and Algeria (among the imperial powers, only authoritarian Portugal resisted the tide more fiercely). Economically, it was outgrown by Germany in the 30 years after the Second World War and by Britain in the following 30 years. The failure of the Suez campaign in 1956, because the us supported Egypt over France, Britain and Israel, resulted in France beginning another long, lonely and futile campaign; this time against us dominance of the Atlantic world. In recent decades, the leveraging of its influence in Europe via the 'Franco-German axis', which allowed it to dominate the integration project in its first decades, is now of little relevance and its influence in the eu has been waning at least since the first round of enlargement in the early 1970s. Perhaps even more important than its actual economic performance in recent decades, which has been considerably better than is often credited, has been its seemingly anachronistic view of the state as a means of taming market forces that would threaten or undermine its ways and values. As there is nothing as unfashionable as yesterday's fashion, the French view of the state was out of step with the post-1970s free-market orthodoxy and symbolised the country's apparent inability to change and adapt (all has changed in recent months and one suspects that derisive, Anglophone sniggering at France will be heard less in the times to come).

If anything, France's capacity not only to survive the upheavals and reversals it has faced, but to remain a leading power and influential country is testimony to its underlying strengths. France retains many of the trappings of great-power status: a permanent seat on the UN's security Council; a nuclear deterrent and a serious military, one of the finest diplomatic corps in the world and the clout, determination and focus to ensure its nationals get to run many of the most important international organisations.[1] The French elite is imbued with a deep self-confidence, flowing from its centuries-long place as a leading power not only in European and world affairs, but intellectually and culturally, too.

But the political and policy-making classes are currently divided on the country's strategic positioning in a manner quite unlike any of the other big powers. On the two pillars of French foreign policy—its position in Europe and its relations with the US—consensus is frayed. Since his inauguration the country's current president, Nicolas Sarkozy, has signalled his intent to abandon France's role as counter-balancer to the US *hyper-puissance* by ending his country's 43-year self-imposed exclusion from NATO's integrated military command. The move is of considerable significance in that it represents acceptance of the reality of US leadership in the trans-Atlantic community. This, in turn, increases the chances of a strong European defence identity being developed within the EU—a long-term objective of France, but one that it has delayed precisely because of its unwillingness to accept US leadership (other countries have long suspected that France aspired to take the US's place at the top of the pecking order). But for many in France, on both left and right, full reintegration into NATO is a bridge too far. And for any French leader to make a change as profound as the de facto abandonment of Gaullism without deep and wide support across the political spectrum carries many risks, not least that the decision could be reversed by his successor. Views on deepening European integration and the country's role therein are also in flux, with scepticism rising across the political spectrum. In many ways, this is unsurprising. France's thousand-year history of independent action and its disproportionate influence over centuries in world politics and international society does not make it a natural candidate to accept willingly the great constraints of the ultimate multilateral mechanism. In this, as in much else, France is similar to Britain. It could yet become as problematic an EU member state.

## BRITAIN ADRIFT

Moving to London in 1998, a year after the most pro-European government in three decades had come to power, it appeared to me as if Britain would gradually be reconciled with Europe. Things turned out very differently. Nothing quite symbolised Britain's drift from the continent so clearly as the decision of the country's prime minister, Gordon Brown, to attend an obscure Westminster committee meeting as his 26 EU counterparts gathered in Portugal in December 2007 to sign the Lisbon treaty. If anything, the pace of drift looks likely to accelerate, and the UK's membership of the EU could come into question if the Conservative Party, now almost entirely bereft of its pro-EU element, returns to power in 2010. Such a position would not meet with much opposition. Opinion polls show Britons to be as unhappy with their country's European entanglement as ever. Most interest groups seem to care little about membership and the media mostly loathe the EU, or ignore it—in Brussels fewer British media organisations are represented than from all the other large countries[2] bar France. The more one observes Britain in Europe, the more one feels compelled to conclude that it cannot reconcile its glorious past with its more modest present and accept the constraints of membership. Since its retreat to island detachment in the middle of the last millennium it has played many roles in Europe; as balancer, dabbler, opportunist, peace-broker, trouble-maker and more besides. But it has never fully engaged. It probably never will.

If Britain has not become bound more closely to Europe, its ties with the US have loosened. Among the hard-heads in the foreign policy community, belief in the 'special relationship' has waned as its costs have proved greater than once thought and its benefits fewer. At popular level, opinion polls show a marked waning in positive attitudes towards the US, no doubt related to the Bush administration in general and the Iraq war in particular. But it is probably deeper than that. Neither country is as Anglo-Saxon as before, both having evolved into far more cosmopolitan societies. The binding effect of a shared view of the Soviet threat has long gone. It has not been replaced. In some ways Britain's isolationism is hard to reconcile with its stature as the most adaptable and most open to outside forces of the large European countries, as evidenced by its welcoming of foreign capital and labour, the most profound forms of openness. Its major companies have been bought up by foreigners in a way no other G7 country would countenance and London is the most ethnically diverse city in the world, never mind Europe. It may be that as the world comes to Britain, Britain ceases to go to the world. For many Britons, it seems, arm's-length isolation can be splendid.

## THE CENTRALITY OF GERMANY

Germany shares borders with nine sovereign states—more than any other country in the world apart from China and Russia. Its location at the centre of the continent, along with its having the largest population in western Europe and the largest-by-far economy, gives it a natural leadership role in Europe. That it has not played a role matching its inherent strengths demonstrates how the country has paid for its attempts to dominate the continent in the seven decades after its unification in the 1870s. Now, in the seventh decade since the end of the Second World War, that rehabilitation process is drawing to a close and it is increasingly becoming 'normal' in the manner in which it asserts itself internationally. In the 10 years since German involvement in the Kosovo campaign became the first time in half a century that its military was deployed beyond its borders, its presence in conflict zones around the world has grown rapidly. Where once its close bilateral ties to the US and France would have prevented serious public spats with either, Germany is now prepared to go its own way, as it did most spectacularly vis-à-vis the US when it vociferously opposed the invasion of Iraq and as it does frequently with France in less dramatic ways—on protectionism, the conduct of monetary policy and environmental standards. Within the EU, it is no longer as '*communautaire*' as it once was, and is now almost as likely as the other big countries to challenge the bloc's institutions.

The question for Europe's future is whether Germany will underplay or overplay its increasingly strong hand. The evidence of overplay is, thus far, limited, but not inexistent. In recent years its targeting of its neighbours' banking secrecy laws included using its secret services to threaten Liechtenstein and some crass bullying of Switzerland. Almost from the moment the current economic crisis erupted in September 2008, the country's leaders have been prone to undiplomatic outbursts on the policy responses of other countries. In 2002, the then Chancellor, Gerhard Schroeder, won re-election on a ticket of opposing the invasion of Iraq by its most important strategic ally, the US.

Yet for all this, and some nervousness about a rising Germany given its history, it is unlikely to push its weight around dangerously in the future. If there ever was anything inherently militaristic and warlike in Germany, it has surely gone now. Culture changes. The traumas of 1914–45 and the deep and pervasive acknowledgment thereafter of the wrongs committed have changed the German consciousness. It is a deeply pacifistic country today and so strong is its desire to avoid confrontation that it is sometimes justifiably considered by its allies to be insufficiently willing to take on a proportionate burden in hard security issues. In Afghanistan, German forces' rules of engagement forbid them from firing on Taliban forces unless fired upon first, even if their allies are under attack. Such a position is untenable for any country, never mind one of NATO's largest and most important members. On Iran's nuclear programme, Germany has consistently been the foot-dragger on ratcheting up sanctions, often to the dismay of France, Britain and the US.

The contrast between Germany's positions towards the US and Russia is perhaps most telling about its orientation. Within the western family it is prepared to disagree sharply with the US, the country which, as the ultimate guarantor of European security, continues to play a role analogous to that of a parent. And it is an indulgent parent—the US does not retaliate when Germany opposes it. The stakes are not so low in the world beyond the embrace of the western family, where standing up to the powerful has potentially far more serious consequences. Germany is not known for its valour in confronting Russia, but instead goes to great lengths to understand its actions, motives and sensitivities, often as a way of not standing up to it. The contrast between the reaction of Germany to Russia's invasion of Georgia in 2008 and the US's invasion of Iraq in 2003 is instructive. Germany criticised the reckless miscalculation of the Georgian president, which, if not quite justification for Russia's invasion, made it comprehensible. There was no such comprehension for the US vis-à-vis Saddam Hussein, whose blundering recklessness made Mikhail Saakashvili appear statesmanlike.

The next decade may see Germany maturing to take on the responsibilities of leadership. But the evidence to date suggests that there is at least as much reason to believe that it will turn in on itself, preferring isolationism over internationalism, and hindering rather than helping its allies. Germany may not have the fortitude, foresight and strength of purpose to play the role that geography and history demand of it. If it does not, a vacuum could emerge at Europe's centre. Such an outcome would invite trouble—there are those who adore vacuums and are adept at quickly taking the opportunity to fill any that open up.

## RUSSIA'S UNRESTRAINT

While the big three western European powers simultaneously co-operate and compete, they do so within a system where the rules of the game are understood and agreed. Underpinning everything is a belief in the centrality of restraint and the knowledge of the costs and risks of overplaying one's hand. Russia shares no such belief or knowledge, largely because domestic checks and counterbalances to the exercise of centralised political power did not evolve as they did in western Europe. There is no tradition of an assertive aristocracy, no tradition of vibrant civil society institutions and no tradition of spiritual authorities challenging temporal power. Against this backdrop, absolutism thrived. As recently as a century ago, Russia's feudal society was more similar to that of western Europe a thousand years earlier, and although the 20th century brought modernisation in some respects, Russia remains a highly centralised, authoritarian, nationalistic state and nation. And that is how most Russians want it to be. Mikhail Khodorkovsky, a former oligarch who is currently serving a long jail term for challenging the Kremlin, described the man who imprisoned him, Vladimir Putin, as more liberal than 70% of the Russian people.

This is reflected in how Russia acts in the world. Where western Europe has become extremely reluctant to project military power, becoming a quasi-pacifistic actor in international affairs, Russia has gone the other way, becoming more aggressive, sometimes resorting to war, as its invasion of Georgia in the summer of 2008 demonstrated (the conflict was the continent's most significant geopolitical event since the end of the Cold War). Russian values are reflected not only in how it pursues its interests, but in how it perceives them in the first place. Where western Europe sees relations with those in the region in terms of 'Neighbourhood Policy' and bilaterally through 'Partnership' and 'Association' agreements, Russia demands a 'privileged sphere of influence'. Where Russians primarily seek prestige and influence in the international arena, west Europeans prioritise peace and prosperity. Where western Europe eschews stick and wields only carrots to achieve what it wants, Russia resorts to intimidation and threat to get its way. Given its sheer size, its great military strength, its enormous energy resources and its sheer will to power, Russia presents not only a challenge, but a threat to the countries of the rest of the continent. Creating mechanisms to manage these challenges and threats are needed, and now more urgently than ever. As Russia's economy suffers chronically from the global crisis and low energy prices, it may not look inwards to heal itself, but lash out to distract from them. If there is real trouble in Europe in the future, it will come from the east.

## AMERICA IN EUROPE

And if there is real trouble in Europe, intervention will come from the west, as it has since the US became a European (and world) power a century ago. It waged hot and cold wars against Nazism and communism and its uninterrupted and permanent military presence in Europe since 1942 defines enlightened self-interest. None of that means that America brings only harmony to Europe. As in any family, differences can run deep. They do on Russia. America has the luxury of distance and has not always appreciated Europeans' need to maintain some sort of accommodation with Russia. These differences existed throughout the Cold War. They were contained, at least in part because the costs of disunity, or even the appearance of disunity, were too high. Cohesion was always the imperative. Since the existential threat posed by the Soviet Union disappeared, differences have been greater and more openly displayed, and the range of opinion in the Euro-American family is greater than ever now that many former communist countries in central and eastern Europe have joined the EU and NATO. Maintaining cohesion vis-à-vis an assertive and forceful Russia will be the Atlantic community's greatest challenge.

The unity of the west is institutionalised in NATO. And institutions matter. 'Nothing happens without men, nothing lasts without institutions,' said Jean Monnet, one of the architects of the European integration project and someone who, incidentally, opposed Gaullism precisely because it was hostile to NATO. Thus, the Atlantic Alliance is both an end in itself and a means to an end (that of providing security). But its role and how it functions can also cause division. The US has long sought more equal sharing of the costs of providing European security. This is reasonable. Less reasonable is that it wants to remain fully in control and is suspicious of European efforts to create security institutions of which it is not a part. The US's war of choice in Iraq in 2003 fractured western unity more seriously than any single act in the post-World-War-II era. In its aftermath, there was much talk of a permanent rift opening up in the Atlantic, so serious were the differences. But, testament to the depth and strength of the relationship, ties across the Atlantic have long since normalised. Interests and values, if not always means and ends, are too closely aligned to sunder the west. America will remain as important a European power in the 21st century as it was in the 20th.

## THE MYTH OF EUROSCLEROSIS

Geopolitical strains among Europe's big powers are always possible. Economic strife and upheaval are now a certainty. In the eight months to May 2009, the global economy has moved into recession at a pace not seen since the 1930s. The ongoing earthquake in the international financial system will affect every country. Those at its epicentre will suffer most and longest, but its tremors will be felt everywhere. Countries likely to recover most rapidly are those with diversified industrial and services bases and without chronic domestic and/or external imbalances. This describes much of continental Europe, which has been and will continue to be among the most powerful engines of the global economy.

Discussion of relative performance economics can be faddish. In the late 1980s, when I first became attuned to these debates in university, Japan's virtues were extolled and its ways were to be studied because it was the model for the future. Almost nobody predicted that its boom would end in bust and a lost decade of economic growth. At the same time, the US looked tired. Focus then was almost entirely on its weaknesses. Its strengths were ignored or downplayed. Few foresaw that it would remain an economic powerhouse; fewer still that it would lead the IT revolution even though the companies that drove it, such as Intel and Microsoft, were already in their second decade of existence.

Discussion of Europe's economic performance from the mid-1990s until recently, and how it contrasts with that of the US, mirrored the Japan-versus-US debate in the 1980s. US strengths were played up and its weaknesses downplayed. Where America's capacity for innovation and its relentless dynamism (both real and enduring strengths) were rightly emphasised, frequently it was as a backdrop against which to portray Europe as unreforming, unreformable, sluggish and—the favoured taunt of the Eurobashers—'sclerotic'. Nothing quite reflected the faddishness of the debate like press depictions of the two continents' central bankers. Alan Greenspan, chairman of the US Federal Reserve, had the status of an oracle and was credited with near-superhuman powers, while the first head of the European Central Bank, Wim Duisenberg, was derided for his poor communication skills and apparent failure to boost growth by cutting interest rates more aggressively. History will surely reverse those contemporary judgments, just as it will on the performance of their respective economies.

Statistics are already doing just that. Despite commonly held perceptions, Europeans grew more prosperous than inhabitants of either of the two other large developed economies—the US and Japan—during the current decade up to the ongoing economic crisis (1999–2007). Per-head GDP growth in the euro area, at 1.7%, exceeded that in both other economies (marginally in the case of the US, and by a wider margin in the case of Japan). One important, if unlikely, cause of misperceptions on relative economic performance between Europe and the US is the manner in which statistics are reported and revised. Where European GDP data tend to be revised upwards after they have been initially reported, those in the US are almost always revised downwards, thus making the small difference in growth appear very large when the initial numbers first make the headlines.[3] As important a reason for the common misperception of economic growth performance are differences between per capita rates of growth and those of overall economies. The US economy did expand more rapidly than Europe's over this period, but only because its population growth was significantly higher. Top-line GDP rates of growth are of course important in determining a country's economic weight in the world, but they tell little about changes in prosperity levels, which are best measured by per capita GDP.

Europe does of course have its weaknesses, many of which are the result of poor policies or policy inaction. Other weaknesses are unrelated or only partially linked to government failings. One is lower levels of innovation than either the US or Japan. Another is the continent's deteriorating demographic outlook, which will create real difficulties as more retirees are supported by fewer people of working age. But the economic outlook of the continent's national economies is diverse.[4] Some peripheral economies in the east, west and south had profound structural challenges even before the current crisis erupted. But Germany, France, the Benelux and Nordics are as solidly based as any economies in the world. When the global recession ends, as one day it must, they can be expected to lead the way back to growth.

## IN GOOD COMPANY

Over the years, at countless conferences, seminars and talks on economic reform in Europe, the focus of speakers has almost always been on government-led reform, both legislative and regulatory. This is of course necessary to improve the conditions for wealth creation by allowing businesses to operate more productively and profitably. But it is not everything. Companies are anything but passive. Businesses are problem-solving entities. They do not sit on their hands waiting for political leadership. In the absence of government action, companies move both to minimise the negative impact of policies that affect their businesses and to overcome obstacles that prevent them achieving their objectives. Corporate Europe has been increasingly successful in doing both, and by any measure it has been more than meeting the challenges of a changing environment. Thus, Europe's economic story is to be found not in the ministries of national capitals, but in the executive suites of its provincial cities: in Munich, Toulouse, Malmö, Turin, Barcelona and Amsterdam.

The *Financial Times'* annual listing of the world's largest companies by market capitalisation was first compiled in the mid-1990s, the decade in which the current phase of globalisation took off in earnest. In 1996 it was dominated by companies from the world's two largest national economies, the US and Japan, which together accounted for 313 of the top 500. As might be expected in a world in which economic activity has spread rapidly, the dominance of the top two has waned. In 2008 both countries' presence in the list had fallen. Europe, by contrast, has not only held its own, but increased its presence in the list, from 119 companies in 1996 to 141 in 2008.[5] The rise of corporate Europe was not only absolute and relative, but spread across the continent. Of the EU-15 countries, 13 registered an increased presence in the list. Interestingly, and despite popular and political scepticism about globalisation, France has been the most successful of the European countries, seeing its presence in the top 500 almost double.

Ranking companies by relative size over time is a good measure of national corporate health. But to understand why European companies are succeeding one needs to dig deeper. One explanation lies in how they have internationalised. With an increasing proportion of global GDP growth accounted for by emerging markets, taking advantage of opportunities in such markets (and other foreign markets) has been, and will almost certainly continue to be, central to any successful corporate strategy. And European companies are internationalising more rapidly and more successfully than those in any other region of the world. The United Nations Conference on Trade and Development (UNCTAD) has, since 1993, maintained a database on the world's largest non-financial companies ranked by their foreign assets. By this measure of internationalisation (one that is probably unbettered), it is clear that European companies are driving the globalisation process, not playing catchup with it. In the dozen years between the publication of the first list, in 1993, and the latest list, covering 2005, European companies have come to dominate the top 100. In the 2005 rankings, EU-15 companies accounted for more than half of the world's large globalised companies, up from just over one third in 1993.[6] If economic well-being in the future is determined by businesses' capacity to internationalise, then Europe is well placed.

## EUROPEANS' CONCEITS AND PREJUDICES
Everyone has his conceits. Europeans are no different. Along with Anglophone contempt for continental socio-economic ways, these conceits have caused me no little frustration over the years. Three stand out: first, a misplaced belief that the continent's peoples have overcome their historic prejudices towards each other; second, a pious belief in Europeans' own multilateral virtue; and third, the persistence of (often open) prejudice towards America and Americans.

Europe has been fragmenting into ethnically based states since the 19th century. That process continues, as demonstrated by the breakup of Yugoslavia and Czechoslovakia in the 1990s, and the seemingly inevitable breakup of Belgium, the unrelenting drive of some of Spain's regions for ever more autonomy and Scotland's slow motion moves to exit the United Kingdom. In each of these cases, the depth of animosity one finds in these regions towards the 'other' shocks this effete observer. It may seem odd to say that high fences make good neighbours when people and products flow largely unimpeded across the continent, but because borders have become far more porous does not mean that they have become politically irrelevant, as all the regions within the EU who seek statehood prove. European structures of common governance are successful not because the continent's people stopped loathing each other, but because they are so solidly based on the nation state. Pretending otherwise is not only delusional, it could be dangerous.

Europeans parade their belief in multilateralism. Within Europe's borders, they practise what they preach, but in the wider world, they act like other countries and are very far from being the 'conscience of the world'. In its security doctrine, set out in the aftermath of the Iraq invasion, the EU placed 'effective multilateralism' at the core of its view on how the world should be organised. The document specifically cited the World Trade Organisation as an example of the sort of effective multilateralism that Europe should support and encourage. Yet in practice, and for all the European talk about its commitment to multilateralism, nothing it does at the WTO, either in positions taken during trade talks or in its respect for the findings of arbitration panels, amounts to any operational implementation of its strategic goal. Other examples abound. In a 2008 ruling, the European Court of Justice ruled that the security council declarations 'cannot have the effect of prejudicing [regional] constitutional principles'. In other words, European law trumps international law every time. The International Covenant on Civil and Political Rights, which is perhaps the most important legal document on human rights, has not been implemented by European governments any more thoroughly than by their American counterpart. On climate change it has become increasingly clear with each passing year that many European countries will fail to meet their obligations to reduce greenhouse gas emissions under the Kyoto protocol. So much for Europeans' unfailing support for multilaterism.

Too often Europeans like to define themselves as much by what they believe they are not than what they are or believe themselves to be. And in too many European minds, their self-image is defined in juxtaposition to the US. Despite the uniquely close relations across the Atlantic, a history of common sacrifice and the sharing of values and interests, anti-Americanism in Europe is rife, reflected in a frequent failure to see the world from a US perspective, the attribution of the worst possible motives to US actions, and the holding of its actions to standards not applied to any other countries. During the run-up to the Iraq war (which I opposed, incidentally) one did not have to look far for European diplomats to vent uncontrollably and undiplomatically against the US, their usual detachment and objectivity abandoned. Much the same was true of others in the wider foreign policy community (one Brussels think tanker became quite alarmingly aggressive when I interviewed him at the time about the state of transatlantic relations). The loss of objectivity reached its apogee with George Bush. He was an awful president of the US—for his country, for its international standing and for the rest of the world—but his time in office was one of two halves, towards Europe in particular. His first administration was characterised by arrogance, dismissiveness and aggression, but his second was little different from any other administration in the previous half-century. Yet so great was European loathing for him that the change went largely unnoticed. Indeed, so blinding was this detestation that many Europeans could not see the facts, never mind allow those facts to impinge on their set-in-stone opinion of him and the conduct of his administration.

## AN ENDURING AND DURABLE EUROPE

Europeans have their foibles, and Europe its faults and weaknesses. But it has been at the global frontier of progress for half a millennium. There is no reason why it will not remain there. Europe is the largest economy in the world and its strengths are far greater than its weaknesses. Its states are at peace and they exploit their peace more effectively than any other part of the world. Domestically, those same states are among the best-functioning in the world. This is significant. The ongoing change in nuance to the economic orthodoxy of recent decades is already incorporating a more positive view of the potential of the state. Well designed regulation provides a framework for market participants, often to the benefit of the conscientious over the unscrupulous; the long-termist over the fast-buck-maker. Europe's welfare state, so frequently derided as being a millstone around the continent's neck, is helping to mitigate hardships and cushion the descent into recession. Efficient markets and effective states are, more often than not, mutually reinforcing, not mutually exclusive. That has always been the case. The economic crisis is making it more obvious, and Europe balances the two better than any other region of the world. That it does so is in part because of its European Union. It is a unique mechanism. Though it will be tested in the times to come and it is subject to no little risk, it is much more likely to be part of the solution to Europe's challenges than part of the problem.

> *'The Creator of Europe made her small and even split her up into little parts, so that our hearts could find joy not in size but in plurality.'*
>
> KAREL ČAPEK

---

## EUROPE AND RUSSIA (I)

*18 July 2006*

It is testament to how stability is taken for granted in Europe that until very recently governments thought little about the threat of an energy crisis. Despite the many warning signs—instability in the Middle East, rising demand from the developing world and persistently high prices— disruption to energy supplies was well down almost all countries' threat lists. That, however, changed dramatically earlier this year. The trigger for one of the most rapid shifts in security priorities in recent times was pulled by the man who is hosting this weekend's G8 summit in St Petersburg.

In the depths of last winter, Vladimir Putin, Russia's president, decided to lean on his neighbours in a dispute over the price they pay for his country's gas. Signalling the seriousness of his intent, he abruptly cut supply. Concerns were compounded in April when the state-controlled gas giant, Gazprom, and its oil pipeline monopolist, Trasneft, threatened to shift supplies from Europe to other countries. The message was clear: Russia is back. The diminished giant wants to recover lost stature. The humiliations of the post-communist era will be tolerated no longer. If regaining influence requires using its vast energy reserves as a tool of foreign policy, then so be it. Just how much national pride matters to Mr Putin can be gleaned from his by now infamous remark that the collapse of the Soviet

Union was the greatest catastrophe of the 20th century. For him, the country's many horrors over the past 100 years, including 20 million dead in a single war, were of a lesser order than the decline from superpowerdom.

The shockwaves of his actions were felt in chancelleries, foreign ministries and energy businesses across the continent, and their effect is difficult to overstate—only 9/11 has caused more change in how countries assess threats in the post-Cold-War era. In one sense at least, though, Mr Putin should be thanked. He has shaken other governments from their complacency and made them think hard about energy. Europeans—at national and EU levels—are scrambling to cobble together responses. But, as all involved know, there are no easy answers. Globally, energy reserves controlled by stable governments are running out fast and the planet's remaining deposits of fossil fuels are increasingly concentrated in its strife-torn regions. The Middle East is in turmoil. There is little prospect of it calming and it is all too easy to envisage a descent further into chaos. Other major suppliers look worryingly wobbly. Nigeria is a borderline failed state. Algeria is little better. Venezuela is already a distance down the cul-de-sac its populist leader, Hugo Chavez, calls '21st-century socialism'.

That oil, coal and gas (in that order) still account for almost 90% of the global energy mix despite the precariousness of supply and despite the polluting effects of these carbon-emitting fuels gives some indication of the limitations of renewables, often mistakenly considered the answer to energy needs. Though they will play an increasing role, a range of factors—cost, pricing structures and reliability factors—will limit their growth and leave the world dependent of traditional (dirtier) energy sources for the foreseeable future. Add growing demand pressures to supply worries and the outlook becomes cloudier still. The main cause of the higher energy prices that businesses and consumers have endured over the past three years has been the boom in demand in the developing world. Wonderful though it is that most of these countries are enjoying their strongest ever period of protracted economic growth, the result is more intense competition for energy supplies. Big fish like China and India are cultivating energy exporters and seeking to secure long-term supply contracts. Competition to lock energy exporters into extended deals is intensifying. Pessimists are even scenario-building for future 'resource wars'.

All of this brings us back to St Petersburg. At the G8 meeting this week-end, British, French, German and Italian leaders will be most interested in the agenda item marked 'energy security'. And on this matter, Mr Putin has them over a barrel. Endowed with more than a quarter of global gas reserves and as Europe's single biggest oil supplier, Russia knows it has what they desperately need. Given its geographic proximity and relative stability compared to alternative source countries, Europeans know that they have no real choice but to buy any additional energy they need from the former superpower.

Optimists argue that this will create mutual dependency—Russia needs a reliable source of revenue as much as it needs a reliable source of energy. But common interests don't always make for smooth relations. Russia is a notoriously prickly customer to deal with. It views the world in old fashioned power-politics terms and continues the heavy-handed traditions of both tsars and Soviets in its dealings with foreigners, as illustrated by the recent history of EU–Russia relations. It brushed aside an offer to join the EU's 'European Neighbourhood Policy'. Last year's 'Four Spaces' agreement has done little to make relations work better. And the Energy Charter Treaty, signed 12 years ago, has yet to be ratified by Russia.

How the continent's democratic EU core handles the issue of Russia and its energy will be a crucial test of its members' common foreign policy ambitions in general, and, more specifically, whether it can join up its foreign and energy policies (something all countries have a curiously hard time managing). For Ireland, it can only be hoped that the strength flowing from unity can be achieved and maintained. The country's unfortunate combination of dependency and weakness means that no country would benefit more from an effective common European policy on Russian energy.

*Originally published in the* Sunday Tribune

———

# EUROPE AND RUSSIA (II)

*22 July 2007*

The latest diplomatic row between Russia and Britain is but one of a multitude of disagreements between the former superpower and the democracies to its west. These differences are largely attributable to a Russia that is reverting to its traditional role in European affairs. The result is tension the like of which has not been seen since the end of the Cold War. Lamentably, these tensions are far more likely to worsen than to ease in the future.

Russia is Europe's largest country by population and territory. It has the second biggest nuclear arsenal in the world and vast energy reserves upon which the rest of the continent is dependent. It has newfound financial and economic muscle to flex thanks to persistently high oil and gas prices. That Russia has the raw capability to play a greater role in European affairs and the will to do so is beyond doubt. Its politics and national psyche suggest that this role will be anything but constructive.

Under its current president, Vladimir Putin, Russia has regressed to centralised autocracy. Parliament and the judiciary are subservient to the all-powerful executive in the Kremlin. Opposition groupings are treated brutally by the forces of the state when they protest and are constantly subject to intimidation and harassment by thuggish youth movements who do the government's bidding. Journalists know that they imperil their lives if they displease those in power.

That Putin is hugely popular despite his curbing of civil liberties and snuffing out of democracy demonstrates a Russian preference for collective national greatness over individual freedoms. Russians feel diminished by the loss of superpower status that resulted from the collapse of the Soviet Union and humiliated by the manner in which other countries have not given the country the respect that they believe it deserves. They are deeply aggrieved that its moment of historical weakness was exploited by the west, a charge that is not without foundation.

Understanding Russia's history helps explain its resentments and its behaviour towards its neighbours today. As a great power from the middle of the 18th century until the collapse of the Soviet Union, Russia participated in every major European conflagration. To its great credit, it twice prevented would-be hegemons from dominating the continent—halting the onslaughts of revolutionary France in the early 19th century and Nazi Germany in the middle of the 20th.

But more often than not it has been a destabilising force as it attempts to satisfy what appears to be an insatiable appetite for influence, respect and glory. The clearest testament to Russia's imperial instinct is its sheer size (by far the largest country in the world). Its vast territories were not acquired in a fit of absent-mindedness, but by relentless acquisitiveness— 'How shall I defend my borders but by expanding them?' Catherine the Great famously quipped.

It is very unlikely that Russia would invade its neighbours today, but its aggrandising ambition survives in a different guise, plain to see by the manner in which it conducts relations with the rest of the world. Those who suffer most are those who are geographically closest. Russia has arbitrarily cut off energy supplies to the Ukraine and Belarus, starved Lithuania of oil, terrorised Estonia over Soviet-era war memorials and attempted to isolate Poland in the EU by discriminating against its exports.

In some of these cases, Russia has had legitimate interests to protect, but in all of them, the manner in which it has done so has been anything but legitimate. Its bullying is not only damaging, but also counter-productive. Precisely because it behaves so threateningly, most of Russia's neighbours have clamoured to join NATO, and it is the encroachment of the Atlantic alliance that Russia sees as the greatest single threat to its security.

Beyond its 'near abroad', Russia has what it describes in 19th-century terms as a 'sphere of influence', in which it works to prevent others acting regardless of motive. This can be seen today in its steadfast opposition to EU and US efforts to grant independence to Kosovo at the UN security council and its blocking of efforts in the same forum to prevent Iran from acquiring a nuclear capability.

As Russia has become more assertive in recent years, its has also become more strident in the conduct of its relations with western Europe. It refuses to sign a long-drafted energy treaty with the EU and has engaged in de facto expropriation of European companies' assets. It has worked to control all energy supplies to western Europe by ensuring no pipelines bypass its territory from the resource-rich central Asian republics. And its continued obstinacy means that the contractual foundation of EU-Russian relations—the Partnership and Cooperation Agreement—will not be replaced when it expires later this year.

Nothing illustrates Russia's increasingly aggressive posture better than the issue which has dominated relations in 2007—the proposed roll-out of a US-designed antiballistic missile shield in Europe. Although Russia is justified in its opposition to the deployment of the system and correct in its analysis of the destabilising effect of the shield on the continent's strategic balance, it has managed to emerge as the loser owing to its wildly disproportionate reaction.

Putin's rhetoric on the subject has been hysterical and demagogic. More worrying still, his talk has been matched by a series of grave threats which include: the reprogramming of the country's nuclear arsenal to target European cities; the deployment of nuclear missiles to Russia's westernmost territory, the enclave of Kaliningrad on the Baltic Sea; pulling out of the 1987 Intermediate-range Nuclear Forces treaty; and withdrawal from the 1990 treaty on Conventional Forces in Europe. This is the giant neighbour with whom the liberal democracies of Europe are obliged to live. After appearing blind to the dangers until very recently, they are quickly waking up to the threat posed by an assertive, aggressive and strident Russia.

Just two years ago, even the most powerful democracies chose to downplay or ignore Russian excesses. Germany's Gerhard Schroeder and Italy's Silvio Berlusconi kowtowed to Putin; Britain's Tony Blair and France's Jacques Chirac preferred to avoid confrontation. All four leaders have now been replaced, and each of their replacements takes a significantly less indulgent line with Russia.

But Europeans remain insufficiently cohesive, coherent and determined in their stance towards Russia. They have no greater foreign-policy challenge than the formulation of a strategic posture towards Russia that encompasses their energy, security and economic interests. This will involve incentivising Russian moderation and disincentivising its bullying and bluster. The EU is good at dangling carrots, but weak on wielding sticks. It will have to do both if it wishes to avoid being bent to Russia's will.

*Originally published in the* Sunday Business Post

———

## HOW BROWN WILL LEAD BRITAIN

*20 May 2007*

Last week Gordon Brown finally secured the prize he has coveted all his political life. At the end of June he will become Britain's prime minister. Apart from the country over which he is destined to rule, his rise to the realm's highest political office will have implications for Ireland, Europe and transatlantic relations. Brown has many qualities that make him suitable to lead, demonstrated not least by the failure of anyone to challenge him for the leadership of his party and the premiership of his country. He has a first-rate mind and the energy and stamina to exploit such an endowment—few finance ministers anywhere are as economically literate, and fewer still are willing to put in the hours on the details of policy.

But his capacity for very narrow focus has not meant that he is incapable of seeing the bigger picture. Although his vision for modern Britain, and of moderate British nationalism, may be unachievable, he thinks deeply about the nature of his country's society and about the relationships among its nations. His capacity for wide angling can also been seen from his nuanced views on Islamist terrorism. In a recent speech he cogently dismissed the multiculturalism-versus-integration debate as a false dichotomy, and spoke about the need to take a full-spectrum approach to the terrorism threat, which he said required a willingness to address concerns of British Muslims and a preparedness to take hard security measures at home and abroad if and when necessary.

There are, however, two factors that give others—particularly those outside Britain—some cause for concern about the coming Brown premiership: the first is the man's temperament, the second the limited knowledge anyone has of his views on what Britain's role in the world should be. Brown is not an easy man to get on with or work with, and his personality and operating style mean he has no shortage of enemies at home and very few friends in Europe. Even his strongest supporters do not deny that he is, at the very least, tetchy and irascible. As is so often the case with those who combine high intelligence with great ambition, he easily becomes impatient with the plodding of lesser mortals and often appears not only arrogant, but aggressively so. There are also concerns about such a dark, brooding, solitary individual and suspicions linger that his marriage in 2000, at the age of 49, was one of convenience, designed to signal to the British public he was not a political and policy obsessive incapable of enjoying life's quotidian pleasures.

His character aside, there is also great uncertainty about his objectives for Britain in the world. At a party in his home just days before the Iraq war, when it was uncertain whether Tony Blair would survive as prime minister, this writer and other guests were at a loss to know what our host would do if the premiership were to fall into his lap. More than four years on no one is any the wiser. Apart from the veto over adopting the euro he appropriated for himself early in Blair's tenure and an active interest in Africa's economic development, he has respected the division of labour agreed with the outgoing prime minister whereby he would not interfere in foreign matters in exchange for the widest possible remit on domestic policy. That will all change on 27 June.

On the European scene, there is no great sense of loss at the departure of Blair, but there is something approaching a palpable air of foreboding in Brussels over Brown's imminent elevation. When he deigns to attend meetings of EU finance ministers (which is far less frequently than most of his counterparts), his utterances often sound like lectures. This would irritate if Britain was a genuine model for others to follow, but it is not, particularly in areas such as productivity, export competitiveness, social welfare and public service provision.

Not only does Brown extol the British way, when he sees fit to tell Europeans the route they should take he suggests they also look to the US. This is particularly curious because although his rhetoric is Boston, his own policy choices have been closer to Berlin: taxation and public spending have risen as a percentage of GDP; the tax and benefit system has become considerably more redistributionist; and his incessant regulatory tinkering has been almost Mediterranean.

His non-policy orientation only adds to the uncertainty. While he spends his annual summer holiday on the Massachusetts coast and has more friends on the other side of the Atlantic than he does on the continent, early indications are he will keep his distance from George Bush. With so many mixed signals it is very difficult to predict his orientation towards the EU and US, and, crucially, which side he will take when disagreements occur. But purely domestic considerations are also likely to influence his foreign policy choices.

The capacity of any leader to play a role in international affairs depends to a very considerable degree on public opinion. And because British public opinion is increasingly isolationist—Euroscepticism is deeper and wider than it has ever been, while opinion polls show a sharp fall in support for the US and for Britain's special relationship with the superpower—his scope to lead on the international stage will be less than Blair's was when he took office a decade ago. In Europe this will limit Britain's influence; in negotiating a slimmed down constitutional treaty for the EU, for example. Internationally, it will greatly circumscribe his ability to use force in conjunction with the only ally that counts in such matters. Even if Brown has clearly defined goals about Britain's role in world affairs, and demonstrates the will to achieve them, he may find that he cannot bring his country along. Such an outcome would not be unexpected. It has been his predecessor's fate.

*Originally published in the* Sunday Business Post

———

## THE FUTURE OF FRANCE

*22 April 2007*

Europe is watching today's first round of presidential elections in France more intensely than usual. Not only is there greater uncertainty about the outcome than in recent contests—any one of three candidates could emerge as winner—but other countries are aware that an insecure and unsure France is potentially a source of friction and instability for the rest of the continent.

Illustrating the uncertainty in the electorate is that late last week, two out of five voters had still not decided who to support today. Mirroring this wide indecision, the French elites are also deeply uncertain about their country's future and its role in the world. The reasons are manifold. France's relative position in Europe is weakening. Most obvious has been the dilution of its influence in an enlarged EU and a shift in the bloc's centre of gravity eastwards. This has been reflected in everything from a loss of clout around the European Commission table to the eclipse of French as the lingua franca in all the EU institutions. Also important has been the normalisation of Germany. For decades after the Second World War, French influence in Europe was strengthened by the willingness of a contrite Germany to acquiesce to France's demands when she stamped her foot.

That willingness has been fading over time and change has been hastened by the emergence of the gifted Angela Merkel as the dominant figure in European politics. It is hard to envisage any of the three possible contenders for the Elysée Palace achieving a position of parity with her. Ideologically, France is on the back foot, too. Belief in market economics has traditionally been weak across its political spectrum, a fact possibly explained by low levels of economic literacy. (A recent survey by the Economist Intelligence Unit of the educational backgrounds of those in the top echelons of public and private sectors in Europe found French leaders were far less likely to have studied economics than their counterparts elsewhere.)

Historical factors also play their part in the ideological makeup of the French psyche, not least the role of the state and nationalised companies in building up the economy after the Second World War. France's instinctive 'dirigisme' (state interventionism) is at odds with the mood of the times in Europe, where belief in the benefits of the market is deep and spans the centre-ground of politics from the progressive left to the liberal right. While other countries occasionally attempt protectionist measures that are at odds with single market rules (Italy, Spain and Poland come to mind), these have tended to be ad hoc and take the form of executive decisions, rather than legislation. France, on the other hand, has enacted laws aimed at keeping foreigners out of swathes of business activity. Such laws are a direct and serious challenge to the freedoms underpinning the

European project. If the next French president attempts to use these laws, or mounts new challenges to Europe's most basic rules, the potential exists for real crisis and conflict.

A second source of potential conflict comes from how to overcome the impasse over the EU's constitutional future—a blockage, incidentally, that was triggered by French voters' rejection of the original plan in mid-2005. A big majority of the 27 member states support the existing 'constitutional treaty' and want only limited change. The presidential candidates have taken very different positions on how to proceed but, with euroscepticism on the rise, France is more likely to be part of the problem than part of the solution.

In these and other cases, the challenge for the next French president will be to readjust the country's ambitions to match more closely the (reduced) influence it wields. This will not be easy. It will require a rapid coming-to-terms with relative decline, something that is always difficult for any country, never mind one with such a profound belief in the greatness of its own heritage and culture.

But all that said, there are some reasons to be optimistic. Many of France's diplomats and thinkers on international affairs are as strategically minded as they are tactically gifted. A hard-headed understanding of the realities of world affairs among the political elite was reflected in the rejection by the main candidates of crude anti-Americanism during the campaign. There is also reason to believe that the fretting about relative decline will pass, not least because France remains a formidable country. Its workers are among the most productive in the world, its companies are in the vanguard of globalisation and its state functions well. Publicly provided services, particularly in education and health, are second to none and its transport infrastructure is enviable.

France is undergoing a crisis of confidence. This has made it a more difficult partner in Europe and even raised concerns about its commitment to the European project. There is little doubt that the shift in relative power in Europe will cause frictions and uncertainties. But France's interests will continue to be best served by the existing system. It is difficult to imagine a realistic alternative.

*Originally published in the* Sunday Business Post

# ITALY IN THE WORLD

*7 November 2000*

In October Italy failed to secure one of Europe's two non-permanent seats on the UN security council despite the country's considerable diplomatic resources. When the UN's 187 members voted instead for two of the continent's smallest countries—Ireland and Norway—it was considered little less than a national humiliation. For many, this miscalculation was par for the course for a country that has never come close to punching up to its economic weight (as the world's fifth largest economy) on either the world or European stage.

To understand why, the country's traditional failings—political and bureaucratic sclerosis—must be understood. In reaction to the wholesale abuse of power during the Fascist era, the 1948 constitution went to extremes to prevent a repetition, diffusing power extensively. The result, though largely successful in its primary objective, was weak, unstable and directionless government. Sprawling and unaccountable state structures, a long historical tradition of patronage, and the absence of any credible political alternative to the hegemony of the Christian Democratic Party (the large Communist Party was excluded from government during the Cold War) compounded government weakness.

While Italy's innovative and creative private sector managed to thrive internationally despite the dead hand of an intrusive, inefficient and often corrupt public sector, the state itself fared poorly. With few exceptions after 1948, the efforts of the political class were focused on politicking, at the expense of policy, as government coalitions were formed only to fall apart at the rate of one a year. Short-termism and plain disinterest in policy were particularly evident in the case of the country's international relations, and all the more so once the twin pillars of the country's foreign policy—NATO and the EU—were put in place. Successive governments tended to react to external events only when forced to do so, avoiding the difficult task of defining and articulating a concept as nebulous as the 'national interest'— the cornerstone of any foreign policy. To compound the lack of political direction, the diplomatic corps suffered from the same deficiencies that traditionally bedevilled Italian bureaucracy, namely: fief-building; internal power struggles; weak command and control structures; and recruitment and promotion procedures that were all too often less than meritocratic.

But the security council defeat notwithstanding, Italy has been getting its foreign policy act together in recent years, partly as a result of the more general shake-up of the political and administrative structures since the early 1990s, which has seen moves towards modernisation, albeit at a slow and unsteady pace. Just as relevant in focusing foreign-policy efforts have been the effects of more rapid internationalisation, presenting challenges that have demanded a more coherent and proactive response than in the past. These have included economic globalisation, closer European integration, Balkan instability and an influx of immigrants.

In many cases, the response has been effective, serving to raise Italy's stature and boost confidence. Most important was participation in economic and monetary union (EMU). Against all the odds, Italy's interest groups rallied to support the often painful fiscal measures that were needed to achieve the major strategic objective of the 1990s. Other successes include taking the leading role in returning stability to neighbouring Albania after that country imploded in 1996, a leading role in Kosovo (after the US, the Italian troop contingent is the largest) and being in the vanguard of bridge-building by the west to countries such as Iran, Libya and North Korea.

Turning to the future, this new-found confidence is likely soon to be tested. If, as we expect, Mr Berlusconi comes to power in 2001, the international spotlight will be placed on Italy owing to the probable inclusion in his government of Mr Bossi's Northern League and Mr Fini's AN. Although, we do not expect measures to be implemented that could be considered incompatible with liberal democratic values, growing concerns about the rise of the extreme right in Europe will result in the records of these parties being pored over. Such scrutiny is likely to produce a negative reaction, to Mr Bossi in particular. On domestic issues, such as immigration, he has engaged in inflammatory and reactionary rhetoric. As regards foreign policy, he has often taken extreme positions, such as opposing Italy's involvement in the Balkans and supporting Yugoslavia against NATO during the Kosovo conflict in 1999.

As a result, we expect a sharp increase in negative comment on Italy in the international media. Alive to the potential damage to Italy's reputation, Mr Berlusconi is likely to seek to limit the role of Mr Bossi in government. However, there is likely to be a wariness on the part of foreign governments in their dealings with a Berlusconi-led administration. This may result in an informal cooling of relations, particularly now that EU member states take a growing interest in the domestic affairs of their partners (that said, we do not expect Italy to be subject to diplomatic sanctions—the response of EU member states when the populist Freedom Party came to power in Austria—not least because of the widespread recognition that such measures were at best tactically ill-advised and at worst counterproductive). In order to manage such a potential negative reaction, the choice of foreign minister will be crucial in order to convince other countries that the new government represents no threat to civil and political liberties and that it is a reliable partner with which to do business. In order to achieve this, Mr Berlusconi is likely to appoint a well-known and internationally respected figure. Although limited in his options, the former head of the World Trade Organisation, Renato Ruggiero, and the current foreign minister, Lamberto Dini, are two possible candidates.

The new government is likely in for a brief period of negative international press and an initial cautious approach by Italy's EU partners, before a full normalisation. It is, however, possible to envisage a less benign outlook. In a worst-case scenario, the government—inexperienced in foreign policy, not instinctively internationalist and less committed to the cause of European integration—could lash out at foreign critics rather than seeking to calm fears. Such a reaction, in turn, could reinforce suspicions abroad that the alliance is extremist. If such a vicious circle were to be entered into, the implications for Italy's standing in the world could be serious, in the short term at least, and affect economic interests such as the possible boycotting of the country's high-profile consumer goods.

*Originally published on* www.viewswire.com

———

# AZNAR'S SPAIN

*March 2004*

After eight years as prime minister, José María Aznar is walking away from politics at the height of his powers. His greatest achievement was to complete the country's transition to democracy by bequeathing to Spain a moderate and modern party of the right. For this alone he deserves his place in Spain's post-Franco pantheon. But greatness, which was within his grasp, eluded him. His character is to blame.

In the first half of the 1970s, as Spain's dictator of more than three decades, Francisco Franco, was nearing the end of his life, discussion of what would replace his authoritarian régime became intense. Echoing today's debates about the universality of democracy, there were those in

Spain, and even more abroad, who argued that a history of autocracy and authoritarianism, an intrusive and inefficient state, and a weak and disjointed civil society had caused democracy to fail in the past, and risked doing so again. José María Aznar, then a precocious twentysomething whose family background had steeped him in the politics of the right, was also unsettled by the prospect of change. A Spanish nationalist first and foremost, he feared that if uncontrollable centrifugal forces were unleashed, the centre would not hold and Spain would be torn apart. For him demands for greater autonomy, and even independence, in those regions with the strongest sense of identity—Catalonia and the Basque Country—posed the greatest threat to Spain after Franco. So exercised was he by this perceived threat that he published articles in the late 1970s which, if not openly supportive of the hard-right, hinted strongly of reactionary inclination and advocacy of continued suppression of regional identities and aspirations.

But despite the warnings of Aznar and the doubters of democracy, the transition after Franco's death in 1975 turned out to be remarkably smooth (a failed military coup in 1981 was the only serious blip), and the negotiation of autonomy statutes with the regions satisfied devolutionists without sundering the country. In 1982, another milestone in the transition to democracy was reached when the first left-of-centre administration since the end of the Second Republic in 1939 came to power. Led by the dashing and charismatic Felipe González, the reform-minded social democrats did not seek retribution for decades of persecution as some had feared, but focused instead on bedding down democracy at home and rehabilitating Spain abroad.

While the 1980s were wilderness years for the right, the devoutly Roman Catholic, ultra-conventional and unflamboyant Aznar rose steadily through the ranks of a fragmented and demoralised party. From governor of Castile-Leon—geographically and historically, Spain's dominant core—he became leader of what had evolved into the Popular Party by the end of the decade. But his elevation initially changed little for the right and its electoral fortunes continued to be affected by widely held suspicions that once in power its authoritarian and illiberal reflexes would re-emerge. Nor were suspicions of a recidivist-right 'secret agenda' baseless. Aznar's early writings apart, the decision after Franco's death not to examine the wrongs of the past for the sake of stability in the present meant that there was no purging of those associated with the régime, who, if they had remained in public life, tended towards the Popular Party.

Aznar's attempt to rehabilitate the right was made easier by a González administration which, by the early 1990s, had lost its way. Minister-sanctioned killings and torture of those suspected of involvement in the Basque terrorist organisation, ETA, and almost daily revelations of corruption raised old questions about whether democracy could ever work satisfactorily in Spain. To gain from the yearnings for change, he self-consciously styled himself as the antithesis of González, whom he loathed and whose mere presence he still cannot abide. Aznar made virtues of his defects. Proudly uncharismatic, rigid and austere, he believed such traits proved his 'seriousness'—a characteristic by which he judges others and with which he appears mildly obsessed. He forged his party in the same image: steady and quietly industrious, peopled by dull but dutiful technocrats. This was, again, designed to differentiate his party from its opponents. By then the governing Socialist Party's regional 'barons' paid little heed to Madrid and many of its ministers all too often appeared more interested in lining their pockets than in effecting change. He promised clean and efficient government, but consensus and continuity, too. Politics would become, he implied, reassuringly boring.

But despite the crafted image and assurances of moderation, he struggled to convince, and lost his first election as leader in 1993. And even when he did overtake the Socialist Party in 1996, he was denied an outright majority. But once in power the then 43-year-old Aznar seemed eager to demonstrate that the hard-handed statism he had advocated in his youth was in the past and that he had been successful in forging his Popular Party into a moderate, centre-right party almost entirely free of the Francoist sympathies and authoritarian leanings that had lingered on the right of the political spectrum after the advent of democracy. This moderation was to be seen in a cabinet of figures mostly young and untainted by Francoism, continuity in most areas of policy and a commitment to preserve Spain's consensual 'social partnership' arrangement to reassure the labour movement (and prevent industrial unrest). But perhaps the most important sign that the right had changed its spots was Aznar's stance on those regions which had traditionally railed against Castilian expansionism and who feared that the iron fist of Madrid would be revealed once the right returned to power.

While still in opposition Aznar had authored a book—*The Second Transition*—outlining his plans for granting almost as many new powers to the regions as they had received in the immediate post-Franco period and more than anything the González government had countenanced. Apart from recognising that regional and national identities were in some cases poorly reconciled, there was also a pragmatic logic. The growth in the size of government and the complexity of its functions in the second half of the 20th century demanded a greater role, if only for reasons of efficiency. Confounding those who believed that the centralising instincts of the right would prove too powerful ever to allow a letting go by an Aznar government, he was as good as his word. Today Spain is by far the least centralised of the large non-federal European countries, and as regards public spending approximates federal Germany, with just under half of the total being accounted for by sub-national levels of government.

Yet despite these changes and the genuine transformation of the Spanish right, Aznar leaves office with relations with Catalonia and the Basque Country as fraught as they have been since the time of Franco. While apportioning blame for the dire state of relations between Madrid and regional nationalists is difficult, it is hard to avoid the conclusion that Aznar deserves his fair share, particularly since winning an outright parliamentary majority in 2000 which allowed him to govern without the support of the regionalists from Catalonia, the Basque Country and the Canary Islands.

His thus-far-and-no-further position on devolution in his second term and his unwillingness even to discuss issues such as reforming the country's ineffectual upper house of parliament so that it acts as a forum for the regions (something he himself once advocated) has fanned regionalists' sense of grievance. As important has been his style. While he has grown more determined and confident during his time in office, he has also shown growing signs of an authoritarian streak and his ability to resist an innate urge to overplay his hand has waned. Never known for his empathy, or understanding of regional sensitivities, his unyielding obstinacy and dismissiveness towards regionalists' aspirations has brought back painful memories of the Franco years. The result has been to strain severely relations with Catalan nationalists and contribute to the complete breakdown of relations with their (non-violent) counterparts in the deeply troubled Basque Country, where militant secessionists have used terrorist tactics for decades to win independence from Spain.

And it is polarisation in the Basque country, where moderate nationalists are intent on seeking de facto independence from Spain and have scheduled a referendum on the question for next year, that will be his successor's least welcome inheritance. During his first term Aznar was careful not to overreact to ETA's campaign of murder and intimidation, often directed at his party (he survived an assassination attempt in 1995). And when ETA called a cease-fire in 1998, he sanctioned face to face talks and made concessions on issues such as relocation to jails in the Basque Country of those convicted of terrorist offences. However, the ending of the ETA cease-fire at the end of 1999 led to a hardening in his attitude. The most immediate manifestation of this was a decision to move against ETA's political wing, Batasuna. The banning of the party, which took effect in 2002, was opposed by a majority in the Basque Country and has made any future talks on an end to violence more difficult by weakening less militant and more political elements (most agree that he has been vindicated in that attacks have effectively ended since the ban). He upped the ante further in 2003 by making advocacy of the proposed referendum on de facto independence punishable with up to five years in jail, an astonishing curtailment of free speech in a democratic society. Although it is non-violent Basque nationalists who have chosen to challenge the authority and indivisibility of the Spanish state and its constitution, Aznar has often appeared almost to be daring them to go towards the brink. By so doing he has increased the likelihood of what he himself has ominously warned of; the Balkanisation of Spain. Basques will probably step back, but if they do, it will not be because Aznar has given them space, let alone because he has been statesmanlike enough to show them a way.

But not only in relation to the regions has Aznar become more strident and his tone shriller. Abroad, he has been emboldened to the point where his now uninhibited plain speaking has caused unnecessary and some-times gratuitous offence. In January he riled the French by describing their cultural exception in trade matters (designed to hold back Hollywood-isation) as the mark of a declining civilisation. He has even been prepared to undermine his relationship with his closest European ally, Tony Blair. By persuading George Bush to raise the ever-thorny issue of UK-ruled Gibraltar, he infuriated Blair and squandered a precious Bush favour, even though he must have known it would bring agreement with Britain on the rock's constitutional status no nearer. At home his with-us-or-against-us nature and castigation of the opposition parties for merely doing their job have caused the venom that had poisoned politics in the mid-1990s, and which Aznar had drawn on coming to power, to seep back. He has also undermined his own support for the collective forgetting of the Francoist past by financing the exhumation of Spanish soldiers who fought alongside the Nazis on the Russian front, while refusing to help to find the bodies of those who were 'disappeared' during the Civil War. His decision to back the war in Iraq, and his unwillingness to take the trouble to make the case to a deeply sceptical public, marked a high point of his new imperiousness.

That he has been able to act in this way says much about Spain. Deference towards authority and a weak culture of accountability mean that he enjoys unquestioning obedience in his party (there were no revolts over Iraq despite profound misgivings). Inadequate institutional checks and balances on the exercise of executive power have allowed him to adopt a style so presidential that at times it appears as if he equates himself with the state. Unlike in Germany and Italy, who endured totalitarianism and carefully diffused power afterwards, Spain's experience of less extreme authoritarianism (and the weak government during the Second Republic that led to it) resulted in fewer qualms about creating strong and stable government. To ensure this, the 1978 constitution created a legislature which is largely subservient to the executive and a judiciary which is insufficiently independent.

It was these factors that allowed Aznar, almost single handedly, to make the biggest break with the past on any policy area. He believes that with the tenth biggest economy in the world, a population of 40 million, a world language and links to the Americas, Spain should be a global player. For Aznar, Spain's failure to punch up to its weight in the world was anathema, smacking of the defeatist mindset in evidence since the Spanish-American war of 1898 (a historical turning point for Spain's right), when the US humiliatingly ejected Spain from her last remaining colonies in Cuba and the Philippines. For Aznar the inferiority complex borne of centuries of decline since the height of Spanish power in the 16th century was the monkey on the back he wanted rid of.

In order to achieve this goal, Aznar did two things. First, when necessary he was prepared to take a more proactive and assertive stance in international affairs, even if this risked the ire of other EU countries used to Spain being a follower, not a leader. The second strand was the forging of closer ties with the US in the belief that only by gaining influence with the superpower could Spain wield more clout in Europe and the world. Within months of taking office he fought (unsuccessfully) to have the EU take a stance on Cuba more in line with the US, and integrated his country's military fully into NATO's command structures (it had remained semi-detached since joining the alliance in 1982). In his second term, Aznar accelerated the move towards the US, facilitated by the coming to power of George W. Bush, with whom he is politically and personally close. (An indication of the success of Aznar's strategy was the decision of the US president to begin his first visit to Europe in Madrid.) While other Europeans opposed US plans to create a National Missile Defense shield, Aznar gave it his blessing and later agreed a bilateral defense agreement with the US which was to provide, among other things, satellite intelligence on Basque terrorists. And it was the issue of terrorism that did more than anything else to cement ties as Aznar recognised as quickly as any European leader the fundamental shifts that the attacks of September 11 had brought about. But it was an incident with neighbouring Morocco in the summer of 2002 that convinced him that if there was a choice to be made between the US and Europe, he would come down on the American side of the Atlantic.

To test Spain's reactions to sovereignty-disputed territory, the north African kingdom landed *gendarmes* on an islet between the two countries. Aznar responded forcefully to the provocation by sending in the military to expel the Moroccans and restore the ambiguous status quo. In the ensuing crisis, he felt let down by his EU partners and believed that France had been nothing less than perfidious in showing as much concern for Third-World country Morocco as for fellow EU member state Spain. When US secretary of state Colin Powell quickly and efficiently ended the crisis to Spain's satisfaction, Aznar decided that the Americans were 'serious' and Europeans were not. In his decision to back the war in Iraq it was this view that was central, not any conviction that overthrowing Saddam would reduce the terrorist threat to Spain, still less that the Middle East could be democratised by régime change in Baghdad.

So while Aznar has undoubtedly raised Spain's international profile and increased its influence with the US, it has come at a cost in terms of relations with France and Germany. Quite apart from appearing to relish antagonising those countries' respective leaders—Jacques Chirac and Gerhard Schroeder—on the war in Iraq, Aznar has isolated Spain by taking an excessively rigid line on changing voting weights in the EU's most important institution, the Council of Ministers, while at the same time fighting fiercely to maintain its massive subsidies (it remains the largest net recipient). These costs, combined with the very limited support among the political and policy-making class for Aznar's redirection of foreign policy, the risks attendant on punching above one's weight in the world and the underlying factors that determine international clout, make a return to a lower-profile, less overtly pro-US position likely once Anzar steps down.

As regards the orientation of Spain's elites, they had bought into the European integration project as enthusiastically as any other even before the end of the Franco régime. Not only did they see EU membership as means by which to rehabilitate Spain after Franco and a symbol that it had taken its place alongside the continent's mature democracies, they share with the wider European mainstream the belief that the EU has become the main vehicle for the pursuit of countries' international interests. The breadth and depth of the commitment was evinced by the unquestioning bipartisan commitment to joining the euro. For Spain's elite, remaining outside the centrepiece of the integration project would have been to be relegated to the second tier in Europe and was simply unthinkable. And while there is little disagreement that Spain should punch up to its weight in Europe and be more assertive when necessary, there is considerable unease, even within the Popular Party, at the costs incurred by the manner in which Aznar has attempted to do this. In relation to popular opinion, doubts are stronger still, perhaps best illustrated when the opposition felt able to criticise Aznar in December over his unbending position on voting weights at the Council of Ministers (this was in stark contrast to Aznar's sole ally on the issue—Poland's Leszek Miller—whose to-the-death obduracy earned him a hero's welcome in Warsaw).

As for the shift in orientation towards the US, support is even thinner and doubts greater. Not traditionally one of Europe's Atlanticist nations, visceral anti-Americanism, of the sort seen in most European countries, is strong on the left, not least owing to US support for the Franco régime. Today the opposition Socialists do not see Spain as part of a Rumsfeldian 'new' Europe and their leader has spoken pointedly of not submitting to Washington if elected in March. Nor has the right traditionally felt close to the US owing to distrust of its Protestantism and an inability to forgive it its role in depriving Spain of its colonies. As regards Mariano Rajoy, Aznar's successor and prime ministerial candidate for the Popular Party, he has avoided talking of foreign policy when he can. Unlike Aznar, who almost seems uncomfortable not taking sides, Rajoy is an altogether more emollient figure and is likely to seek to avoid making choices between Europe and America if at all possible.

Finally, as regards the underlying determinants of international clout, Aznar's ambition looks like overstretch. Militarily, Spain is a minnow, spending less than one tenth the UK's defense budget. Economically, it is not yet a model for others, being dependent on EU subsidies and with per capita wealth among the lowest in the EU. And diplomatically it is under-resourced and lacking a strategic thinking capability (the foreign ministry is still jokingly referred to in Madrid as the Ministry for Gibraltar for its once obsessive focus on the territory).

While Aznar broke with the past on foreign policy, he promised to continue the gradual liberalising direction of his predecessor, reflecting the convergence of left and right in Europe to a centre ground where consensual pragmatism, not ideology, is the principal determining factor in framing policy. Paradoxically, however, and despite being of the self-styled 'reformist centre' and loudly proclaiming himself to be in the vanguard of structural economic change in the EU, he has ended up being far less of a liberaliser than the Socialists. As regards the two dominant issues for Spain, as for other continental economies—reform of labour markets and public pensions systems—Aznar's tenure has been marked by tinkering. The result: unemployment remains the highest in western Europe and the pension system could still face crisis as Spain's birth rate is now the lowest in the world. That his reforming record has never matched his rhetoric was evinced as recently as January 2004, when Spain was grouped among the Union's reforming laggards by the EU's arbiter-in-chief in these matters, the European Commission. Moreover, that taxation as a percentage of national income (though still below the EU average) actually rose during his tenure is further evidence to undermine claims of reforming glory.

The failure to make significant changes to labour laws owed in large part to a fear of confrontation with the trade unions. In Aznar's first term this was explained by the need to prove the right's moderation and a desire to maintain the consensual 'social partnership' arrangements between labour and employers. There was also an economic motive. Although Spain's social partnership does not influence policy-making to the extent it does in the Nordics, the Netherlands or Ireland, for example, it has ensured wage moderation throughout Aznar's tenure. Had a more confrontational approach been taken the competitiveness gains of non-inflationary pay awards could have been lost. That said, Aznar won a clear mandate for reform and in his second term, having proved that he was not simply out to do the bosses' bidding, he might have put his authority behind change. In the event, he did the opposite. The only reform package of the term was abandoned in the face of trade union opposition and the minister who had drawn it up fired.

The lack of enthusiasm for more profound reform also says much about how the continental right differs from its more economically liberal, Anglo-Saxon counterpart. The right in Spain, as in most countries where the Christian Democratic tradition is strong, has limited faith in market outcomes and has always stressed a collectivist 'social market' dimension. Also working against the urge to liberalise was the country's long history of statism and patronage. Links between politics and business have always been unhealthily close and political influence over the corporate sector remains strong despite a massive privatisation programme. The government retains 'golden shares' in some privatised companies (found to be illegal by the European Court of Justice) and even today boards are still packed with government appointees. The fact that regulators remain weak and lack independence while the anti-trust authority is under-resourced and toothless demonstrates that in Aznar's Spain the interests of well-connected producers still trump those of consumers.

Nowhere has maintaining control and dispensing patronage been more a priority than in the media. Not only is the sort of stand-off that occurred between the British government and the BBC over Andrew Gilligan's radio reporting unthinkable in Spain, the state-run broadcaster, RTVE, tailors its coverage to avoid offending the government of the day. In 2003, for example, its news bulletins downplayed massive street protests against the war in Iraq and a year earlier simply ignored the only general strike of the Aznar years, which brought whole swathes of the economy to a standstill. But the Aznar administration has gone further than its predecessor in using its powers to influence the media. The advent of new media technologies— satellite and digital TV in particular—has opened up opportunities for the private sector, and the Aznar government has unashamedly used its legislative and regulatory powers to favour media groups that lean right-wards and hinder those of a leftist orientation. Within a year of coming to power, the government used its decree powers to delay the Prisa media group launching its digital TV service, while encouraging the then state-owned telecoms company, Telefonica, which was run by an Aznar loyalist, to expand into the medium. In 2002 it again changed the law to allow its friends in private television—Telefonica and Mediaset (the jewel in Italian prime minister Silvio Berlusconi's business empire)—to wrestle controlling stakes in private TV channels. Given the extent of government interference in media, Aznar has been fortunate to avoid even a fraction of the inter-national opprobrium that has been heaped on Berlusconi for curbing media pluralism in Italy.

But like their Italian counterparts, Spaniards appear little exercised by government interference in the media and care more at election time about their material well-being. And if, as appears likely, the Popular Party wins a third term at the March general election, it will be because of strong economic growth over the past eight years, when Spain has expanded more rapidly than any of the other big European countries. But how much this can be attributed to sound policies and strong management? By far the most important reason for the strong growth of the past eight years has been the euro. By abandoning the soft peseta for the hard euro at a highly competitive level, Spain gained a strong currency and permanently lower and stable interests (the cost/benefit analysis of adoption was far more clear cut for Spain than it would be now for the UK, for example). It was this massive monetary stimulus, more than anything else, that was the cause of the long consumption and property boom that Spain has enjoyed for almost a decade.

Nor does Aznar's administration deserve all the credit for ensuring Spain's qualification for the single-currency project in the first place. He was fortunate to inherit an economy on the cusp of boom and doubly fortunate in that Spain's large budget deficit, which threatened to exclude it from participation, began to fall as a result. This triggered a virtuous cycle: improving public finances increased confidence that Spain would make it to the cut, which caused Spain's traditionally high interest rates to fall towards those of historically low-interest-rate Germany. This, in turned, caused debt servicing costs to fall. The cycle of fiscal and monetary virtue was complete. A budget deficit painlessly cut in half in just two years allowed Spain to become a founding member of the euro. In terms of managing the boom, fortune again smiled on Aznar. With European Central Bank interest rates being set too low for the fast-growing Spanish economy, the OECD (among others) advocated an off-setting fiscal tightening to damp things down. The advice was ignored. But unlike fellow 'Club Med' countries who had also see interest rates plummet Portugal, where overheating turned boom to bust, and Italy, where the economy never heated up in the first place—Spain's economy became neither too hot nor too cold. Though it is hard to fault any politician for taking more credit than is his due when things go well, Aznar's failure to take advantage of his good fortune to have been in power when the economy was booming was his greatest failing of his time in office. Had he overcome his lack of interest in economics and shown his characteristic determination to cajole and push the unions he might have removed more of the rigidities that keep unemployment so high.

Yet for all this, it is hard not to sense that the opportunity for greatness was missed. Had he been able to resist the temptation to show such hostility to regionalists, the threat of serious confrontation between Madrid and the Basques might be less than it is as he leaves office. Had he been less willing to alienate France and Germany, he might have placed Spain's foreign policy on a firmer footing.

*Originally published in* Prospect

———

## PORTUGAL LOOKS NERVOUSLY TO THE FUTURE

*November 2003*

For a month from 12 June, eyes in Europe, and far beyond, will look to Portugal. Euro 2004, a 16-nation soccer tournament, will be this smallish country's first time hosting a big sporting event. Running the year's biggest show after the Olympics will cause 10 million Portuguese hearts to swell. Those same hearts will be ready to burst if, come tournament's end on the fourth of July, the country's ageing 'golden generation' of stars become champions of Europe. For the likes of Luis Figo, Rui Costa and Fernando Couto—household names to soccer-lovers everywhere—it will probably be their last chance to live up to the expectations generated when, as teenagers in the late 1980s, they twice won the youth World Cup championship.

But despite a soaring profile next summer, some in Europe's western-most nation fear that once the floodlights are turned off, their country will be forgotten about. The reason: the eastward enlargement of the European Union on 1 May. Historically minded Portuguese know that half a millennium ago Europe's centre of gravity moved from the Mediterranean south to the Atlantic west when treasure and trade routes to the new world were opened up. Their country grew powerful and rich as a result. But now, long peripheral since that centre moved northwards, they fear an eastward shift will cause their country to drop off the continental shelf, at least as far as foreign investors and the subsidy-dispensing EU are concerned.

For those who want to register disgruntlement with the EU over enlargement (or anything else for that matter) they will have an opportunity the morning after the football begins. If the prime minister, José Manuel Durão Barroso, is as good as his word, voters will have their say on the EU's new constitution, due to be agreed no later than the spring of 2004, in a referendum on 13 June.

A motley two—the unreconstructed communist party and a rag-bag, populist-right outfit—will probably campaign against. But in the poorest country in western Europe, few dislike the EU. Most Portuguese believe that membership has brought prestige and extra influence in the world, while few contest that subsidies have been anything but generous. And despite being, by common consensus, Europe's oldest nation state, the Portuguese have never been unduly sensitive about sharing some of their sovereignty. If the EU constitution is put to a vote, expect a solid majority in favour.

But being enthusiastic European integrationists has never stopped the pragmatic Portuguese from being as pro-American as the other great seafaring nations on Europe's Atlantic coast—the Netherlands and Britain, Norway and Denmark. And in 2004 they will be as stalwart in their Atlanticism as they were in 2003 when Portugal's government backed the us-led ousting of Saddam Hussein. Though the war, as elsewhere in Europe, was not popular, opposition was as muted as anywhere in the western part of the continent, and few doubt that whatever happens in the us's 'war against terrorism' in 2004, Portugal will be there with moral, if not always military, support.

On 25 April the Portuguese will mark the 30th anniversary of the ending of their own dictatorship. Though not quite velvet, the revolution that ended almost half a century of authoritarian rule occurred with next to no bloodshed, something for which Portuguese give thanks each year. But the three-decade anniversary will not be cause for extravagant celebration, less still for a bout of protracted introspection.

With little time for picking at old wounds, most attention in 2004 will be paid to the centre-right government's efforts to revive the recession-mired economy. After two years of stagnation, a return to growth, however modest, should take place. But even as the economy splutters back to life, there won't be much cheer, for two reasons. First, the government's finances are in a mess. A third year of spending cuts is in store, not least to prevent another breach of its commitments under the euro area's Stability and Growth Pact (Portugal was the first country to break the rules when its budget deficit exceeded 3% of GDP in 2001).

The second reason for the lingering feel-glum factor in 2004 will be more 'structural' reforms of the kind so often advocated for other slow-growing countries in Europe. Though beneficial in the long run, their more immediate effect will be to continue causing uncertainty, thus denting consumer confidence. Thickets of labour regulations, some unchanged since the 1930s, will be trimmed a little more. The civil service and public healthcare will face further shake up. Social welfare and state pensions will be cut to reduce costs and, it is hoped, get the jobless into work and keep more older folk there.

And as if the government was not already risking overstretch by fighting so many reform battles, new fronts will be opened up in 2004. Privatisation will move up the agenda. TAP, the national airline, will go back on the block after a first attempt to offload it failed in 2001. Gas and electricity infrastructures are also pencilled in for disposal. The unions will resist, warning of ownership falling into the hands of the Spanish, their much larger Iberian neighbours. This will touch a raw nerve far beyond the labour movement. Many fear that Spaniards, by snapping up stock in privatised companies, will nibble away at the country's independence and achieve through corporate acquisition what they failed to do when they tried to swallow the country whole more than four centuries ago.

But such fears will be brushed aside by the prime minister, an almost jesuitically zealous reformer who rarely stops preaching to his compatriots about the need to embrace change. By taking advantage of the sense of crisis generated by recession, big budget deficits and the challenges of EU enlargement he should manage to push through many of his much needed reforms. But for all the upheaval and another year of fiscal hairshirt, after a year to forget in 2003, things should be a little better in 2004 thanks to an end to recession, falling unemployment and lower inflation. And, who knows, if Fernando Couto leads his team to footballing glory during the summer, it could even turn out to be a year worth remembering for the Portuguese.

*Originally published in* The World in 2004

———

## EUROPE AND AMERICA: THE CLINTON YEARS

*6 June 2000*

The role of the US in the world during the past century, although far from unblemished, has been unlike that of any other great power. Not only did it lead the defeat of 20th-century totalitarianism, in both its fascist and communist guises, but it allowed the countries in its sphere of influence a unique degree of freedom to pursue their own interests. However, with the demise of the Soviet Union, the US went from being one of a pair of super-powers to became the sole global 'hyper-power'. Now, in the absence of a meaningful security threat, the US is unchecked by anything other than its in-built (democratic) self-restraint.

But this has not always been sufficient, as the US is presented with an irresistible temptation to go it alone in the world. American unilateralism in recent years has included attempts to impose its domestic laws on foreigners (most contentiously to punish non-American firms for doing business with Cuba and Iran), cruise missile attacks on Afghanistan and Sudan and a refusal to sign up to the International Criminal Court.

Recently, a plan to create a missile shield, primarily to protect the US, has unsettled most non-Americans by threatening to decouple US security from that of Europe and undermine the nuclear deterrents of Russia and China.

The passing of the Soviet threat has also lifted the lid on competing domestic interest groups in the US, who now exercise greater sway over foreign policy. This has contributed not only to increased unilateralism, but also created greater unpredictability. Congressmen, unrestrained by a strong whip system and insatiable in their appetite for election campaign contributions, are easy prey for such interest groups and their lobbyists. In 1998, protectionists for the first time denied a president 'fast-track' trade negotiating powers—in that case to expand the North American Free Trade Area to include poor Latin American countries. In 1999, isolationists refused to ratify an international treaty to ban nuclear weapons testing.

While US foreign policy becomes less coherent, progress towards co-ordinating the external affairs of 15 EU countries advances at a snail's pace (it will inch forward again at next week's Feira summit in Portugal). In concrete terms, the advance is often imperceptible. Even today, their over-riding collective objective—bringing the former communist countries into the EU—is being lost sight of as the narrower concerns of individual member states take precedence. As a result, enlargement seems further away than ever.

Nor have the EU's chaotic institutional arrangements for external relations made progress any easier. Javier Solana, the former NATO secretary-general, occupies the still ill defined role of the EU's 'High Representative' for Foreign Affairs. At the European Commission, responsibility is frag-mented, with four departments dealing with various aspects of external relations. To make matters worse, the carve-up of competences between Mr Solana and his Commission colleagues is far from clear cut.

Despite these handicaps, some progress is being made. As an aspiring political union, the EU has moved the development of a defence capability rapidly up its agenda. In late 1998, France—ever-alert to ways of counter-balancing the influence of the US—persuaded a new and unusually pro-European British government of the need for a stronger role for Europe in defence. Since then, the EU has committed itself to the establishment of a 'European Security and Defence Identity' (ESDI), including a 60,000-person corps capable of deploying in humanitarian crisis situations beyond its borders.

However, as defence increasingly preoccupies the EU, it has become a matter of contention with the US, exacerbating tensions over trade matters. True to recent form, neither side is entirely coherent in its position. Although Americans have long pressed Europeans to share more equally the costs of defending their continent, they fret that ESDI will undermine NATO, the main pillar of European security. But Europeans believe that what Americans really fear is a loss of influence if ESDI succeeds. Moreover, they suspect that the US wants to have its cake and eat it—maintaining its influence over European security through NATO, but having Europeans pay for the privilege.

Financing issues aside, Europeans also say that they cannot be sure the US will always be around to guarantee their security, pointing to the US pursuit of invulnerability with its missile shield as proof of its isolationist impulses. Americans are on firmer ground when they question the ability and willingness of Europeans to formulate common policies and then back them with meaningful military muscle. They ask whether 15 countries with very different histories and interests can ever hope to agree common positions on security and defence matters—matters that go to the very core of national sovereignty. They also point to ever-shrinking defence budgets in Europe which create a gap between the EU's grand rhetoric and the readiness of member states to pay for expensive military hardware.

But the need for greater balance to the international system will focus European minds on what must be done to co-operate more closely. The only question is how far and how fast it will go. A European counterweight to US global dominance has obvious advantages for all non-Americans. But it is also in Americans' interests. Our shared constitutional heritage is founded on the need for checks and balances on those who wield power— a recognition that unrestrained power is bad not only for those upon whom it is exercised, but also for those who wield it.

Incoherence on both sides of the Atlantic will make the shift towards a more equal relationship difficult. And with a plethora of issues already causing transatlantic tensions, there is more turbulence ahead in EU–US relations. However, despite a decade of doom-saying, our shared values of democracy, freedom and reason, along with broadly similar interests, have ensured that there has been no return to the shallow peace of 19th century balance-of-power geopolitics. Despite disagreements about defence and squabbles over trade, fundamental similarities will ensure that the transatlantic partnership endures in the 21st century.

*Originally published in the* Irish Times

## EUROPE AND AMERICA: THE BUSH YEARS

*March 2007*

Four years ago this week, the US-led war in Iraq began. The invasion triggered the most serious rift in transatlantic relations since 1945 and caused some of the deepest ever divisions among the EU's members. The anniversary of the invasion provides an opportune moment to assess the state of transatlantic relations. The happy conclusion is that though some fall-out from the split remains, talk of the continents drifting apart has proved very wide of the mark and relations between Europe and the US are now close to normal.

### Transatlantic values: more to unite than divide

During the traumatic days of early 2003, a great deal of analysis and comment focused on explaining the divisions that had emerged by reference to attitudes towards the use of force, perhaps most vividly captured by a US academic, Robert Kagan, in his essay (and later a book) 'Of Paradise and Power'. Mr Kagan (an advocate of the Iraq invasion, incidentally) described Europeans as inhabiting the world of perpetual peace envisaged by the German enlightenment philosopher Immanuel Kant. As a result, they had become incapable of dealing with other states that did not play the international relations game by their rules, whereby disagreements are solved in the committee rooms of Brussels by grinding out reasoned compromise.

There was and is much to this analysis. Europeans countries spend far less on defence than the US and they are often reluctant to engage in military activity even when they agree that such action is both justified and necessary (in the 1999 conflict between NATO and the régime of Slobodan Milosevic, many European members of the alliance declined to participate, while the US undertook the overwhelming majority of the military action). To the US, this unwillingness to resort to the use of force, even in a region as proximate to the EU as the western Balkans, remains a source of frustration. But it would be wrong to overstate this as a factor in undermining transatlantic ties, mainly because this difference has existed for decades—in the 1960s even the UK declined to involve itself in Vietnam, in the 1970s German '*Ostpolitik*' towards the Soviet Union was far too placatory for American tastes and in the 1980s many Europeans feared that the US plan for a 'star wars' missile defence system risked upsetting the strategic balance in Europe (this latter difference is in evidence again today in relation to a new anti-ballistic missile system that the US is offering its allies). It is hard to argue, therefore, that there is a widening gulf between the sides on resort to force in international affairs. Rather it is one that they have managed to live with for decades. It would also be an error to overstate European pacifism. Sizable European contingents fought along-side the US in the first Gulf War in the early 1990s, 25 of the EU's 27 member states have forces of some kind deployed in Afghanistan and 12 still have a presence in Iraq. Moreover, Germany, the EU's largest member state, is gradually increasing its military engagement after decades of non-involvement in such matters. This makes the prospect of Europe punching up to its economic weight in the world more likely in the future.

And what of the US: is it becoming more belligerent and bullying, as some in Europe and elsewhere claim? The case to be made that the US is becoming more aggressive is certainly stronger than the case for an ever more cowering and cowardly Europe, but this is based almost entirely on the Iraq war, which was an aberration rather than the beginning of a new unilateralist trend. To see why, one need only consider briefly the context in which 9/11 took place.

Although the Cold War had been over for a decade by 2001, the US was still seeking to define a new posture in a world without a Soviet threat. Competing ideas existed, but the emergence of the Al-Qaeda as a serious menace to the American homeland and the rapid victory over the Taliban in Afghanistan gave credence to the views of those who had long argued that the US had underestimated and under-used the unique power that it wields. These neo-conservative voices won President Bush around to the idea that with such preponderance, the US did not need to shore up unpleasant régimes, but could sweep them away, leaving fertile ground for democracies to flourish. And this, they argued, was the only way to guarantee American security in the long run because in democracies people are far too busy enjoying freedom to engage in terror. But the neo-conservative account of the transformative potential of US power has been discredited by the failure of Iraq, and, if to a lesser extent, by the success in free and fair elections of Hamas in the Palestinian territories and Hezbullah in Lebanon. The moment of America attempting to impose democracy on the point of a bayonet is well and truly over.

## More humility and less hubris in Washington
This comes as a great relief to Europe, where even the most hard-headed and staunchest Atlanticists in diplomatic circles were appalled by the hubris some of their US counterparts displayed at the height of the

neo-conservative moment. In the second Bush term, the sort of humility in foreign affairs that the president had promised when campaigning for election in 2000 has become evident, and a determined effort is being made to mend fences. Mr Bush's first foreign visit after re-election, for instance, was to the EU. This was significant not only because he was the first US president to recognise the EU in this way, but also because it signalled a definitive rejection of 'disaggregation', a policy of divide and conquer towards the EU advocated by some in his first administration.

American efforts at extending an olive branch have been enthusiastically accepted. Those Europeans who opposed the war, arguing that it would open the Middle East's Pandora's box, feel vindicated, but they are careful not to appear to gloat, not least because they have no wish ever again to see relations with their American cousins plumb the depths of 2003. They are also determined to demonstrate that they can be taken seriously when it comes to hard security issues, which explains the intense efforts they have made to halt Iran's nuclear programme and their close co-operation with the US at the UN to impose sanctions on the Islamic Republic. Though there are differences—the US wishes to ratchet up those sanctions rapidly, while the Europeans prefer a more gradual approach—they have remained united in the face of the threat, despite Iran's best efforts to divide them.

## Transatlantic economic interests are eternal

Because Europeans know that their clout in hard security issues internationally is limited, they have often focused their reconciliation efforts in other spheres, most notably in economic affairs. Current proposals by the German chancellor, Angela Merkel, to use her country's presidency of the EU in the first half of 2007 to launch a major initiative aimed at deepening economic integration in the transatlantic space is only the latest example. But even without considering Ms Merkel's big idea, huge energy is already being expended at the political and policy levels to remove many of the remaining obstacles to doing transatlantic business. Though disagreements are plentiful—some intractable, others merely technical—the two sides are talking about the Doha multilateral trade round, bilateral trade issues, competition policy, harmonisation of accounting standards, public procurement, aviation, financial services regulation and a lot more besides. Little illustrates the normality of transatlantic relations better than the daily interaction between European and American officials as they go about their problem-solving business.

**Business as usual**

If transatlantic relations are back on an even keel at the official level, the damage done by Iraq remains at popular level. Positive European sentiment towards the US is far lower than it was before the Iraq invasion according to opinion polls and many of the continent's media often display a visceral dislike of President Bush which distorts reporting of his administration's actions and its dealings with other countries. Four years on, it seems unlikely that he will ever find a place in European hearts. But he is not long for the White House and a new president should see levels of pro-American sentiment rise again, not least because Europeans know that they share values and have common interests that are unlike those with any other region. Although disagreements inevitably exist given the unique scope of the relationship, there is very considerable political will to solve them. Despite much portentous talk of European and American drifting apart, this has not come to pass. Nor is it likely to. The ties stretching across the Atlantic are too many and too strong to allow that to happen.

*Originally published on* www.viewswire.com

———

## EUROPE'S FAR-RIGHT: SHEEP IN WOLVES' CLOTHING

*January 2004*

The rise to power of Dutch populists in mid-2002 looked dismayingly familiar to Europe's moderate majority. By bringing to four (of 15) the number of EU states in which the reactionary right had a say in government, the advance of illiberalism seemed irresistible. But the routing of Jörg Haider's Freedom Party in the Austrian general election on 24 November, the implosion of The Netherlands's Lijst Pim Fortyun in September and the inability of these parties, and others like them, to implement their agendas of intolerance strongly suggest that they will remain a largely insignificant force in European politics.

The coming to power of the Freedom Party (FPO) in Austria at the beginning of 2000 was the first in a string of success for populist parties in western Europe in recent years. But even before Austria's 14 EU counterpart states had time to impose diplomatic sanctions on the country in response, there was considerable evidence to indicate how little sway the FPO would have in the governance of the country.

Before being deemed an acceptable coalition partner by the centre-right People's Party, the FPO was forced to abandon the raft of populist promises made in opposition, including its commitment to halt immigration, block EU enlargement and slash taxes. With the coalition's legislative agenda bearing no resemblance to the FPO's populist election manifesto, the party's chances of wielding real influence were confined to executive decision-making functions. But inexperience and, for the most part, ineptitude allowed the FPO to be outmaneuvered by its coalition partner at almost every turn, resulting in a slew of ministerial resignations and sackings during the 30-month life of the coalition. As regards the FPO undermining democracy or eroding civil and political liberties, even the opposition, as well as human rights groups, agreed that it had not done so.

The failure to deliver, for ill or good, resulted in the loss of one third of the party's support by the end of 2000. Jörg Haider, who formally stepped down as leader after the election but remained in charge, distanced himself from his fellow party members in government. Unwilling or unable to change the habit of a lifetime, he continued to act as if in opposition. His constant sniping opened up a division with those who wished to transform the FPO into a respectable party of government. Unlike the personality clashes that caused most of the party's unsightly public in-fighting while in office, this fissure was more profound. As Haider went to ever greater lengths to grab headlines, he became a growing embarrassment for his colleagues. As the party's poll ratings remained in the doldrums, Mr Haider gambled. By deposing the nominal leader and championing tax cuts he believed that the party's fortunes could be reversed. But the plan backfired and the government collapsed. A premature election, a party in disarray and an abysmal record in government resulted in erstwhile supporters abandoning the party in droves.

But this internal instability is not unique to the FPO. To a greater or lesser extent it is a feature of all populist parties, as the case of the Dutch anti-immigration party, the Lijst Pim Fortuyn (LPF), illustrated during its far briefer period in government. When the colorful Fortuyn burst onto the Netherlands's usually unchanging political scene earlier this year, he struck a chord with surprisingly many voters, mostly by demanding a halt to immigration. Despite being left leaderless by his assassination just two weeks before the May election, the LPF went on to become the country's second largest party, earning it a place at the cabinet table.

But from the moment the LPF entered government to the time of its departure its members were absorbed with internal power struggles. When LPF ministers did focus on their jobs, they had a tendency to shoot from the hip, sometimes requiring embarrassing back-tracking. Stormy meetings were held to give the party purpose and direction. But little came of them other than frayed tempers and demoralising public squabbling. Without leaving any significant legacy the party fell apart after just four months in office, precipitating the collapse of the coalition. It now faces electoral oblivion on 22 January (2003) when the Dutch return to the polls.

The implosion of the LPM and the FPO says much about the nature of such parties. Like other populist movements in western Europe, they advocate incoherent and often contradictory policies, ranging from libertarianism to authoritarianism, neo-liberalism to statism. To compound the difficulties of running a political organisation so politically confused, these parties tend to attract an unusually heterogeneous range of mavericks, eccentrics and opportunists. The result is something akin to an in-built self-destruct mechanism.

But if in-fighting and ineptitude prevented the FPO and LPM from posing any threat to liberal democracy and the civil and political liberties of citizens, what of other, more cohesive parties normally classed as far-right that are still in power? Consider first Italy's Northern League, led by the demagogic Umberto Bossi, and the National Alliance, whose illiberal antecedents include Mussolini. Despite both seeing their vote-share decline on the 1996 election, they joined the right-of-centre government dominated by the moderate-right Forza Italia in June 2001.

Bossi's often virulent tirades against immigrants have been toned down since taking on a cabinet post. His rhetoric seems more hollow than ever now that the government has decided to grant the biggest ever amnesty to an estimated 700,000 illegal immigrants after pressure from business organisations in areas suffering labour shortages. As for the one-time neo-fascists of the National Alliance, its authoritarian 'social right' wing was roundly defeated at the party's most recent congress, confirming the dominance of Gianfranco Fini, now deputy prime minister and architect of the party's move away from extremism.

Although the centre-left opposition maintains that there is no question of Italy moving back towards its fascist past, worries about the role of the police would appear to be the only real cause for concern in any of the countries surveyed here. Sympathisers of the far-right in the security forces were accused of colluding with like-minded elements in the government at the Genoa G7 summit in Genoa in the summer of 2001 when excessive force was used against demonstrators. Although relations between the government and anti-globalisation organisations have improved, allowing a large rally in Florence in November 2002 to pass off peacefully, a more recent case of protestors being held on remand on trumped up charges suggests that there is still some cause for concern.

In Denmark, the People's Party made sufficient gains in the 2001 election to force the centre-right minority coalition to look to it for support in parliament. It backs up its claims to be the friend of the 'little man' by using its influence for more public expenditure on health and pensions and, predictably, by engaging in sometimes shrill anti-immigration rhetoric. And this has translated into action. Though the People's Party is the least extreme of the five parties, Denmark's recent tightening of its laws probably includes the harshest measures anywhere in western Europe—children over the age of 13 will no longer be allowed join their legally resident parents nor non-nationals under 24 their spouses. And the Danes are not alone on this touchstone issue. In Austria and the Netherlands, immigrants have not only been forced to take language lessons if they wish to stay, they are obliged to pay for the privilege. In Italy the taint of criminality will attach itself to all immigrants by proposed compulsory finger-printing.

But however heartless or petty, none of the measures proposed or implemented breach the obligations of these countries under the 1951 UN convention on refugees, nor has any country in which anti-immigration parties have influence seriously considered withdrawing from the convention. Moreover, these more restrictive laws are being matched across western Europe, even in countries where there are no anti-immigration parties such as Spain and Ireland, suggesting that it is wider grassroots intolerance of current levels of immigration, rather than these parties themselves, that has triggered the tightening.

### Here to stay
While all this means that the atmosphere is now more hostile towards immigrants, negatively affecting the lives of all non-native peoples, there has been no recorded increase in violence against newcomers in the countries of concern. Nor has the presence in government of xenophobes meant that those who share their bigotry in the institutions of the state—the police and judiciary, for example—believe they have a green light to indulge their prejudices in the absence of evidence to suggest that immigrants now suffer higher levels of unjust treatment when interfacing with legal systems or are more likely to be maltreated by police forces.

However regrettably, such parties are unlikely to disappear. They have been a feature of European politics throughout the post-war period, enjoying sharp increases in support in Germany in the 1950s, Scandinavia in the 1970s and France in the 1980s. They have a seemingly enduring presence in Switzerland and Flanders and appear to be on the rise in Norway. Given declining party allegiances, frustration with mainstream politicians, the narrowing of ideological differences leaving little apparent choice for voters and the inevitability of increased migratory flows, the rate at which they come to prominence will probably be more rapid in the future than in the past. But as the Austria and Netherlands example illustrate, they may be exposed more quickly too.

*Originally published in* The World Today

## JÖRG HAIDER: EUROPE'S POPULIST PAR EXCELLENCE

*7 July 2000*

When it comes to elected representatives scape-goating impoverished immigrants for electoral gain, the erstwhile leader of Austria's xenophobic Freedom Party (FPO), Jörg Haider, leaves most in the ha'penny place. In her examination of the rise of Haider, Hella Pick, forced to flee Austria when the Nazis annexed the country in 1938, is careful not to dismiss the FPO as a one-issue party. The former diplomatic editor of the *Guardian* recognises the frustration engendered, particularly among the young, by the cosy carve-up of patronage by Austria's two main moderate parties, who together have dominated government in the post-war period. Such clientelism created a thick seam of resentment which has been masterfully mined by Haider, Europe's populist par excellence.

However, other aspects of the FPO's appeal go under-elaborated. Chief among these is Austria's strain of anti-globalisation feeling, born of economic insecurity and rising levels of job turnover. However misplaced (unemployment has remained below 5% for 50 years), these concerns have led to working class voters abandoning in droves their traditional party of choice, the Social Democrats, for the protest politics of Haider, a self-appointed champion of the 'little man'. While entirely justified in her distaste for Haider and his antics, Pick fails to communicate his Clinton-like charisma. In the beer tents of provincial Austria, his pulpiteering venue of choice, he is protean, metamorphosing in the course of an evening from put-upon martyr to champion of Austria's interests to authoritarian leader-figure. The beer-drinkers, among them bigots and backwoodsmen, the disgruntled and the marginalised, lap it up.

But the book is more about the aftermath of the Holocaust than Haider (despite its title, there is disappointingly little attention paid to any link between the two) and the threat, if any, posed by his nasty brand of politics to civil and political liberties. *Guilty Victim* focuses on the failure of post-war Austrians to face up to, and atone for, their involvement in Nazism. It also examines the post-1945 injustices heaped on those who suffered Nazi depravities, including niggardly compensation for confiscated assets and callous indifference towards many exiles who sought to return to Austria. Moreover, the author's evidence strongly suggests that the cruelty of the state towards Jewish victims was, at least in part, the result of institutionalised anti-Semitism.

Although clearly unconvinced, Pick does set out the arguments that Austrians used to rewrite history and avoid culpability for their part in Nazi atrocities, including the case for collective amnesia, advocated by most in post-war Austria in order to focus on the future and avoid dredging up a divisive past. The important role of the wartime allies in concocting the fiction of victimhood, in order to drive a wedge between Austria and Germany and discourage Austrians from seeking re-absorption into a Greater Germany, is also recognised. Pick appreciates the irresistibility of this opportunity for Austrian politicians, including those who were genuine victims of the Nazis, as a means of avoiding international opprobrium and costly restitution claims.

The author is generous, too, in her praise for the country's many achievements, not least its consensual style of politics that papered over, and eventually healed, many of the wounds of both the Nazi era and the deeply divisive civil war in the 1930s (though it is difficult to see how such consensus could have been arrived at without the amnesia that is much maligned throughout). Frequent mention is also made of the country's excellent record on offering asylum to victims of tyranny and war, from Hungary in 1956 to Kosovo in 1999.

On balance for Pick, Austria's shameful behaviour towards its wartime victims since 1945 outweighs all else. But this is a curious conclusion. The author readily admits that despite being in full possession of the facts, she believed Austria a model society for most of her life. That her views changed during the 1990s, precisely when amends were belatedly being made to victims and collective guilt acknowledged, is all the more perplexing.

*Originally published in the* Irish Times

---

# WHAT'S IN STORE FOR EUROPE IN 2008?

*6 January 2008*

Europe had a good 2007: a second consecutive year of above-trend economic growth; new jobs in spades; the avoidance of crisis (so far) in the Balkans; better transatlantic relations; the unexpected ejection from office of the daftest government this side of the EU's eastern border (Poland's); and the ending (finally, it is hoped) of wrangling on EU institutional reform. Alas, 2008 will be less benign. Economically, politically and geo-politically, Europe faces more challenging times in the year to come.

**Economic slowdown, or worse...**
After growing by almost 3% in 2007, the pace of the European economy's expansion is already cooling. The causes are many. The economic cycle has passed its peak. The euro is over-mighty. Consumers are warier of splashing out. And businesses are reining in their investment plans. But, even taken together, all these factors suggest a moderation rather than a halting of growth. We at the Economist Intelligence Unit are forecasting a still-solid rate of expansion in 2008, with the euro area expected to grow by 2% and the wider EU-27 by 2.2%.

But our forecasts, like all others at the current juncture, come with more than the usual health warnings because the risks are unusually great. The world's economic worries are centred on the US. It is teetering on the brink of recession. If it goes over the edge, Europe will feel the drag. Americans will demand fewer European exports and supply less invest-ment. This side of the Atlantic will also be affected via financial markets, and more than might normally have been expected. Although the credit crisis has been causing an inter-bank funding crunch since August, there is almost no hard evidence of it yet affecting the real economy. But that is unlikely to last. Higher short-end market interest rates will, sooner or later, start affecting investment spending and consumption. If confidence can be restored quickly, and banks gradually rebuild their balance sheets, the impact should be limited. If, however, uncertainty continues or deepens, the possible effects on the economy range from bad to catastrophic.

## The ECB's quandary

In 2008 the European Central Bank will face its most difficult balancing act since it took control of monetary policy in 1999. Euro zone inflation hit its highest rate in six years as 2007 ended, and the bank now expects to miss its inflation target by the largest margin ever in 2008. Given persistently high food and energy prices, tightening labour markets, greater capacity constraints and strong growth of broad money, rates would normally be hiked. But these are not normal times.

Despite clear and present upside inflation risk, the job of the ECB has been complicated by the big downside risk to economic growth already discussed. The bind the bank is in was plain to see at its December meeting when its rates decision was not unanimous—for the first time ever. With upside inflation risk and downside growth risk, official interest rates could go either way in 2008.

## Kosovo and the wider Balkans

After almost a decade in limbo, Kosovo will unilaterally declare independence in early 2008. Most EU member-countries will back the move as the least bad option. But redrawing borders always causes instability. Too often it leads to bloodshed. Since the Balkans were dragged from their 1990s abyss, much has been done to lay the groundwork for sustainable democracy and sound economies. But ultra-nationalism dies hard. Hatreds and tensions still glow. Given how combustible the region is, a declaration of Kosovan independence could cause violence to flare again—in Kosovo itself and in Bosnia, where efforts to foster reconciliation have been largely unsuccessful.

At stake is not only the peace and stability of the immediate region; the reputation of the EU is also on the line. The EU seeks to become an actor of real clout in international affairs with its common foreign and security policy. If the bloc cannot manage relatively minor squabbles on its own doorstep, its hopes of becoming a serious actor on the world stage will be gravely undermined. To watch for in 2008 will be whether the EU's 27 member states can stand together on the Balkans, and particularly if a crisis erupts.

## More Russian recidivism

The chief reason for the failure to allow Kosovans to attain statehood under international law is Russia. It wielded its veto as one of the permanent members of the UN security council for a range of reasons, including its need to exercise power and influence even when its own interests are undermined in the process. The list of disputes between Europe and Russia continues to lengthen. No moderation in Russia's aggressively assertive posture can be expected in 2008.

If anything, relations with the rest of Europe will deteriorate further. At worst, Russia will use the threat of withholding gas and oil from the western part of the continent. Interruptions in supplies are unthinkable to those who think rationally. But as Russia has so often been prepared to shoot itself in the foot if it believes its honour and prestige are at stake, such an eventuality can't be ruled out in 2008.

## Eyes on the Irish

The EU celebrated its 50th birthday in March 2007. By the end of the year it was celebrating the ending of a saga that felt as if it lasted most of that half-century—its latest round of institutional tweaking, now known as the 'Lisbon treaty'. There were sighs of relief all round in the Portuguese capital earlier this month when the infernal thing was finally signed off. During 2008, presidents and prime ministers of 26 member states will endeavour to push it through their respective parliaments. One—Bertie Ahern—will have to campaign to persuade the average Joe to buy it.

Irish diplomats are muttering darkly to anyone who'll listen that a Yes vote can't be taken for granted. This is clever. If Irish voters choose not to rain on the euro parade, the achievement of winning over the people will be all the greater (one shudders to think how Dick Roche will regale his euro-minister counterparts with tales of his heroics on the hustings). But if voters thumb their noses at it, others countries will not be as shocked as they were when the Nice treaty was initially rejected. Even so, a rejection would cause consternation after so much time and energy has gone into the reform process. This would be bad news for Ireland. The brutal truth is that if a big country, such as France, fails to ratify, it is a European problem; if Ireland blocks ratification, it will be an Irish problem.

## Europe à la Sarko

French president Jacques Chirac's long goodbye was ploddingly completed in 2007. By contrast, the 'hyperactivity' of his successor, Nicolas Sarkozy, is already the stuff of journalistic cliché. His activism on the international stage has been as marked as it has been domestically, and the pace is set to become even more frenetic in 2008. His presidency of the EU in the second half of the year will place him at Europe's centre stage. He is typically ambitious in his objectives.

Chief among his goals will be to give Europe some real military muscle (despite the guff Ireland's anti-EU brigade has spouted for years about the 'militarisation' of Europe, the bloc still couldn't muster sufficient force to fight its way out of the proverbial wet paper bag). With Sarkozy's plan to rejoin NATO's core military structure after a 40-year absence, Atlanticists worry far less that France is plotting to manoeuvre the Americans out of their central role in Europe's security architecture.

But it is the misfortune of the most pro-American post-war French president to have as his counterpart across the English Channel a British prime minister who is less engaged with Europe than any since the UK joined the bloc. Gordon Brown has already forbidden his foreign secretary, David Miliband, to mention the possibility of deeper defense co-operation. On this issue, and many others, Brown and Sarkozy could clash. For human drama on the political stage in 2008, no duo will be as compelling to watch.

*Originally published in the* Sunday Business Post

––––

# REASONS TO BE CHEERFUL ABOUT EUROPE'S ECONOMY

*23 November 2006*

The recent strengthening of European gross domestic product growth has given cause for optimism about the Continent's economy. This is long overdue. Despondency has been overdone. Between 2000 and 2005, GDP per head—the most important indicator of economic well-being—grew by one fifth among the 15 pre-accession members of the European Union. In the US, the figure was a marginally higher 21%. Given such similar performances, it is curious that the US is lauded for its strengths, while Europe's weaknesses tend to be the focus of most comment about its economy.

One reason for this negativity has been the slow pace of legislative and regulatory reform. More reform is needed, but it is only one part of the equation. Change at the corporate level is at least as important. If some European politicians view globalisation as a threat, the Continent's corporate executives are in its vanguard. Restructuring across the single market has progressed with increasing speed, as evinced by the number and size of mergers and acquisitions. This has led not only to consolidation within Europe, but also to continued expansion beyond the Continent's borders. According to the United Nation's Conference on Trade and Development in 2003, of the world's 20 biggest non-financial multinationals ranked by foreign assets, 13 were European. The internationalisation of the European company has since accelerated. In 2005, direct investment out of the EU-15 reached €172 billion ($223 billion), over 20% higher than 2003.

The global expansion of European business could be interpreted as a vote of no confidence in their home region—if the facts did not suggest otherwise. EU-15 merchandise exports are growing strongly and their world market share (excluding intra-EU trade) increased from 17.6% to 19.2% between 2000 and 2005, and this in spite of the rise of China. Another favourite claim of the euro-despondents is that a pair of government dead hands—one in Brussels, the other in national capitals—crushes the enterprising and wealth-creating. While greater efforts are needed to ease the regulatory burden, this could be said of any economy (think of Sarbanes-Oxley in the US). More importantly, such claims overstate the problem. If European conditions for business were so dire, foreign investors would shun the region. The reality is that they flock to the continent. Between 2000 and 2005, inflows of foreign direct investment to EU15 countries amounted to almost half of the global total.

Old Europe is an investment magnet because it is the most lucrative market in the world in which to operate. As suggested by equity returns in Europe having out-performed those in the US over decades, it should be no surprise that corporate America is Europe's biggest source of inward investment. US companies' affiliates in the EU-15 booked profits of $85 billion in 2005. This was far more than any other region and 26 times more than the $3.3 billion they made in China.

The Economist Intelligence Unit's Business Environment Rankings show that, even at government level, some reform progress is being made. Between 2006 and 2010, we expect improvements in the business environments in all the EU-15 economies. More could be done, but it would be wrong to believe that Europe suffers total reform paralysis.

None of this is to say that Europe need not urgently address its challenges. The two most pressing are sluggish growth in labour productivity and insufficient job creation. Since the mid-1990s, the rate of labour productivity growth has slowed as many countries' innovation systems fail to fire on all cylinders. Europe's under-funded and under-reformed universities are a real weakness. Too few of them are world-class centres of research and teaching excellence. It is becoming ever harder for the EU to attract and retain the best and the brightest.

Labour market reform is also needed, though for reasons of justice more than efficiency. Since 2000, net employment in the EU-15 has risen by 6.5 million. But this has been inadequate. While almost half of the EU-15 economies have enjoyed effective full employment during this decade, France, Germany and Italy need more radical reform to give the jobless a chance of finding work.

Much of the derision about Europe echoes comment in the 1980s about economic models. Then, Japan was the future and the American model written off. This ignored Japan's weaknesses and exaggerated its strengths. The opposite mistake was made about the US. The same pessimism is in vogue in Europe, fuelled by visceral Europhobes who are only too happy to talk up the 'sclerotic' Europe thesis.

Political leaders would do well to match their corporate counterparts' drive and self-belief. They should explain to voters that change is needed, but reassure them that this does not mean doing anything as radical as abandoning the European welfare state. Europe has challenges. But they are neither as profound nor as intractable as is usually claimed. Recognising this would make facing them far easier.

(Co-authored with Aurora Wanlin)

*Originally published in the Financial Times*

——

## THE MARKET AS A MECHANISM FOR SOCIAL JUSTICE

*October 2006*

Citizens of the European Union have never been more prosperous than they are today and have never enjoyed such a range of rights and liberties. They inhabit an usually safe corner of the world and have never lived longer and healthier lives. The appeal of life in Europe can be seen by the number of immigrants it attracts and by the desire of almost every country in and around Europe to join the EU.

Despite this, Europe is suffering a crisis of confidence. The rejection of the EU constitution by French and Dutch voters in mid-2005 came at a time of growing concerns about the region's economic performance. Over the past decade the EU has not matched its potential, not matched the strong rates of economic expansion enjoyed by the US and come nowhere near matching growth in the most dynamic parts of the developing world, notably China and India. Confidence has been further eroded by failing efforts at EU level to raise the continent's game in the shape of the ambitious Lisbon reform agenda. Extrapolated into the future, current trends would see Europe's importance in the world decline. Pessimists warn that the continent could become a stagnant backwater. Many argue that the European economy is afflicted by terminal sclerosis and, relatedly, that the welfare state is no longer affordable.

Such claims lack perspective, and, happily, neither of these latter two gloomier assertions is correct. On the first count, while it is true that *some* European economies have serious problems (e.g. Germany and France), many do not (Ireland and the Nordics) and of those that do only a small number (Italy and Portugal) face profound challenges (and, for comparison, even these latter countries have fewer and less serious problems than Ireland in the 1980s). But not only is the European economic picture mixed and declinist talk much exaggerated, Europe's many strengths have been understated: the continent's workforce is highly educated; its physical infrastructure unbettered globally; its currency strong and stable; its balance of payments with the rest of the world sustainable; and its companies in many of the most important sectors world-beating.

The EU's essentially solid economic fundamentals and continued high levels of wealth creation mean that there is nothing inherently unaffordable about the level of European social spending, and claims about the demise of the welfare state are, at best, premature. Another reason to believe in the sustainability of the welfare state is that much (but not all) of the resources allocated to creating and maintaining European countries' social safety nets actually contribute to better economic performance by reducing the costs of risk taking (this boosts wealth creation by, for example, increasing business start-ups and encouraging the movement from secure jobs to less secure but more rewarding ones).

### Ideology is dead: long live evidence-based policy-making

None of this is to say that Europe does not have serious problems which need to be addressed. But here, too, there is reason for optimism. By and large, governments are fully aware of their economic weaknesses and there is general consensus in most countries about what needs to be done (limited success in moving ahead has more to do with the strength of opposition from those negatively affected and the political weakness of many governments than with disagreement about what the problems are and how to address them).

The demise of old-style left–right ideology is to be thanked for the broad consensus on the European reform agenda, as embodied in the Lisbon Agenda. While evidence-based policy-making has always played a greater role in Europe's democracies than ideology, it has triumphed since the collapse of communism and the subsequent failure of ultra-minimal government experiments in former communist countries. Today serious thinkers and commentators agree that the secret to economic success is to have both well functioning markets *and* well functioning states, because when they both work they become mutually reinforcing. Nowhere is this to be seen more clearly than in thinking in the field of development economics. The watchword among the policy and scholarly communities is now 'Good Governance', i.e. that an effective and efficient state is essential if market economies are to generate the sort of wealth that can lift their people out of poverty and towards prosperity. A non-ideological analysis of economic history supports this: almost every country in the world today that enjoys high standards of living has achieved success by a combination of market and state working in tandem. (Ireland is no exception: the role of the state in supporting foreign multinationals to create jobs, widen the export base and generate tax revenues is a textbook example of smart government.)

When one considers what governments actually do today (ignoring their spin), left–right ideology plays little role. Socialist governments liberalise and privatise, while governments on the right increase taxes and add to environmental protection legislation. When countries consider how to organise their education systems, social welfare benefits, healthcare, pensions and transport they assess what has worked in existing policies, they examine what has failed and why and they look at international experience (in the EU, a system of peer review is designed to tease out best practice so that policies that work in one country can more easily be assessed for suitability in others). At EU level, legislation and policy choices traditionally associated with both left and right are the norm (it is, incidentally, for this reason that ideologues on the right can find evidence to support their paranoid view that the EU is a plot to impose socialism on Europe by stealth, while their counterparts on the left can simultaneously point to things that support their equally paranoid charge that the EU is a neo-liberal conspiracy for the benefit of rapacious multinational corporations).

So what can Europe's countries do to solve the problems they face and put their economies and welfare systems on a firmer footing for the future? Solutions are (and should be) both market-centred and state-based. Of the latter type there are plenty of good proposals about, with many forming part of the Lisbon Agenda, including greater public investment in education and training, more expenditure on research and investment, and the implementation of the EU's Environment Technology Action Plan. But for the EU as a whole, the direction needed today is, on balance, towards more market. Not only will this help strengthen economic growth, it will make for greater social justice. In three of the most important areas—jobs, food prices and the freedom to compete—more market and less state intervention will make a more prosperous *and* fairer society.

### Worker protection: a fine balance

While high unemployment in Europe is confined to a minority of countries (over the past decade just six of the EU-15 have had levels of joblessness averaging above 8%), it afflicts most of the big economies—France, Germany, Italy and Spain. Given the number of people affected there is almost universal consensus across the political spectrum that this is Europe's major socio-economic failing. It is not hard to see why. Joblessness not only means material deprivation, it deprives people of dignity, of social interaction, of self-reliance and of hope for the future. In those countries afflicted, young people are particularly badly affected, with up to a third of under-30s suffering the frustration of spending their youth in a vain search for employment.

Why, then, are some countries successful in generating employment and others less so? The answer lies mostly in how governments intervene in their labour markets. While too little protection for employees means unnecessary insecurity, the social harm caused by excessive regulation can be just as great. Though this may sound counter-intuitive, the injustice of over-protection is incontestable. Excessive employment protection legislation (EPL) means that because it is very difficult or very costly to lay off workers, employers hire fewer people. The evidence clearly shows that the higher the levels of protection, the lower the levels of employment. The result of excessive protection is that those on the inside are very secure, while those without a job have far less chance of finding one. A second injustice also inevitably flows from cosseting labour market insiders, and can be seen in all the high-unemployment countries. Where people are locked out of the labour market, desperation to find a job pushes more people into the black economy, where wages are lower, benefits few and protection non-existent.

The Lisbon agenda recognises all this, as did the 2004 Kok report by a cross-section of European experts, which included trade unionists, academics and business people. However unpalatable it seems, those countries with high unemployment need to make it easier to fire workers. But while this may sound harsh, it does not mean a slippery slope to a Dickensian world in which people can be sacked on the whim of a boss, as often suggested by opponents of reform. It is, rather, a rebalancing of labour law to give as much protection to those in work as possible without damaging the prospects of those without a job of finding one. And the sort of labour market arrangements many advocates of reform have in mind, including the Kok group, is Denmark, a country well known for its egalitarian ways. The Danes recognise that economic change is inevitable and will inevitably bring with it a degree of insecurity. But they also recognise that this insecurity cannot be legislated away. Their system of 'flexicurity', which is seen by most to have got the worker protection balance right, has low levels of EPL, giving flexibility to employers who in a time of rapid change need to be able to restructure their companies to remain competitive. It also gives security to employees by equipping them with marketable skills and offering high unemployment benefits to protect against hardship when people are between jobs (the evidence suggests that higher benefits do not act as a significant disincentive to returning to work).

As in the case of many of Europe's current socio-economic ills, the answer to joblessness and its attendant injustices is to be found in allowing the market to operate more freely.

## CAP: fits farmers; hurts the poor

While the importance of having a job can hardly be understated, access to food is an absolute essential. And in the market for food in Europe, state intervention, in the guise of the EU's Common Agricultural Policy (CAP), is excessively tilted towards those who are doing well, with the cost falling disproportionately on the poor. The transfer of resources to farmers is engineered in two ways. First, by artificially guaranteeing high prices for farmers, consumers pay higher prices for food than they would if it were imported from farmers elsewhere who can produce it more cheaply. The second mechanism is direct transfers to farmers (the cheque in the post). This money is raised by taxing others in society, including the poor. The CAP benefits some farmers to the tune of as much as €6,000 a week, while the average family in the EU picks up the tab with, by some estimates, an extra €1,000 added to its annual grocery bill. For families struggling on low wages or social welfare, this amounts to a far higher proportion of disposable income than for richer families—a thoroughly regressive mechanism.

The effects of the CAP on the developing world are also considerable. Market intervention by Europe drives down world prices of food and cause greater price fluctuations elsewhere. This directly undermines the farming sectors in developing countries with negative effects for food supplies in those countries and for their prospects of accelerating economic development. Not only does this policy work against the EU countries' development programmes, it exposes Europe to justifiable accusations of double standards in trade policy.

Europe, like all developed countries, intervenes heavily in its market for food. The rationale behind this system of agricultural subsidies and protection, as it is elsewhere, is mostly to ensure that there is always enough food produced locally so that no matter what happens elsewhere in the world there will not be an interruption in supply. It therefore makes sense to have a degree of self-sufficiency, and this security dimension, ignored entirely by some opponents of the CAP, remains important today in an unstable world. But Europe produces more food than it needs, and exports the surplus. As in the case of labour laws, described above, the balance has tilted towards excessive and damaging government intervention in the market for food. While the CAP has been partially reformed, the case for deeper reform is strong. It is overwhelming when one considers its regressive redistributive effects in Europe and its development-retarding effects globally.

The argument made here, therefore, is not one of abandoning the CAP, but a rebalancing, allowing the market a greater role so that the more equitable outcome it would produce can be attained.

### The freedom to compete: giving everyone a chance

There is little disagreement that a significant reason for Europe's recent economic under-performance is a result of government-imposed curbs on the freedom to set up businesses and on the freedom of existing firms to provide goods and services where they believe there is a demand to be satisfied. While sometimes these curbs are sensible, a necessary evil, or just a least worst solution, most are either anachronistic or exist because of the power of a lobby group to influence policy. Such barriers have a number of negative effects. First, by protecting insiders, they unjustly exclude outsiders. Second (and relatedly), they usually mean fewer jobs. Third, they always result in higher prices, impacting most on those on lower incomes. Fourth, they raise other companies' costs, thus making them less competitive.

The examples of what happens when markets are liberalised is indisputably beneficial (this argument is not to be equated with privatisation.

Evidence suggestions that ownership of firms is far less important than the competitive framework in which they operate). While air travel was once the preserve of the super rich it is now available to everyone thanks to opening up of the European market. Liberalisation has also transformed telecommunications—in most European countries up until the 1980s having a telephone installed took months and calls were far more expensive. Today prices are a fraction of what they were and almost every adult owns a mobile phone. These benefits are now taken for granted, and it is hard today to remember just why the state banned people from freely offering these services. On a macro level, liberalisation of economic activity between countries has made Europe more prosperous, with no country benefiting more than Ireland (it can be persuasively argued that the Celtic Tiger might never have come to life if the EU's single market had not been created in 1992).

Despite the successes of liberalisation, vested interests in sheltered sectors continue to lobby against fair competition, foretelling doom for everyone if they have to compete fairly. This can be seen in the debate about the liberalisation of services which ignited in the run-up to the French referendum on the EU constitution. Previously, the services directive had been an uncontroversial piece of law working its way through the EU's legislative process, being amended and changed to iron out its imperfections. Just how uncontentious it was can be by the endorsement given it in late 2004 by the Kok report, whose authors included the heads of the Austrian and Swedish trade union federations. Given that two thirds of Europe's wealth is generated by services providers, the potential for creating jobs and driving down prices is great if barriers can be broken down as envisaged by the directive.

Also high on the list of Lisbon Agenda reforms is the removal of government curbs on entrepeneurship. These are to be found mostly in countries with strongly statist traditions, particularly in southern Europe, where the freedom to set up a business is severely curbed by onerous quantities of regulation and the requirement to apply for multiple permits. Jumping through these hoops takes much time, money and effort, often resulting in the exclusion of those with more limited means from setting up a business. According to the World Bank, founding a company in Greece costs a quarter of average per capita income and in Portugal takes 54 days. In Denmark, the state does not charge aspiring entrepeneurs to start a business and they can be up and running in just five days. Just as in the case of excessive labour market regulation, Europe's barriers to entrepreneurialism drive those with business ideas into the black economy where no regulations apply. The result is bad for entrepreneurs, their employees and their customers.

## Markets: much maligned; poorly defended

To begin, this paper rejected arguments usually made by the ideologically right-leaning about Europe's economies and their welfare systems. To conclude, a word on criticisms often made by the ideologically left-leaning, because support for the reforms advocated above is undermined by their anti-market arguments. The three most commonly made and serious charges are that markets result in greater inequality, increased social atomisation and an erosion of standards and rights.

Inequality first. One does not need to search far to find statements such as this made in a recent newspaper comment article: 'the inherent tendency of unregulated capitalist economies [is] towards ever-wider inequalities'. This assertion and variants thereof are repeated so frequently by those hostile to markets that they have come to believed as true by many non-ideologically-minded people. The truth about inequality, which is determined by many different factors, is that there are no iron laws. That said, some observations can be made. First, empirical evidence suggests that when countries begin to develop relative income inequality rises, but then tends to fall (so frequently is this pattern observed it has been named: the Kuznets Curve). In short, and contrary to the assertion above, a mass of evidence suggests that markets do not tend towards 'ever-wider inequalities'. Second, evidence from around the world shows that the most unequal countries (Latin America in particular) are those in which the market is prevented from working because vested interests have captured policy-making for their own benefit. In effect, those at the top have used their influence to kick the ladder away, preventing those at the bottom participating fairly in the marketplace in a way that would allow them to become more prosperous. In many ways Latin America today looks like Europe in the late 19th century and it is often forgotten now that the European left then was pro-market precisely because it understood that market forces would break the stranglehold of the powerful, thereby lessening inequalities.

But does recent Irish experience undermine this point? There is a common perception that Ireland has become a more unequal society during the boom (shared by this writer until disabused by exposure to the evidence while researching this paper). According to Prof. Brian Nolan of the ESRI, there are only three data sources available. Data published by the CSO found a very slight widening of income inequality between 1994 and

2000. ESRI data show a very slight narrowing over the same period. The most comprehensive and timely numbers, published annually by the European Commission, found not only that between 1995 and 2001 relative income inequality in Ireland fell sharply, but that the narrowing was by far the greatest of any EU-15 country. The perception that Ireland has become more unequal during the Celtic Tiger years, whether perpetuated wittingly or unwittingly, is simply not supported by the evidence.

A second frequently made charge is that market exchange atomises society, causing the erosion of social cohesion. Robert Putnam, perhaps the leading expert on causes of decline in social capital, says this of the US context: 'America has epitomised market capitalism for centuries, during which our stocks of social capital and civic engagement have been through great swings.' He succinctly dismisses the charge. 'A constant can't explain a variable.' Serious thinkers, such as Putnam, also recognise that market exchange, far from eroding social capital, actually enhances it. Commercial life, a vital element of civil society, brings people together to interact, co-operate, solve problems, socialise and build relationships. Few more eloquently and authoritatively make the case for the centrality of market participation than Nobel laureate and the brains behind the UN's Human Development Index, Amartya Sen.

A third, more moderate charge is that the globalisation of economic activity has intensified competition to such an extent that countries, whether they like it or not, must cut social provision and reduce standards to stay competitive (often described as a 'race to the bottom'). Developments in the EU over the past two decades provide laboratory conditions to test this hypothesis (the single market has been the greatest ever experiment in proactive market integration among states). The intensification in competition in Europe as a result of the removal of national barriers to trade has not been accompanied by any decline in health and safety or environmental standards but an increase, nor has there been any decline in tax levels, with government revenues remaining around 45% of GDP over the past 20 years. A slight downward trend in corporation tax rates is about all the evidence that exists to support the 'race to the bottom' thesis.

## Conclusion
While Europe is not in crisis, it does need to change and adapt. On balance, the market must play a greater role and state intervention should be reduced. This should not been seen as the thin end of a 'neoliberal' wedge or a foot on the slippery slope to a society without state-provided

welfare—the role of the state will remain central both to improving economic efficiency and social provision. But a strengthened role for the market is essential. The result will be a stronger economy and a fairer society.

*Originally published in* Studies

*Chapter v* ∿

# THE EUROPEAN STATE SYSTEM: AN UNLOVED MIRACLE OF MULTILATERALISM

*'There will never be a United States of Europe... I refuse to identify myself with those who promote the disappearance of the nation state.'*

JACQUES DELORS

## INTRODUCTION

The evolution of Europe's political and economic union is a development of world-historical significance. It is all too easy to lose sight of this when one watches it functioning. Having spent two years working for the European Commission and many more years writing about how the bloc operates, I know that it can be exasperating, perplexing, complicated and exceedingly dull. But it is most probably the future. It is by far the most successful mechanism for managing relations among states the world has even known. It smooths interaction, builds trust, provides security, leverages influence, spurs economic growth and widens opportunity for those who participate. Little wonder, then, that almost every country in Europe, and some further afield, want to join; and, once in, they stay in, because they get far more out of it than they put in. Without the European Union, its members, alone and collectively, would be less stable, less secure and less rich.

But for all its strengths, there is much to be critical of—just as there is of any system of government. And it is a real pity that the Union and its workings are rarely analysed and critiqued that way. This does not happen for a number of reasons. The most important is what the EU does and how it does it. Government in nation states has human drama. In TV studios and on the airwaves, instantly recognisable big beasts of politics thrash out issues that everyone understands and cares about—crime, jobs and taxes. The EU is different. When there is drama in the European Parliament, it is more multi-lingual circus than theatre. Beyond the parliament, in the bloc's other institutions, it is not the done thing to raise voices, barrack or engage in other staples of normal politics. A once-in-a-blue-moon ministerial walkout is about as dramatic as it gets. At the level of officials, where most deals are agreed and tied down, a fly-on-wall outside observer would have difficulty recognising a full-blown diplomatic crisis if it were happening under his nose, such is the restraint and formality of meetings.

It is not only *how* things are done in the EU, but *what* countries do collectively within it that results in lack of voter interest. So much of what is decided on and legislated for at European level is utterly un-newsworthy—breakthroughs in food labelling and soil protection directives, the complexities of competition policy, daily diplomatic declarations on trade missions to almost every country in the world, the never-ending saga of agreeing an EU-wide patent and countless other such examples. Such things, regardless of their importance and how much sense it makes to agree them at an international level, will never engage people with jobs, families and busy lives.[1]

## A CAGED BEAST

Observing the power dynamics of the EU is usually more arresting than examining its end products. The real power remains firmly with the member countries and their representatives in Brussels, the national ambassadors. These 'permanent representatives' remain central to the entire process. And though the EU context is different from other international organisations in that the intensity of interaction is higher and more constant, these diplomats (and almost all come from their respective foreign ministries) operate a quite traditional diplomatic bargaining model. But what makes the EU different from all other international organisations is its 'European' institutions. Of these, the European Commission is the most interesting (the European Parliament is something of a shambles and the European Court of Justice too small and too closed to be easily observed).

It is uncontested by anyone who follows what is happening in Europe that the Commission has declined in influence since its heyday, a period from the mid-1980s to the mid-1990s. During its decade of glory, as the proposer and drafter of legislation to put the EU's single market in place, its profile soared and an aura of omnipotence surrounded it. For well over a decade since then, however, its role has been much less as a player in its own right and more that of an unglamorous referee, ensuring that the member states stick to the rules that they themselves have set and agreed to. This is by far its most important role because no rules-based system can function without an arbiter who is impartial, and who is seen to be impartial. And in this role it is fiercely independent and ready to pounce on member countries who stray into the territory it has been given.

But the Commission is ultimately a creature of the member states, and it is kept firmly caged to ensure that it does not challenge them excessively. That, however, is not to say that it does not test the bars. The Commission is never slow to volunteer itself when it believes that it could have a greater role in anything, and pads around restlessly waiting for opportunities to expand its influence to drop within its reach. In this, the Europaranoiacs are not at all far off the mark. But just as all paranoiacs see only what they want to see and ignore anything that does not fit their delusions, they ignore the relative powerlessness of the Commission and how tightly circumscribed are its powers. Few incidents demonstrate its relative weakness better than the resignation of the entire college of commissioners in 1999. All 20 members stood down over minor jobbery by just two of their number, the sort of scandal that would not have brought down any national government in Europe. A decade on, the Commission's political weakness can be seen in the context of the financial and economic crises engulfing the world. It has waved through bank rescues and company saving measures in the member states that in normal times would be subject to far greater scrutiny. It knows that in times of real crisis, people still look to national governments and that it would make a stick for its own back if, in its attempts to protect the single market, it was charged with worsening financial instability or pushing workers out of jobs. If ever anyone believed the Commission omnipotent, recent developments have surely punctured that myth.

Internally, the Commission operates as any other bureaucracy in many ways: there is no shortage of manoeuvring and in-fighting, particularly among the Commissioners themselves; it can be excessively hierarchal and has its quotient of unsackable deadweights; and its officials often a exhibit a detachment from the world most average people inhabit. So far, so normal. But two things—one good, one bad—set it apart from other bureaucracies. The first is the quality of its people, the second its ideological uniformity. The calibre of its staff is the highest of any bureaucratic institution, national civil service or international organisation anywhere. There are two reasons for this. First, its recruitment procedures are influenced little by money or nepotism, something that is certainly not the case in many member states. Second, as the numbers taking the entrance exams run to the tens of thousands, and as there are few openings in an institution that is smaller than even the smallest member state's public service, each opening is massively oversubscribed. The result is that only the very best get hired. The second feature that marks it out from other bureaucracies is the depth and uniformity of the ideology that pervades every nook and cranny of the institution. It is rare to find an official who does not believe that 'more Europe' is the answer to every public-policy challenge faced by the continent. This knee-jerk response, like all such reactions, is worrisome. Ideologues of any hue—leftist, rightist, nationalist or environmentalist—see the world in rigid frameworks. European integrationists do, too. That the Commission is full of such true believers is not good for Europe, the integration project or the institution itself.

## THE FUNCTIONS OF STATE

An enormous amount of nonsense is written and spoken about the EU. Misconceptions, misunderstandings and prejudice abound. It is not hard to see why, given the limited media coverage, the inherent complexity of many of the things it does and the magnitude of the changes in governance that it represents. It is easy both for its advocates to attribute to it all the wonders of modernity and for its opponents to claim it is a baby step away from casting a totalitarian blanket over the continent. To make sense of it all a framework of analysis is needed. Its critics provide such a framework. They frequently claim that it is, or is becoming, a 'superstate'. It is unclear what the 'super' part means, but comparing what it does to the functions of the average state is as good a framework as any to think about it, to understand what it does and to see how it is changing. The modern developed state does three big things: it redistributes wealth; it regulates all sorts of human activities; and it provides security. What role for the EU in each of those functions?

Redistribution has become the biggest role of the modern developed state, from straightforward transfers of cash, in the form of welfare payments, pensions and allowances, to a vast range of services: to assist the ill, unfortunate and under-skilled; to boost business and the arts; and to widen access to education and science. To pay for all this, European countries tax their citizens more than those in any other part of the world. This has been the case for decades and is likely to be the case for decades to come (the spectacular and unprecedented increases in public spending in response to the ongoing economic and financial crises will see to that).

But this almost all happens at national level. The EU's redistributive role is minuscule. Its budget is a little over 1% of the bloc's aggregate national income. Not only is this a fraction of what unitary states spend, it is tiny even compared with what is spent by central governments in real federations. The US federal government, for instance, spends approximately 20% of GDP, 20 times Brussels' budget. So the EU is a redistributive pygmy. But could it change? The answer is 'No', emphatically. The most important reason is that none of the member countries wants to give more spending powers to Brussels. That, in turn, is partly because none of the big areas of public expenditure—health, education, pensions and welfare—is suited to centralisation: healthcare systems are being decentralised within countries; education is far too culturally and linguistically specific; and pensions and welfare payments reflect the very different price levels across the bloc (a pension that would be wildly generous in Latvia would leave a Luxembourger in near-penury).

If there is no prospect of the EU getting its hands on more tax revenues, there is the separate but related issue of setting rates of tax. The demand by some EU countries for harmonisation of corporation tax is seen by its opponents as the thin end of a fiscal wedge—with harmonisation followed by higher tax rates followed by revenues being diverted to Brussels. But the harmonisation debate has gone on for many years. It has become predictable. It is now something of a choreographed set piece. Those in favour make their case and those against shoot it down, as their veto powers allow them to do. They all move on to the next agenda item. The most significant change in the choreography in recent years has been the number of performers. The stage has become more crowded since the accession of 12 new member states earlier in the current decade. But as they have mostly joined the anti-harmonisation group, the prospect of any substantive shift in tax-setting powers from the states to the centre is as remote as ever.

But if countries' tax-setting powers are unlikely to be centralised any time soon, it is possible that the current economic crisis could unleash a new and different centripetal force. There are now real strains on the currency union. The 'peripheral' countries in particular—Greece, Ireland, Italy, Portugal and Spain—have not taken seriously the obligation to manage their public finances soundly. This has made them vulnerable in a time of crisis. It has, too, created vulnerability for the currency itself. Having abdicated their responsibilities as members of the euro area, they could see their rights affected if the situation goes critical. A worst case scenario is that one or more participants goes bankrupt, or comes to the very edge of that abyss, and requires rescuing, at some point in the future. At time of writing, in May 2009, the chances of the worst case scenario coming to pass are worryingly real.

In response to this a political willingness to bail out any euro area member appears to have emerged in the early months of 2009 among those with the wherewithal to do so, notably Germany. Assuming that the EU's largest member state remains in a position to backstop bailouts in the future, the question would arise as to the design and conditions of any rescue package. Little can be said with certainty at this time, but there can be little doubt that those throwing the lifeline would impose harsh austerity measures on those being rescued. In the medium term, the rescued would almost certainly face a more intrusive role for non-national entities (the European Commission and peer member states) in their budgetary processes. This would differ from the relatively toothless after-the-fact sanction process as it currently exists (called the 'Stability and Growth Pact'). It could involve, for example, all national budgets being signed off by the other member states and the Commission before they are put in place, and powers for peers and the Commission to demand changes before implementation if a member's budget targets appear unrealistic. But none of this intrusiveness, if it were to come to pass, would be likely to involve controlling levels of taxing and public spending.[2] These levels are mostly a political issue, not an economic one. Sweden taxes and spends a great deal, but is competent enough to balance the two. Greece spends and taxes relatively little, but rarely comes close to ensuring that revenues cover outlays. If there is greater centralisation in the future, it will involve more external discipline on errant member countries. And this would be no bad thing, for the countries involved and the currency.

## A REGULATORY SUPERSTATE

If the EU is a redistributive pygmy and likely to remain so in the future, it has long been a regulatory superpower. The widening and deepening of rules-based frameworks for human activity has been a notable characteristic of all societies over time, and this process has accelerated in recent decades. In Europe, national governments have collectively decided to do much of their regulating together at EU level, not least because a genuine single market could not have been created otherwise. Much of the most voluminous regulation enacted today is the sort of technocratic stuff that European countries have agreed to do together. By some estimates, more than half of the new laws placed on national statute books annually are made at EU level.

Short of the entire integration project falling apart, regulating at European level is here to stay. As and when new regulation is needed—for new types of businesses and new types of products—the EU will be there or thereabouts. But that does not mean that some invisible force is driving everything towards the centre and that bureaucrats in Brussels are taking ever greater control of the lives of Europeans. Since the single market was launched in the 1990s, the division of labour between national and EU-level regulators has settled down and is broadly stable, with the latter becoming mildly more important. The slight bias towards the latter is mainly because the member countries see it as being easier to make rules together when so much activity takes place across borders—having a single set of rules makes life less costly and complicated (even if common regulation is less than perfect, it is more efficient than having 27 different sets of perfect regulation). But there are limits to the further centralisation of regulatory power, in part because there is not that much further it can go. It is hard to envisage what aspects of life not already subject to EU regulation could be subject to it in the future. Of course, debate about the precise extent of regulation will continue.[3] But that is what politics, and interest-group politics in particular, is all about.

Common rules also give Europeans more influence in the wider world. Not only have EU product standards become the global benchmark, EU-level competition authorities are capable of influencing behaviour of firms far beyond their jurisdiction in a way that individual member states could never do alone. Perhaps the best example of this came in 1999 when the European Commission concluded that the proposed merger of two American multinationals, General Electric and Honeywell, would result in a reduction in competition in Europe, and thus risk pushing up prices for European consumers. Even though both companies were headquartered in the US, they were forced to cancel the merger because they could not run the risk of being locked out of the biggest market in the world.

Yet another advantage of EU-level rule-making is that it reduces the costs of regulatory competition. These costs are to be seen in regulation that is inadequate or excessively lax for fear that it could, however rationally and objectively framed, undermine a country's relative competitive position. The inadequacy of financial services regulation is a topical example. As recently as early 2007, Germany, as chair of the G7 countries, attempted to put on the agenda more stringent regulation of financial services. The proposal went nowhere because Britain and the US would have none of it. Their financial services industries were world leaders and increasingly important sources of employment and wealth creation. They refused to take any measures that might in any way shackle the industry. The refusal has come home to roost with a vengeance. Within Europe, the regulation of chemicals shows how this problem can be overcome. The REACH directive, which is the most comprehensive form of chemicals regulation in the world, would never have been enacted by a member state acting alone, despite the health and environmental risks of excessively lax laws on chemicals.

## SECURING EUROPE

So with little in the way of an integrative leap in the areas of redistribution or regulation, will there be 'more Europe' in the third major role of the modern state—the provision of security? Security was the original function of the state. In a more peaceful world it has become less central, but security abroad and order at home must always be provided for. On the former, Europeans have being trying to act together for decades. In recent years they have intensified co-operation. Collective institutions to conduct a common foreign, security and defense policy have been expanded and the culture of co-operation that has served Europeans well on economic policy issues has been fostered in security matters. Increasingly, the EU speaks with one voice on external security issues and the very perception by outsiders of greater unity magnifies it in the eyes of others.

The existence of the EU and of its policies towards non-member countries has enhanced Europeans' security in some ways. The transition to market democracy in the former communist countries in central and eastern Europe was both accelerated and steadied by their desire to join the EU. The 'carrot' of membership gave, and still gives, the bloc a very considerable stabilising influence in its neighbourhood. On soft security issues further afield, the EU wields clout: Europe accounts for the lion's share of aid flows to the developing world; on international trade issues, the EU is a superpower with an exercisable veto power on all aspects of world trade negotiations;[4] and on climate change, the EU has been the most active of the large powers in pushing for greater action globally.[5] On harder security matters, deployments of EU-led missions, of various civilian and military kinds, have made some contribution to stabilising conflict areas around the world.

But despite these efforts, an effective and credible common foreign, security and defense policy remains distant. This reflects, in part at least, the inevitable difficulties in unifying the positions of 27 countries whose concerns, interests and outlooks differ. This is in evidence at even the most basic level of how such a common policy should be organised and what relationship it should have with NATO, the region's most important security-providing institution. But even taking into account the enormous difficulties of attempting to forge common positions on structures and issues as sensitive as those related to foreign policy, Europeans, through miscalculation, blunder and wishful thinking, have frequently undermined their own security objectives.

Divisions among the 27 over Turkish membership of the bloc, a matter of genuine strategic importance, have contributed to that country's accession negotiations being mired in a near-constant state of crisis since they were launched in 2005. The failure to end the division of Cyprus before its accession to the EU may have been inevitable, but by offering Greek Cypriots membership regardless of whether they accepted a UN plan on reunification, Europeans guaranteed that they would fail to achieve their own objective. The continued failure to curb Iran's nuclear ambitions has been little short of a humiliation. It has been the bloc's most concerted diplomatic effort ever and was undertaken despite Europeans not having within their gift the one thing that has the only chance of ending the Islamic Republic's bomb programme—a security guarantee. To be sure, Iranian deviousness and American dunderheadedness have placed the EU in an invidious position. But these constraints were obvious in 2003 when the EU decided to place itself in that position. The result, thus far, has been no gain in slowing down Iran's nuclear programme and considerable pain in terms of reduced credibility. A lower-profile but equally unsuccessful initiative has been its framework for relations with the countries of north Africa and the Middle East, known as the Barcelona Process. It has sputtered along for 15 years, and no one would claim it has done much to achieve its stated objective of fostering greater stability and prosperity around Europe's 'soft underbelly'.

It could be argued that it is not necessarily how successful Europeans have been when acting together, but how much value-added has been created by common action. By this measure the balance sheet appears somewhat better. There can be little doubt that Europe is greater than the sum of its parts when it agrees a common position, be it on climate change, trade or regulatory affairs. More specifically, on Iran, it may be better to be a player in negotiations, even an ineffective one, than not to have any role—the likely position if Europeans had not been acting in concert. On north Africa and the Middle East, a minimally productive Barcelona Process may be better than no process at all, and who knows when the institutional shell that has been created could come into its own?

Two ongoing challenges should provide clearer answers as to whether Europeans can enhance their own security by collective action:

state-building in Kosovo and bear-wrestling with Russia. Kosovo is in some ways Europe's Iraq. The big three powers—Britain, France and Germany—led the move among European countries to allow the Serbian province to declare independence in early 2008. Though NATO will continue to provide the brawn, the EU has taken for itself the role of providing the brains to design and build a new state in that unruly territory. Just as the US cannot afford to fail in Iraq, the EU cannot fail in Kosovo. It will have to stay as long as it takes. Given the magnitude of the challenges, it would not be surprising if it is still running the place decades from now.

The greatest and most serious failing of European foreign and security policy has been the inability to handle a changing Russia. Russia's sheer size and power, its energy resources, its disputes with its immediate neighbours and its unEuropean brand of assertive nationalism make it by far the biggest and widest-ranging foreign-policy and security challenge facing Europe. To date, individually and collectively, EU countries have not met that challenge and have frequently undermined their own strength in numbers by diverging from the common EU position, usually in order to secure some national goal vis-à-vis Russia. This does not augur well for the future.

## SAFETY AT HOME

Law-breakers are internationalising, along with everyone else. This has led to Europeans applying their unique form of international co-operation to the domestic dimensions of security. Cross-border crime, terrorism, financial fraud and illegal immigration have come to be among the most important issues on the domestic agendas of most European countries in recent years. For this reason, strictly national responses to international phenomena are increasingly inadequate, or so say most governments and reflex integrationists. The EU-level response has been its Justice and Home Affairs (JHA) initiative, the fastest-growing branch of EU activity in recent years, with more than 1,200 laws enacted over the past decade. New agencies and bodies have sprouted: Europol is a mechanism for enhancing co-operation among police forces; EuroJust is a framework for the continent's public prosecutors to work together on cross-border investigations; Frontex is a collective effort to secure the bloc's borders.

It is difficult to evaluate the effectiveness of JHA as it remains in its infancy, but it is in the field of home affairs and justice, more than any other area, that deeper European integration in the future is most likely, mainly because it simply makes a great deal of sense. If criminals and terrorists use borders to their advantage, those who protect populations from them must respond. Lessening the importance of those borders is the easiest way to achieve that objective. The integrationist logic is powerful. But what of civil liberties? If police, prosecutors and security agencies are given new powers, they need new forms of accountability. In their haste to catch internationalising villains, it is far from clear that the architects of JHA have put in place sufficient checks and balances to ensure that new powers are not abused. It would be wrong to exaggerate, but anyone who believes liberties are fragile must feel some sense of unease. That said, whether the EU increases its role further, in the short term at least, will depend a great deal on whether the Lisbon treaty, the latest change to the bloc's basics laws and structures, ever enters into force. Among its most important innovations are mechanisms to allow closer (and more accountable) JHA co-operation. Without it, JHA will go back to the drawing border, for a few years at least, or proceed, as it often has to date, on an ad hoc basis of willing coalitions.

## CAN THE CENTRE HOLD?

All human constructs are fragile. Many will be shaken during the economic earthquake that the world has been experiencing since late 2008. Along with other governance structures, the EU is sure to suffer damage. How serious that damage will be will depend on the depth and duration of the crisis, something that is, at time of writing, far from clear. Much clearer are the European edifice's points of vulnerability. There are three significant weaknesses: the bottom-up, foundational problem of the limited attachment voters have for it; the top-down overburdening of the system; and the domestic weaknesses of some of the member states which constitute the bloc's pillars.

Many observers have long believed that there is a disconnection between the EU and the voters whom it is designed to serve and benefit. This 'legitimacy deficit' is cause for concern because all systems of government, if they are to endure, need citizens to have faith in their institutions and to trust them to act in the broad public interest. It is a view almost universally shared among students of political systems that governments with limited legitimacy are more vulnerable in times of crisis. In Europe, it is easy to envisage Brussels becoming the focus of popular ire if competition rules are blamed for preventing the implementation of measures to save jobs or the European Central Bank in Frankfurt comes to be perceived as prolonging recession by setting interest rates at levels that are believed to be inappropriate. National governments may find it expedient to pass the buck to Eurocrats and central bankers. And even if mainstream politicians, who broadly support integration, resist that temptation, there will always be demagogues and populists lurking in the shadows to take the opportunity. In times of uncertainty and fear, the desire to look for scapegoats is strong. Foreign scapegoats are all the more appealing. If voters come to see the EU institutions as part of their problem, rather than part of any solution, governments will, at the very least, come under pressure to ignore or break the rules of the EU game. If the rules are ignored, the system's *raison d'être* will quickly be undermined. There is no doubt that there are centrifugal forces at play in Europe, as evidenced by the desire for devolution of power to regions within many countries. If those same forces are unleashed on the EU, it is not inconceivable that it could be torn apart.

It could also collapse under its own weight. The EU is designed to be part of the solution to many of the challenges of modern governance. But any system can crack if overloaded. There is some reason to believe that EU structures have been overburdened over time, resulting in tensions among the member states that would not have come about if the structures designed to bind them more closely together had not existed. Attempts to create a common foreign and security policy are one major area of possible overburdening, as the divisions over the invasion of Iraq demonstrated. Had Europeans not had ambitions, structures and systems to act together in foreign affairs, the poison which paralysed relations among them at that time would not have been as venomous. One need only look to other regions of the world to see this. While Japan supported the invasion, its neighbour China did not. This caused no deterioration in their bilateral relations because neither had the expectation that the other would or should take the same position. The same could be said for Latin America and Africa, where some countries backed the invasion and others opposed it, without causing regional recriminations.

But falling out over relations with an ally who poses no direct security threat is one thing. If EU countries split on Russia the consequences could be far more serious. Russia's assertiveness is triggering very different responses among the 27. Many of the members who were once subject to Soviet domination feel directly threatened. Others, mostly longer-standing members, have signalled repeatedly that they will not confront Russia regardless of its action. Increasingly, the former group does not trust the latter. Any deterioration in the security situation in central and eastern Europe would see countries such as Poland and the Baltic states shift their foreign policy emphases from the EU to NATO in the knowledge that, ultimately, only the US is able and willing to stand up to Russia. If such divisions were to emerge they would be far more serious than those over Iraq and would likely affect all aspects of the EU.

The euro is another case of possible system overload. Many economists warned that by creating a currency without shock absorbers—a centralised budget and labour mobility—the project would be difficult to sustain. In the euro's first decade in existence, differences between France and Germany over the conduct of monetary and exchange rate policy contributed to the deterioration in their relationship. In the early months of its second decade, the single currency is being tested as few ever thought possible. There is a pervasive sense in the air that something, somewhere will have to give. If that leads to the breakup of the euro project (still very unlikely), it could well bring the entire EU edifice down with it.

The third point of weakness is the former communist member countries. Although they have made great strides since 1989, in many cases their economies and democratic structures are extremely fragile. In early 2009, two members—Hungary and Latvia—reached a point where the EU and International Monetary Fund moved to bail them out. Others will surely follow. And even if they do not, the effects of recession will drive up unemployment and cause much hardship. In countries where cynicism about politics is deep and wide, the risks of serious instability are considerable (there have been only a handful of incidences of governments winning re-election in the 10 former communist states now members of the EU in the two decades since the advent of democracy). A scenario in which a government collapses and the vacuum is filled by a non-democratic alternative is possible to envisage. This would cause a real crisis. In 2000, when Austria's reactionary-right party, led by the arch-populist Jörg Haider, was brought into government, the then 14 other member states introduced bilateral diplomatic sanctions, citing the perceived threat he posed to Austrian democracy. The Nice treaty, which came into effect subsequently, included a clause that would allow for a suspension in the event of a serious slippage in democratic standards. Triggering that clause would bring the bloc into uncharted waters.

## A TIME TO TEST METTLE

Over more than half a century, the drive to integrate Europe has become an immensely powerful dynamic. It may even be as powerful as other great dynamics in European history—the religious zeal that drove the continent to crusade in medieval times and the urge toward absolutism and nationalism in modern times, which, respectively, forged the state and the nation. Although integration may be reaching its limits and the impetus behind widening membership of the bloc running out of steam, the European integration project is not like a bicycle, as ideological integrationists have often claimed. It will not topple over if deeper integration comes to a halt. A steady-state EU is perfectly possible. The habit of European co-operation has become deeply embedded. For Europe's political and administrative classes it is almost as normal a part of how they govern and administer as national-level institutions. No state has ever left and many want to join. Other regions of the world have modelled aspects of their co-operation structures on it. The current extreme economic conditions will have serious political consequences. Each of the three weaknesses identified above will be tested. But if the project can survive the current economic earthquake, it will have proved its durability. It almost certainly will. We will know soon.

> '*There is nothing more difficult to take in hand, more perilous to conduct, or more uncertain in its success, than to take the lead in the introduction of a new order of things.*'
>
> NICCOLÒ MACHIAVELLI

## EUROPE NEEDS A FINANCE MINISTER, NOT A FOREIGN MINISTER

*15 October 2003*

Europeans want their European Union to be a superpower in world affairs. Figures as disparate as Tony Blair, the British prime minister, and Romano Prodi, the head of the European Union's executive-cum-civil service, agree on that. So what are they doing to achieve this ambitious end?

Twenty-five European countries have begun months of intergovernmental bargaining to finalise a constitution for the EU. Among the many matters up for discussion is the creation of the position of EU foreign minister, his remit and resources, and how he will speak and act for the Union in the world. It is hoped that by having a foreign minister Europe will finally be able to punch up to its economic weight in the world. Some even believe that with a foreign minister, divisions such as those that tore the EU apart earlier in the year could be avoided if there were ever again to be a crisis as grave as Iraq.

But this is wishful thinking, because while Europeans will the end, they are unprepared to will the means. For an EU foreign minister to have a real foreign policy to work with, member countries would have to forgo their vetos on EU action in foreign and security matters. They would also have to merge their armed forces to a far greater extent and convince their electorates to pay much more for defense spending. But no such proposals are in the draft constitution. Nor is there even the remotest prospect that they will be added in the months ahead. Although the Union's efforts to forge close co-operation in defense, security and foreign policy have not been without success, Iraq showed how differently EU countries perceive and pursue their interests in foreign and security matters when the chips come down. The creation of an EU foreign minister would not change these fundamental differences. It would, at best, raise unrealisable expectations. At worst, it would invite ridicule if divisions were to re-open. The Union's prestige would suffer further as a result.

But none of this is to say that the EU does not have a role to play in the world. It has; and it can best fulfill this if it eschews sovereignty-sensitive high politics for what it does best—economics. The EU was built from the ground up, starting with humdrum economic matters, and so too should its foreign policy be. And because the Union has genuinely common economic policies, in contrast to security and defense, this is eminently achievable. The EU should, therefore, postpone the creation of a foreign minister indefinitely and instead establish the role of minister of international economic relations. The EU has a single currency, giving it real clout in the international monetary system. Its antitrust powers are enormous, giving it as much sway as the United States on global competition issues. Collectively it has the world's largest aid budget by far, giving it a big say in the developing world. But most important by far is trade. And it is not only desirable for Europe that it should show leadership here, it is imperative for the rest of the world too, because the international trading system is now in grave danger.

Traditionally, the enlightened self-interest of the United States underpinned that multilateral trading order. But since the end of the Cold War, the United States has become increasingly like other countries, pursuing its interests narrowly. It has strayed from the one true free trade path of multilateral agreement into the thicket of bilateral and regional deals. It has resorted to the protectionist ruse of 'antidumping measures' far more than any other rich country. Last year it imposed old-fashioned tariffs to protect jobs in its steel industry and then massively increased protection for its farmers.

And the future is bleaker still. As the u.s. trade gap breaks new records each year and hyper-competitive Chinese imports are snapped up by American consumers in preference to domestically made goods, protectionist voices in Congress are growing louder. Some American lawmakers advocate ignoring World Trade Organisation rulings that are unfavourable to the United States. Some even want to pull out of the wto altogether. If the United States does not again become the indispensable nation of the rules-based trading system, there is a real danger that the spectre of 1930s protectionism will return.

It is therefore imperative that the eu fill the vacuum. And although to date it has shown precious little of the sort of vision required, an eu economics minister would be well positioned to do so, for three reasons. First, such a minister would have the necessary tools at his disposal. Trade policy in the eu was long ago denationalised and is decided in Brussels, unlike security and defense matters. Second, a half-century of belonging to a common market has lessened Europeans' mercantilist instincts. Since 1995 the eu has resorted to antidumping measures less than half as frequently as the United States and its politicians do not clamour for protection in their parliaments and the media. Even in agriculture, though they continue to move far too slowly, the Europeans are going in the right direction by reducing trade-distorting subsidies. Finally, even if Europe's industries and trade unions were to bring pressure to bear to pull up the drawbridge to imports, they would have less chance of success than their American counterparts because the political process is far better insulated from moneyed lobbyists, largely because of the very different nature of political party funding in the eu.

If the eu wants to have real clout in the world, it should make a start by showing leadership where it is capable of doing so. A foreign minister without a foreign policy and without military capability is bound not to lead, but to fail. An economics minister, in contrast, would have real clout at meetings of the Group of Eight, the International Monetary Fund and, most importantly, the wto. The eu was built on a foundation of free trade. Its foreign policy should be, too.

*Originally published in the* International Herald Tribune

# EU EXPANSION: SLOWLY DOES IT

*15 June 2006*

In a little over nine months' time, the European Union will mark the half-century since the signing of its founding treaties in Rome on 25 March 1957. But that anniversary looks set to be celebrated under a cloud of uncertainty. This week Europe's leaders will agree an open-ended extension to the 'period of reflection' on the bloc's future, which has been going on since the rejection of the EU constitution in referendums in France and the Netherlands a year ago. To lift the fog and end an unnecessary existential crisis about the EU's future, a clearer sense is needed not only of the Union's continued usefulness, but also of its limitations and of its vulnerabilities.

There is a growing sense that the central rationale of the European project—to supply peace and prosperity to the continent—now has a hollow ring. Europe would still be prosperous without integration, even if it would be less well off than it is today. It would, too, remain free of war—profound changes in politics, economics, society and military affairs have caused a marked decline in interstate conflict globally since the middle of the 20th century. It would be hard to conclude that the European integration project has caused this worldwide change.

It is the quality of Europe's peace, however, that marks it out from other regions; and this is attributable directly to the EU's unique, and uniquely successful, multilateral mechanism for managing its states' interactions. Although war is resorted to less frequently in every region, destabilising rivalries, suspicions and tensions mean that peace is not exploited elsewhere as fully as it is in Europe. The success of the European arrangement for smoothly managing international relations is to be seen in flattering imitation. Regional arrangements inspired by the EU have sprung up across the world, from Asean in southeast Asia to Mercosur in Latin America to the more recent African Union. Closer to home, the EU's success is evinced by the clamour of its neighbours to join it.

But this very success in attracting so many applicants for membership has contributed to the EU's current crisis about its future. High on the agenda as leaders meet this week is the question of how many new countries the bloc should accept as members and whether the EU has the 'absorption capacity' to include those lining up to join. Arguments against further enlargement are all too often made by those vainly seeking to cordon off the outside world's troubles or by those who believe that the EU should exclude states of a non-Christian tradition. These are bad arguments. But it is not only the opponents of enlargement who can get it wrong. Some of those in favor of rapid expansion can also sound unpersuasive, making seemingly naïve arguments about the undesirability of excluding any country.

Avoiding the prejudices of many exclusionists and the pieties of some inclusionists has proved difficult. A calm debate on future enlargement—who should join and when—has been hard to conduct as a result. It is beyond dispute that the lure of EU membership has been a hugely effective means of exporting stability to countries consolidating democracy. But because stability has been successfully exported in the past does not mean that it should be taken for granted that it will work in every case. Turkey and the countries of the western Balkans differ in important ways from previous aspirants. Membership and its lure may not extinguish the extreme nationalism that is not only alive and well in some corners of the Balkans, but is of a virulence that exists nowhere else within the Union. Nor can the prospect of EU membership be certain to convert Turkey's Islamists to secularism or guarantee civilian control of the Turkish military in perpetuity.

It would also be wrong to assume that significant instability could not be imported into the Union if enlargement happens too soon and the EU's democratic values are not fully internalised by new members. The countries of the western Balkans remain frighteningly close to the abyss from which they were dragged in the 1990s. If, once members of the EU, their disputes were to reignite, or if Turkey were to take a turn away from democracy, the EU mechanism would be tested as never before.

None of this is to suggest that Europe's leaders should definitively exclude any aspirant, let alone set final borders for the EU, as some have suggested. But there are risks as well as rewards in further expansion if it happens too hastily. A candid recognition of the risks would mean that, in the long run, enlargement works to the benefits of those now seeking to join and those already members. Proceeding cautiously should help ensure that the EU is as successful in the coming decades as it has been in its first half-century.

*Originally published in the* International Herald Tribune

———

# EUROPE'S FOREIGN POLICY PRIORITIES FOR THE YEAR AHEAD

*December 2007*

With Europe's global influence in decline for more than a century, the continent's countries have been trying to halt and reverse that trend by formally co-operating on foreign policy since the early 1970s. Efforts to strengthen their shared institutional capacities and widen the range of issues that they deal with collectively continue apace.

But despite these efforts the European Union is still far from punching up to its economic weight in the world. The reasons are manifold: differing interests and values among the 27 member states, inadequate resources, a limited strategic-thinking capability and more besides. The result, all too often, is fudged policy formulation and poor implementation.

In 2008 there are likely to be opportunities aplenty for the EU and its 27 sovereign states to test their ambitions to become an international actor of real clout. And there is nothing to test such ambitions like a crisis. Of the foreseeable flashpoints, the Balkans and Iran loom large.

Despite big differences, EU cohesion on supporting an independent Kosovo, and wider Balkan issues, has been solid thus far. But real differences exist among the 27; and with tensions in the region rising, these could be exposed. Having failed so disastrously to prevent the former Yugoslavia's descent into the abyss in the 1990s, a second failure to contain extreme nationalism on its own doorstep would gravely undermine the EU's hopes of becoming a player in international security matters.

Iran's nuclear programme also retains the capacity to generate crisis. Though the urgency of dealing with it appears to have waned following recent US intelligence re-assessments of the Islamic Republic's bomb-making programme, the EU will keep up the pressure. Engaging Tehran on the issue has been the EU's most intensive diplomatic offensive ever. The big three of Britain, France and Germany, along with the bloc's foreign-policy supremo, Javier Solana, will continue to work for a halt to uranium enrichment.

But even if crises are avoided, or successfully handled, longer-term matters will require at least as much management. Of the three countries with which the EU has genuinely strategic relations—Russia, Turkey and US—each will present its own challenges and opportunities in 2008.

With Vladimir Putin certain to remain at the Russian helm— one way or another—no change in that country's external posture can be expected. That can only spell trouble for the EU and its members, having had such limited success dealing with recent Russian recidivism. It will take all the forcefulness, unity of purpose and guile that the EU can muster to prevent the energy superpower pushing its weight around to the member states' detriment.

While Russia insists on playing a 19th-century Great Power game, Turkey is closer to the 21st century in its dealings with the EU. But it has its own problems, and deep divisions in the bloc on whether it should become a member have complicated its ongoing negotiations to join. These talks have been in a state of half-suspended animation since December 2006. They are unlikely to be much revived in 2008.

Transatlantic relations, by contrast, are in surprisingly good shape. George Bush's stance towards Europe in his second term has been as pro-EU as any post-war US president. The final year of his presidency could see closer co-operation with the Europeans on a number of issues, most notably world trade talks, climate change and Iran.

As the US president begins his long goodbye in 2008, France's new president will be getting into his stride. All European eyes will be on Nicolas Sarkozy as he takes the EU presidency in the second half of 2008. He has already shown himself to be as energetic in foreign matters as he is in domestic affairs. But he has also been erratic and unpredictable, causing irritation among allies.

If he wishes to advance his (typically ambitious) presidency agenda, he will need to hone his diplomatic skills. Nowhere will calm reassurance be more needed than if he is to convince Britain to deepen EU defense co-operation—a major objective. Despite being the most Atlanticist French president in post-war history, he faces across the channel a British prime minister who is less engaged with Europe than any since the UK joined the bloc.

Given Brown and Sarkozy's different world views, national interests and personalities, the prospect of a bust-up between the two in 2008 is real. Free trade is one issue on which they could easily clash. If the Doha round of trade negotiations were to move towards conclusion, Britain and France would bookend the spectrum of EU opinion on offering concessions to secure a deal.

With the Lisbon treaty signed, institutional change is now off the EU agenda. This will free up time and energies. Greater focus on making Europe's common foreign and security policy more creditable is therefore likely. But, as is almost always the case in EU affairs, expect advances to be measured in baby steps, not giant leaps.

*Originally published in* 'European Union: Policies and Priorities', Financial Times publications

———

## REFORM STARTS AT HOME—NOT WITH EU TARGETS

*28 March 2004*

Terrorism and constitutional affairs may have dominated the headlines surrounding the gathering of European leaders presided over by the Irish government last week, but dismal economics was, as usual, the topic that most exercised those present. As they have done for four years, the EU's leaders considered progress on reform goals originally set out in Lisbon in 2000. Predictably, their conclusions on achievements to date were not happy. Designed to make the EU 'the most competitive economy in the world by 2010', the Lisbon agenda set a string of targets—for everything from spending on research and development to unemployment rates to reform of pension systems—in the hope that the success of the Maastricht criteria (when targets brought down runaway budget deficits in the 1990s) could be repeated.

Alas, things have not turned out that way. Not even the most sanguine would deny that progress on economic reform goals has been at best disappointing. Though Europe does not have the deadbeat economy that it is often portrayed as possessing, some countries (particularly the big ones) have problems. Failure to tackle these is time wasted and a postponement of the inevitable. The result is economic growth forgone. So why is the Lisbon process failing and who is to blame? The answer to both questions is the member countries themselves. To see why, consider the nature of the problem and the source of the solution.

Although there is a single market in Europe, it is unhelpful from a reform perspective to talk of a single European economy because the reforms needed in Ireland are very different from those needed in, say, France. This is because national rules, regulations and ways of doing things—not decisions from Brussels—determine economic performance. The lesson: reform must begin at home. A cursory glance at how things differ from one country to the next shows why national laws and actions remain far more important in determining economic outcomes than legislation enacted in Strasbourg or executive decisions taken in Brussels.

Member states' differences are most broadly reflected in the ultimate measure of performance—economic growth. While Italy and Germany have propped up the OECD's growth league over the past decade, Ireland has topped it, outpacing all others, including the Asian tigers and America. These differences, by the by, also debunk the myth that made-in-Brussels red tape is throttling Europe's entrepreneurs (if European directives and regulations were so business-unfriendly how could a country where they are applied have grown so fast?).

But perhaps best to illustrate the variance within the union are the differences in the functioning of labour markets, the improvement of which is a central objective of the Lisbon agenda. While some states have chronic problems, others are already world-beaters—six of the EU-15, including Ireland, have lower unemployment rates than America and four have more of their working age populations in jobs (the Republic is not yet in this club owing to its legions of stay-at-home older women). As regards the productivity of workers, five of the EU countries recorded stronger growth than America since 1995.

While Ireland heads the productivity growth race by a furlong, and faces fewer of the painful reform hurdles confronting most other countries, our government has paid about as much attention to its Lisbon commitments as have its 14 counterparts in power elsewhere. For Ireland it is not a sticky labour market or unaffordable pension system that handicaps, but unfree product markets that rein in growth. From providing professional services to serving up pints, the interests of producers continue to trump those of consumers. And where change has taken place—taxis and pharmacies—it was because, respectively, of a court decision and the advice of the Attorney General, not EU efforts and not because the government matches its liberalising rhetoric with action to break up state-created cartels.

So if economic ills can be remedied only by national governments taking tough decisions at home, why was the EU roped into the Lisbon reform wheeze in the first place? The answer is the Euro habit. Governments have got so used to doing things together in Europe that there is a tendency to involve it when domestic efforts to get things done flag. Advocates of the Lisbon process add that setting targets at EU level helps, if nothing else, to embarrass governments out of their reform inaction (the basis of this belief is the success achieved by targets in the 1990s to qualify for the euro).

But this is misplaced. Quiet apart from the evidence over four years, there are two fundamental differences between Lisbon and the euro project. First, in the case of the euro the prize of participation and sanction of exclusion focused minds. Lisbon involves neither punishment nor reward. Maastricht-style targets for reforms have other limits, too. In economic reforms, as in most aspects of human affairs, it is easier to stop people doing bad than to make them do good. While targets stopped fiscal recklessness in Europe in the 1990s, using them to bring about virtuous structural reform shows little sign of making reform laggards change their ways.

There is a second big reason to believe Lisbon is misguided. By linking the EU to reforms that, however necessary, cause uncertainty for many and pain for some, it undermines the union's fragile foundation of legitimacy by (wrongly) giving the impression that meddling Eurocrats are in some way responsible for imposing painful reforms. This is not good. Whether you loathe it or love it, member countries join the EU (and stay in it) because they calculate that they can do things inside that they cannot manage alone, from fighting terrorism to cutting pollution. If more Europeans become unsatisfied with membership, it will become more difficult to use the EU for other things it is better suited to, like freeing trade and putting manners on monopolists.

While national politicians have always found it hard to resist the temptation to blame Brussels for unpopular decisions they agree together in Europe, the Lisbon process is the formalisation of this vice and allows governments to invoke the EU when introducing unpopular reforms, as Silvio Berlusconi is now doing in his attempt to change Italy's unsustainably generous pension system.

Externalising domestic political costs (as political scientists inelegantly put it) may make life easier for national politicians in the short term, but the danger for the EU over time is that feelings of resentment will be directed towards Brussels by those who see their pension entitlements reduced or lose their jobs as hire-and-fire rules are loosened.

None of this is to say that the EU should not have some role in the reform process. But the Lisbon agenda should be scaled back in both its content and its ambition to include only EU-determined objectives, such as ironing out wrinkles in the regulatory framework for the provision of services across borders and facilitating the transfer of pension rights to increase labour mobility between member states. Let member states take sole responsibility for reforms that only they can decide on and implement. After all, is that not what the principle of subsidiarity is all about?

*Originally published in the* Sunday Times

# EUROPE IS WINNING THE WAR FOR ECONOMIC FREEDOMS

*30 March 2006*

Economic freedoms, no less than other liberties, are eternally vulnerable, and never more so than when governments are weak or prone to populism. The 'four freedoms' underpinning the European integration project—the free movement of goods, services, labour and capital—are no different.

In the aftermath of the rejection of the European Union constitution in referendums in France and the Netherlands in mid-2005, the Union's single market appeared to be at risk if member states interpreted the votes as a rejection of liberalisation. The failure of many member governments to implement reforms and recent efforts by three governments to prevent foreign corporate takeovers have added to concerns that the half-century of (unsteady) progress towards European market integration is going into reverse.

The evidence does not support such a conclusion. Consider first the free movement of capital. Only a handful of cross-border deals have attracted unwanted government attention in recent times, while thousands have not. In 2005, almost 5,000 EU businesses were acquired by non-national firms. This represented a two-thirds increase on 2003 and includes sectors, such as energy, which have until recently seen limited pan-European corporate consolidation. Further restructuring will be facilitated, to some extent at least, when a new takeover directive comes into force in May.

This reflects the balance of forces between vestigial interventionism and market liberalisation. The latter is not only stronger but getting more so. Businesses are becoming more assertive in exercising their right to move capital freely within the EU. The European Commission, though a shadow of its former self in its influence over policy formulation, has seen its regulatory power strengthen and has never been more ready to stand up to member states that break or bend the rules. More member governments are opposed in principle to interfering in corporate restructuring than those willing to resort to such action.

Today there is no intellectually respectable case for protectionism. This is in contrast with the spirit of 1914, evoked recently by Giulio Tremonti, Italy's finance minister. The decades of global catastrophe that took place after that date, caused in part by protectionism, and the successes of the post-1945 liberal order leave those with protectionist instincts in the uncomfortable position of defending the indefensible.

As a consequence, the forces of protectionism are also failing to prevent freer movement of goods and services. Imports to the EU continue to grow strongly. In 2005 they surged, with 15 of the 25 member states registering a record high in imports as a percentage of gross domestic product.

This deepening import penetration is in part explained by China's emergence as an exporting superpower. Though the rise of the Asian giant has been hindered by the occasional EU resort to protectionist measures, such as last year's ill-judged decision to re-impose quotas on Chinese textiles, these amount to little more than tinkering. China is set to overtake the US as Europe's largest supplier of merchandise goods in 2006 after years of high double-digit export growth to the EU.

The market-opening trend in the EU's bilateral trade relations is mirrored multilaterally. At the World Trade Organisation's ministerial meeting in December 2005, the EU agreed to phase out its agricultural export subsidies and accepted that its tariffs on such goods must fall further. Trade in services in Europe is also on the rise, despite measures that hinder cross-border provision. While the services directive has been watered down, it represents a still-significant step towards greater liberalisation.

The freedom to work in other member states was partially denied to citizens from the 10 new members when they joined in May 2004. This was the most egregious case of protectionism in the EU in recent years. But even here there are positive signs. The three member countries that allowed full access to workers from the newly joined 10—Ireland, Sweden and the UK—show no sign of reversing their decision and three more countries—Finland, Portugal and Spain—have committed to extending the freedom to the newcomers this year.

None of this is to say that the EU single market is not fragile. The risks of opportunistic protectionism are ever present and vigilance is always necessary. However, the evidence shows that Europe continues to go in the right direction, however slow and hesitating that progress may be.

*Originally published in the* Financial Times

# THE SILVER LININGS OF FRANCE'S 'NON' TO EUROPE'S CONSTITUTION

*31 May 2005*

With the rejection of the proposed European Union constitution in France's referendum on Sunday, and the likelihood of a similar result in the Netherlands on Wednesday, a half-century of deepening European integration appears to have hit the buffers. Some warn of a crisis of confidence in the EU, while devoted advocates of integration fear that without forward momentum, the European project will topple over.

That the constitution is now a dead letter is undoubtedly a setback for the EU in some ways: Its prestige has been damaged and the prospect is now remote that the many sensible reforms contained in the document will be implemented any time soon. But not only are these downsides not as great as they appear, the upsides of the referendum—empowering voters who have not been brought along in the integration process—have been all but ignored.

While the European project has been a boon for Europe politically and economically, it leaves most ordinary people cold. And many of those formerly enthusiastic are falling out of love fast, according to successive opinion polls since the early 1990s. This is unsurprising. As the EU has become more important in the governance of Europe, it has not become any less elite-driven. At a time when trust in ruling classes and popular willingness to defer to politicians and bureaucrats is falling in most countries, an EU 'legitimacy deficit' has opened up.

Experience across the continent shows that it is only when the EU is put centre stage in referendums—imperfect though they may be—that elites and electorates engage with each other and start speaking the same language on Europe. As the French and Dutch campaigns, and referendums in other countries in the past, have shown, when people get to vote on changes to the way the EU works, passion is injected into a debate which, if even audible, is usually dull and technical. Voters attend rallies, ask questions and actively inform themselves, as France's best-seller list shows, with books on Europe dominating the top 10. 'If you want to build a crowd, start a fight,' said the 19th-century circus impresario P.T. Barnum. He was right. The referendums have in recent weeks generated far more public interest than the convention that drafted the constitution received in its 18 months of tortuous consensus-building.

None of this is to ignore the disadvantages of direct democracy. It is true that much of the debate in France and the Netherlands has had little to do with the constitution and that the referendums have given demagogues, scaremongers and political opportunists a platform to whip up fears. But it is for political leaders to understand voters' fears, explaining them away if they are baseless and building consensus on how to face them if they are real. If they cannot do this they are not doing their job. Referendums have proved to be the only effective discipline to force Europe's leaders to make the case for Europe. That they have failed to win over voters this time does not mean that voters should not be trusted on EU matters, but that politicians must try harder next time.

But while the process may have re-empowered voters, what of the downsides of not having a constitution? Many constitutional advocates argue that the rules governing the EU need to change if Europe is to avoid gridlock now that the union has 25 members, and is set to grow even bigger. These concerns were perfectly plausible before 10 new members joined in May 2004, but all the evidence since says otherwise. More than a year after enlargement, gridlock is the dog that didn't bark. The EU's institutions are functioning better than almost anyone expected, decisions are still being taken and EU legislation is being enacted. The rules may be complicated, but they work, and there is nothing to suggest that the system cannot go on functioning.

Finally, there is also a geopolitical bonus from the French 'no'. Had France not torpedoed the constitution, Britain would almost certainly have done so. For a country that has been semidetached from its continent for centuries to be the one to kill off the constitution would have pushed Britain to the EU's margins, or even precipitated withdrawal. To have one of Europe's great powers disengaged from the mechanism for reconciling the interests of the continent's countries could be seriously destabilising. However irksome Britain's congenital lack of enthusiasm for mucking in with the rest may be, it is simply too important a country not to be kept closely locked into the system. It is better, surely, to have less integration with unity than more integration and disunity.

Direct democracy is awkward, unpredictable and easily exploited by opportunists, but for a political entity that is so disconnected from voters, it has proved to be the only effective way to give voters a say. Two cheers for referendums.

*Originally published in the* International Herald Tribune

# TACKLING EUROPE'S LEGITIMACY DEFICIT (I)

*16 June 2005*

The French and Dutch referendums have intensified debate about how to reconnect electorates and European elites. But if this debate is to have any chance of success, the nature of the problem must be clearly defined. And nowhere is definitional clarity needed more than in the distinction between the EU's (small) 'democratic deficit' and its (very large) 'legitimacy deficit'. These terms have often come to be used interchangeably, yet they are profoundly different.

An absence of democracy allows rulers to take actions arbitrarily, for their own benefit or for the benefit of those they favour. The result of a democratic deficit is that people with power abuse it to the detriment of the rest. In the EU system it is hard to find examples of people's interests being trampled upon in the half-century since the project was launched.

What's more, many of the obvious democratic flaws have ready solutions and almost no one disagrees that the changes contained in the constitution to address them—citizens' initiatives, more say for national parliaments and public scrutiny of legislating ministers—should all urgently be implemented, and be seen to be urgently implemented. But televising 25 ministers debating the regulation of, say, the chemicals industry in halting interpreter monotone will not engage voters, give them a sense of ownership of the project or reassure them that the whole enterprise has not run out of their control—all needed to bolster legitimacy.

This shows that different types of deficits require different solutions. While democratic deficits can be addressed by reforming institutional structures, narrowing a legitimacy deficit is harder because changing voters' perception involves a permanent change in the behaviour of politicians. And engineering such a change is daunting, not only because it would require inventive, determined and sustained political leadership of a sort that seems in woefully short supply in Europe, but because the EU's mostly technocratic functions will never easily engage voters.

The (relatively) easy part of changing politicians' behaviour is what they should stop doing: expediently blaming Brussels for unpopular decisions and policies that they themselves have often been involved in making; doing things at EU level because it is less politically difficult than at national level; and speaking in impenetrable Eurojargon when talking about the union.

The much harder part is what politicians should start doing to change the way they make the case for Europe, not least because here there are not many ideas about. Among the few is Ireland's permanently instituted 'National Forum on Europe'—a sort of travelling circus that pitches up in towns and cities across the country with MPS, MEPS, Eurocrats and academics in tow. They take the floor to listen and be quizzed. People roll up to inform themselves, argue their points, and be reassured that their voices are being heard.

But there is little to suggest that EU leaders see the need to put reconnecting with voters to the top of their agenda by coming up with more ideas like this.

The Commission's '1,000 debates' initiative—an attempt to generate discussion in town-hall forums in all member countries—has flopped because politicians have not run with the idea. Despite the shock of the French and Dutch rejections of the constitution, EU leaders are now expending their energies fighting each other over the tiny, 1% of GDP, EU budget, and referendums are being busily derided even though they are the one proven way of getting politicians to sell Europe and voters interested in buying.

Leaders ignore or underestimate voter alienation at their peril. Legitimacy deficits, like weaknesses in a building's foundations, are usually only exposed when things go badly wrong. If the EU were to face a real crisis it might not withstand the shock. The entire edifice could conceivably be at risk. The referendums have provided a salutary wake-up call. They should not be ignored.

*Originally published in the* European Voice

——

# TACKLING EUROPE'S LEGITIMACY DEFICIT (II)

*6 August 2008*

One does not have to be a paranoid Europhobe to fear that what politicians and officials get up to in Brussels is bad for democracy. Such fears were much in evidence in Ireland during the recent referendum on the Lisbon treaty. They have not been assuaged by the subsequent reaction to the vote across the continent. But to see whether a democratic deficit really exists at the heart of the EU, a long view is needed.

If European political history has a central theme, it has been the slow and unsteady circumscribing of the exercise of state power. In the past, monarchs and despots ruled their subjects arbitrarily and absolutely. Today, government is limited and accountable, and rulers are constrained by a tangle of checks and balances. The democratic system of government enjoyed by the peoples of west and central European states today—though far from perfect anywhere, and better in some countries than in others— is the happy product of centuries of evolution. But in those same states that long process of evolution has in recent decades undergone one of its most significant mutations ever. The creation of a layer of government above the state, otherwise known as the European Union, is a historically unique development.

Debate about this development and its implications usually creates more heat than light, dominated as it is by uncritical pro-integrationists on the one hand and opponents on the other who attribute to the EU all manner of ills. Such polarised views are one reason why the EU and its works are not as scrutinised as any other layer of government (another is that much of what it does is detailed, technical and indescribably tedious).

Such a lack of scrutiny is unhealthy, not least because any change to the infrastructure of government of the magnitude seen in Europe in recent decades needs to be understood and accepted by voters if it is to have a firm foundation of legitimacy. Because this does not happen as it should, suspicions abound that opportunistic politicians and 'faceless Eurocrats' are up to no good and, at worst, are working to reverse the long trend towards making the wielders of power more accountable to the people.

Such suspicions are well founded in principle. It is always unwise to assume politicians and officials have noble intentions, even if many do much of the time. Healthy scepticism about the motives of those driving the integration project is warranted, just as it is about all those who exercise power in any context. But even if one assumes the worst—that politicians support deeper integration because it allows them to operate with less scrutiny and officials because it increases their power—examining motives alone is insufficient to determine whether an EU democratic deficit exists. Most important is what the EU actually does.

Though the EU has many flaws, a democratic deficit is not among them. The proof is easily demonstrated. If you are on the sharp end of a demo- cratic deficit, be it in today's Russia, the Northern Irish state of yesteryear or countless other examples, you do not have to be a political scientist or legal theorist to know it. Your rights are ridden roughshod over and woe betide you if you attempt to do anything about it. This is patently not the case in Europe today. Over a half-century of European integration one will not find any country or group who has suffered such a fate, even among the smallest and most powerless countries, And it is not mere happenstance that the EU functions as it does. The reason is simple: manifold checks and balances. The most important is the hawk-like manner in which 27 member countries look out for their own interests and watch the actions of the other 26. Ministers in national capitals spend much time shuttling back and forth to Brussels to push their interests and protect their patches. Swathes of national civil services and their entire diplomatic corps support them, scanning the radar screen for anything that threatens their national interests or those of a constituency in their countries.

When alarm bells ring, even the smallest countries can veto, block, hinder and delay regardless of motive. Tiny Luxembourg has long prevented changes to EU-wide banking laws to protect its financial services industry, and this in the face of almost all of the other members wanting such measures to curb tax evasion. At the other end of the continent, little Cyprus has wildly disproportionate and often pernicious influence on the entire bloc's relations with Turkey, a country of real strategic importance for the union.

The manner in which countries conduct their affairs in the EU is in many ways little different from most other international organisations. But the EU differs in that it has a second layer of checks and balances that entities such as the UN have not. Where most intergovernmental organisations have toothless institutions, the EU's are anything but. The commission, parliament and court of justice all have significant powers in the limited areas where they can act. They are in an endless struggle for influence, unceasingly seeking to prevent each other and the member states from encroaching on their turf, and each is permanently poised to spring on the others if there is the slightest suggestion that the mark is being overstepped. Though this endless squabbling among institutions is sometimes petty, it ensures everyone is kept in check.

The EU's most urgent task is not to deal with an illusory democratic deficit, but to close its yawning legitimacy deficit whereby voters are willing to believe wild and often baseless accusations against it. As recent referendums in Ireland, France and the Netherlands have shown, this is not easy. Unless it can be addressed more effectively, the union's long-term future may be in doubt.

*Originally published in the* Irish Times

———

# THE LISBON TREATY: MUCH ADO ABOUT LITTLE

*January 2008*

For most of the current decade the EU has been consulting, debating and negotiating how it should tweak its institutions and structures to make them more efficient and legitimate in the eyes of its citizens. This has taken place in the context of the enlargement of the bloc from 15 economically developed, mature democracies to include 12 new members, most of which are considerably poorer, administratively weaker and politically less advanced in their democratic cultures. Advocates of change have argued that the bloc's ground rules need to be changed if its decision-making capacity is to continue to function with 27 heterogeneous member states. Although there is no evidence to suggest that the EU has become less efficient since enlargement took place in May 2004 (a comprehensive academic study has recently proved this beyond any doubt), the gridlock argument has remained the logic for the protracted and time-consuming efforts expended to amend the EU's founding treaties.

In December 2007 the product of this long period of introspection finally emerged as the 'Lisbon treaty'. Should the document be ratified during 2008, it is scheduled to enter into force in 2009. On balance, its measures are likely to improve overall effectiveness, but will be far from radical. As regards the second objective of boosting political legitimacy of the EU among voters, the prospects of achieving this end are far more limited—both because the changes designed to achieve it are few in number and scope and because of the inherent difficulty of endearing so technocratic a structure to citizens.

Changes contained in the Lisbon treaty designed to improve policy-making and policy implementation are focused mostly on two areas: external relations and justice and home affairs (JHA). In the field of foreign relations, the role of the EU representative is to be beefed up by giving the office greater powers and something approaching a fully fledged diplomatic service. Institutional overlap will also be reduced, as the new office will incorporate the existing foreign-policy office located in the secretariat of the Council of Ministers and the European commissioner responsible for external affairs (the newly created figure will also have the title of vice-president of the European Commission). While these changes are mostly commonsensical, they are unlikely to make as significant a difference as has been heralded. Agreeing and implementing common external relations policies has long been hindered by differences in interests and values among the member states. These fundamentals are by far the most important factor in determining the effectiveness of the EU's foreign policy. The Lisbon treaty will change little in this regard, and the bloc's effectiveness as an actor of real standing on the world stage is likely to improve only gradually as a result.

The second major area of change will be in the field of JHA. In recent years EU-level activity on internal security has expanded more rapidly than in any other area. The cross-border nature of many of the new security challenges being faced, notably large increases in the legal and illegal movement of people across borders, as migration levels have risen sharply, has been the driver behind greater common action. To overcome the disagreements that have tended to limit severely the effectiveness of EU-level action on JHA issues, the member states have agreed two major changes. First, they will forgo their vetos on many issues and subject most JHA questions to a qualified majority vote (QMV). Second, they will share with the European Parliament legislating competence in all these areas.

These changes should enable a meaningful common asylum policy to be put in place and lead to a more co-ordinated management of the bloc's external borders. The body tasked with this role—Frontex—is to be given greater powers under the terms of the Lisbon treaty. Also of note will be a greater role for Europol (the EU-wide policing body); the creation of a foundation upon which an EU prosecutor's office could be established; and moves to make national criminal laws interact more effectively. It is perhaps in this area, more than any other, that the Lisbon treaty can be expected to make a significant difference to the effectiveness of the EU.

Apart from specific policy areas, the treaty also seeks to improve the overall management of the bloc's affairs by creating better leadership structures. The most eye-catching change in the treaty in pursuit of this end is the creation of a permanent president of the European Council, ending the long-standing tradition of rotating the job among the member states for periods of six months. The end of the system of twice-yearly rotation is designed to bring greater consistency, continuity and long-term focus to EU leadership and put an end to the constant rejigging of priorities that comes with each presidency change-over. This is likely to lead to some overall increase in efficiency (although the existing system has the merit of constant reinvigoration that comes with a new leader at the helm every six months, which will now be lost).

The presidency issue illustrates one of the conundrums facing the architects of the EU, i.e. that an increase in efficiency can at times reduce legitimacy. Ending the rotating presidency system illustrates this well, because it will, if anything, put a greater distance between citizens and the bloc's political structures. Whatever inefficiencies were associated with rotating the role, it did generate a sense of ownership, as each country, regardless of size, had its time at the helm. The period in charge almost inevitably raised the profile of EU issues in the country exercising the role. Its abolition, and the moving of the role to Brussels, will insulate the EU's capital further from the goings-on outside its own bubble.

The issue of the EU's legitimacy has risen up the agenda in recent years owing to its growing importance in almost all areas of government in Europe and signs of grassroots discontent (the rejection in referendums of the precursor to the Lisbon treaty in France and the Netherlands was the most obvious manifestation of this). As a result, consensus has formed around the need to narrow this 'legitimacy deficit'. Proposals contained in the treaty designed to do this include the televising of Council of Ministers' legislative sessions, more input into the EU legislative process for national parliaments and the creation of 'citizens' initiatives'.

The first is designed to counter the valid argument that legislating in all democracies should be an open and visible process (in the world today only North Korea and Cuba, it is sometimes noted, legislate behind closed doors). In future, debates and votes among ministers will be done in the conventional democratic way. The second is the granting to national parliaments of the power to strike down proposals by the Commission if it is deemed to have exceeded its authority (in Eurojargon, if it has failed to respect the principle of 'subsidiarity'). However, this power is carefully circumscribed, in that even a majority of national parliaments would not be able to trigger the mechanism. In order to do so, the support of 55% of member states (on the basis of existing voting weights) or a simple majority in the European Parliament would also be required. The third major change designed to increase legitimacy is the creation of a 'citizens' initiative'. This will give the status of draft legislation to any proposal signed by one million people. The EU institutions would then be obliged to put the proposal through the legislative machinery. Again, this change is more limited than it might at first appear, given that there will be no obligation on either the Council of Ministers or the European Parliament to pass into law anything contained in such initiatives.

More generally in terms of making citizens feel closer to the EU, advocates of the Lisbon treaty also suggest that a more effective union will, in and of itself, make the entire project more legitimate. While there is undoubtedly merit to this argument, the same advocates are usually less willing to acknowledge that at times the two objectives may be subject to trade-offs (as in the case of the current and future arrangements for the presidency).

In sum, the Lisbon treaty amounts to a limited overall change to the EU with the exception of the JHA area. While the EU should function more effectively once the treaty enters into force, it will have rather modest effects. Moreover, citizens' feelings towards the European institutions are very unlikely to be changed much either way. As such, the net overall effects will be limited, and indeed, if the document were to fail the ratification test, the only serious consequence would be a blow to the prestige of the union and its leaders.

*Originally published in* European Policy Analyst

*Chapter* VI ∿

# WAR, DEMOCRACY AND PROSPERITY

*'The pursuit of commerce reconciles nations, calms wars, strengthens peace and commutes the private good of individuals into the common benefit of all.'*

HUGUES DE SAINT-VICTOR (CIRCA 1125)

*'All societies have the capacity to generate spontaneously the institutions they need to function.'*

AUGUSTE COMTE

*'From the crooked timber of humanity, nothing straight can ever be fashioned.'*

IMMANUEL KANT

## INTRODUCTION

Ten years ago, as the 20th century drew to a close, its final decade seemed a golden age. The end of the Cold War, economic boom across much of the planet, increased prosperity beyond the developed world, advances in international law, the advent of the internet, and much else besides augured well for the world. The new millennium dawned with the belief in human progress as strong as it had ever been. But the omens were bad almost from the beginning. In March 2000 the dotcom bubble burst and in September 2001 the era of hyper-terrorism dawned. Troubles mounted as the decade progressed. Conflict in the Middle East erupted. Climate change accelerated. Food and energy insecurity increased. The spectre of pandemic lurked. And in late 2008 the global financial system collapsed. At time of writing in May 2009, the world is in the deepest recession since the 1930s. Uncertainty abounds. Little can be taken for granted in the years ahead. Yet despite so many causes for despair, there are good reasons to retain a belief in progress. Three stand out above all others.

## THE PACIFICATION OF HUMAN AFFAIRS

Any TV montage of modern times will include flashed images of violence and war: Flanders' trenches, swastikaed panzers, mushroom clouds and napalm fireballs. It will not include graphics showing falling instances of violence, murder, conflict and war. The first and most important reason for optimism about the direction of the world is that it is becoming less violent. Despite copious evidence, there is no 'big' fact that has so conspicuously failed to seep into public consciousness. From anthropology, archaeology, criminology and history we know that the probability for an inhabitant of this planet of dying violently at the beginning of the 21st century is lower than it has ever been. The annual murder rate in western Europe, the safest part of the world, ranges from one in 35,000 in Finland to one in 131,000 in Greece.[1] This contrasts with hunter-gatherer societies—the oldest forms of human society—which were and are the most violent, with as many as 60% of male deaths attributable to violence.[2] Over centuries, in those countries where records have been kept, the level of violent crime has trended downwards.[3,4]

If interpersonal violence has declined gradually over centuries, interstate violence—war—has seen a much sharper decline in a much shorter period of time. Since the end of the Second World War, conflict between states has become rare. Since the end of the Cold War, there have been only a handful of such conflicts, and this despite the proliferation in the number of states[5] (reflecting the increase in their number, UN membership has risen from 50 in 1945, to 159 in 1990, and to 195 in 2009). If interstate conflict has been on the wane for decades, the falling incidence of conflicts within states is more recent. The number of civil wars and occurrences of ethnic conflict has been declining over the past 20 years.[6]

What has caused the pacification of human society? The urge to violence evolved in response to an environment in which its use was indispensable. Early humans killed to survive. But as humans gradually began to master nature, first by agriculture, the usefulness of violence declined and its disruptive costs rose. In response, societies that move from hunting to farming generate new traditions, institutions and mechanisms to contain and limit violence. But if interpersonal violence declines in such societies, it usually becomes more prevalent in its organised forms. Most agrarian societies create groups who specialise in violence. These warrior classes defend territory. They also fight to acquire the territory of others because power, glory and wealth are determined by the possession of land. But the shift from agriculture-based economies to knowledge-based ones (and the increased destructive capacity of modern weaponry) changed the cost/benefit calculus of the use of violence as much as the earlier transition from hunting to farming. This has resulted in the sharp decline in war since the middle of the 20th century. Given how fundamental are the changes underpinning this decline, there is little reason to believe it will go into reverse.

None of this is to say that war and violence will ever end. There will almost certainly be new wars. The clamour for access to resources, compounded by the impact of climate change, is an obvious cause of possible conflict in the future. The proliferation of weapons of mass destruction will increase the potential impact of any conflict that does break out, whether by design or miscalculation (nuclear conflict between India and Pakistan tops the list of real risks). Then there is terrorism. It may well buck the trend towards peace. The nature of modern weaponry and its falling cost makes unconventional warfare much cheaper and easier to conduct. This empowers ever smaller groups. It also increases the havoc that any given group can wreak. At its most extreme, the chance of a terrorist group getting its hands on a nuclear device and detonating it in a city somewhere in the world over the coming decades is considerable. Such an event would transform our world, affecting not only global security, but the world economy, travel and transport, civil liberties, how we plan and build our cities and much else besides.

## DEMOCRACY'S UNSTEADY ASCENT

The second big reason to be optimistic about the world's direction is the success of democracy. Over the past century each wave of democratisation has left a new high-water mark—the first taking place after the First World War, the second when European imperialism receded in the decades after the Second World War and the third in the 1980s and 1990s when Latin American authoritarianism went out of fashion and communism collapsed. Today, there are more democracies in the world than authoritarian régimes.[7] The reasons for the success of democracy go beyond Churchillian cliché—that it is the worst form of government excepting all others. Democracies outperform other systems of government on every level. They are, on average, more stable, less violent, more efficient and more legitimate. Almost without exception they give those who live in them more liberty and prosperity than any other system.

But the global democratisation process is far from complete. Many countries have adopted only some democratic characteristics and a significant number show few signs of advancing further. Such countries have become mired in a 'grey area' between despotism and democracy (societies divided on ethnic or religious lines are particularly vulnerable). But this should not be cause for despondency. It took Europe centuries to abandon autocracy and absolutism. The habits and values of democracy have to be acquired. Such a culture change takes time. But as long as there is no serious intellectual case for a better system of government, democracy looks set to continue its long and unsteady ascent.

In the shorter term, though, the democratic tide could recede. Three forces pose a threat to democracy: apathy, extremism and economic crisis. The first is the least serious. Occasional fretting that voters in developed countries could become detached from politics invariably proves unfounded. Electorates disengage and re-engage over time depending on the issues and the often unknowable zeitgeist. No democracy has ever failed because of voter apathy. A second, far more serious risk is that extremists use elections to clamber to power, but then cancel subsequent votes. This has happened frequently in past and will happen again. The third risk to democracy comes from crisis, such as the economic mael-strom in which the world is currently mired. This will threaten all forms of government—elected and unelected.

## PROMETHEUS BOUND, UNBOUND AND (PARTIALLY) REBOUND

The third reason to remain optimistic about the world's outlook is the boundless human capacity to innovate and create wealth. Not only has this allowed the population of the world to multiply, but a rising proportion of the planet's people live in countries where mass prosperity is enjoyed. That process will almost certainly continue over the longer term, even if it is likely to be patchy and uneven. The spark of innovation—the magic ingredient that allows ever more to be squeezed from a given amount of inputs—is so inherently part of human nature that it could never be extinguished. It is to be seen everywhere: by the advances in farming that allow more than six billion to survive on a planet that Thomas Malthus famously, assuredly and wrongly stated could support no more than 800 million; by the medicines that allow most of the planet to live longer and healthier lives; by the ever greater energy-intensity of the world economy; and by a thousand other examples. Moreover, the accumulation of scientific and technological knowledge is self-reinforcing and accelerating. The more knowledge that exists, the more new knowledge is generated, as evidenced by, among many other things, the rising number of patent applications each year.[8]

The market plays a central role in incentivising the generation of knowledge and disseminating it—the commercial-technological nexus that has transformed the world. It will not be changed by the financial and economic crises that erupted in 2008. A profoundly serious flaw in the system has been revealed. There can now be no doubt that a free market in finance produces fewer gains and far greater costs than it does for widgets. The unavoidable conclusion, therefore, is that finance cannot be allowed to function like other markets.[9] Now, the central challenge is to restructure, reform and re-regulate the global financial system to ensure that it does not pose a threat to the rest of a generally well-functioning market economy. This adjustment, however costly and painful, will take place, just as adjustment happened after the Great Depression and the crises of the 1970s, when earlier flaws were exposed.

The new doubts about how the market system functions add to longer-standing ones. The most important and controversial relates to its distributional effects. Many voice concern that globalised markets are bad for both the developed and developing worlds. But such doubts are woefully misplaced. This globalisation process has not only seen hundreds of millions lifted out of abject poverty, and given hope to many more that they will follow suit, it has created new markets for rich countries and supplied them with cheaper goods. This change, like all other economic changes, to a greater or lesser extent, has caused some dislocation, but the view that the developed economies are being damaged in any significant way by others' advances is wrong. The scare-mongering that jobs are leaking ever more quickly to Asia and elsewhere does not survive even the briefest encounter with the facts. Of the G7 large industrialised countries, six registered their highest ever numbers of people at work in 2007. Moreover, joblessness was either non-existent, in the cases of Canada, Japan, the UK and the US, or at its lowest rate in decades, in the case of France, Germany and Italy. The seemingly more plausible thesis that high-wage countries are losing their manufacturing bases to the developing world is almost as wide of the mark as the same charge on jobs. Despite much talk of deindustrialisation in the 1970s and outsourcing and off-shoring in recent years, the rich world has never manufactured so much. By 2007, five of the G7 economies reached all-time highs in industrial production and the two that did not—Britain and Italy—were only marginally off previous recent peaks.

Co-operation and interaction, including most importantly in the context of competitive commercial endeavour, usually generates benefits for both contracting parties. There is no more important insight from economics, or any other social science, than that of the positive sum game.[10] If this insight were more widely and deeply understood, so many of the fears and concerns about globalisation, and economic change more generally, would dissipate.

## A NEW WORLD ORDER: BRIC BY BRIC

The waning resort to arms, the inherent strengths of democracy and the general robustness of the market mechanism are the deep underlying trends that should ensure that the world remains on the path of greater security and widening prosperity over the long term. Another underlying trend (and reason for optimism) is the diffusion of power from the Atlantic world to the rest of the planet. There can be little doubt that a global rebalancing of power, returning to the more even distribution that existed up to the 18th century, is inexorable as rapid economic develop- ment of many poorer countries takes place. This is one of the most positive developments of modern times, allowing as it does a greater share of humanity access to a decent standard of living and the promise of prosperity. This trend also has potential to enhance the security and stability of an interconnected and globalised world by giving more of its states and peoples more say in how it functions, both in existing institutions, such as the UN, and in new ones, such as the G20. But the process will be slow and unsteady, in contrast to the assertions of the breathless 'The Rise of...' and 'The End of...' genre of analysis. The dull truth is that in the absence of war or environmental catastrophe, geopolitical change is almost always gradual (the collapse of the Soviet Union being the great exception). To see why this should also be the case in the 21st century, it is necessary to survey the poles of this new multipolar world, starting with the emerging 'BRIC' powers, a term coined by an investment banker in 2001 to refer to the populous, fast-growing countries he believed would be increasingly influential in the future—Brazil, Russia, India and China.

In many ways Brazil is the mirror image of the US in the southern part of the western hemisphere: it is vast and rich in natural resources; it is populous and ethnically diverse; it has a history of independence from Europe of similar duration; and it is a decentralised, federalised polity. Despite these similarities, the country has continuously failed to live up to its potential. So consistent has this failure been, a cruel put-down has been around for decades: 'Brazil is tomorrow's country—it always has been.' But in recent years there has been reason to believe that it would finally live up to its potential. Its democracy has strengthened and transfers of power have become smoother; economic policy-making has improved and fewer mistakes mean the country is less at risk of boom and bust; reforms have opened its cosseted sectors and allow some real corporate success stories to emerge.

But, alas, for every step forward, Brazil continues to be dragged back and down. It still suffers the perennial Latin American weakness of under-investment, in both public and private sectors, owing to rock-bottom savings rates. The result is decaying infrastructure and companies who too often use outdated plant, machinery and equipment. Weighing even more heavily on the country's efforts to advance is its education system. Teaching is too focused on rote learning and mantra-like repetition, and despite being inadequate, most resources go to teachers' pay rather than buildings and books. Also relevant has been Brazil's lack of meritocracy (income inequality is among the highest in the world). Among other things, this has allowed the country's elites to remain complacent and parochial. São Paulo is a long way from anywhere—and it feels it. Debate and intellectual life appear only partially influenced by ideas from else-where and Brazil remains a country that prizes appearance over ideas. Numbering 180 million, Brazilians filed just 451 international patent appli-cations in 2008, but underwent plastic surgery 47,957 times in 2002, the last year for which data are available (the comparable numbers for the us in the same years were, respectively, 53,521 and 90,9920). The limited inter-est Brazilians appear to have in the world may also be illustrated anec-dotally—over the 10-odd weeks I have spent in the country, I never once saw anyone reading a book. Little wonder that it has been the economic growth laggard among the BRICS over the past two decades.

Russia is different. It is a deeply intellectual society. In science, math-ematics, literature and the performing arts its people have frequently excelled. Its human resources are one of its two greatest strengths. But this resource is being depleted. Its demographic outlook is among the worst in the world. From a population of 142 million in 2007, it is expected to shrink to 126 million by 2030.[11] Russia's other great gift was endowed by nature, and its economy remains heavily dependent on these natural resources—energy accounted for two thirds of its exports in 2007. Despite this dependence, the country hinders itself by chronic underinvestment in its oil and gas fields. As a result, extraction infrastructure is aging rapidly. This will result in output in the decades to come declining, despite greater demand globally. And in spite of all of this, rather than co-operating with foreign energy companies to ensure the oil and gas continue to flow, Russia's regular expropriation of their assets has precisely the opposite effect.

This is in keeping with Russia's unerring determination to undermine its own interests. A stand-out example came the day after the 2008 US presidential election. Rather than taking the opportunity to attempt a fresh start with the new Obama administration, Russia's opening gambit was to announce the stationing of missiles in its Baltic enclave of Kaliningrad as part of its dispute with the US over the latter's deployment of a missile shield in central Europe. Although the decision was subsequently rescinded, it is difficult to see by what rational calculation Russia believed it would advance its cause by making this announcement. There are many other examples of Russia acting against its own interests, including its by-now almost annual mid-winter interruption of energy supplies to its neighbours and its opposition to UN-centred efforts to ensure Iran complies with the nuclear Non-Proliferation Treaty. Meeting and talking with Russian officials and diplomats helps to explain the country's curious international posture. They wear on their sleeve their sense of being a diminished giant and often appear never to have recovered from their decline from superpower status after the collapse of the Soviet Union. Despite a much reduced role in world affairs since the early 1990s they still demand to be listened to and react harshly to any word or deed—real or perceived—which questions their country's greatness. They can be hyper-sensitive and tetchy and, at the same time, over-bearing and strident. With only a modicum of empathy, one can easily see why. The US and Europe have often addressed post-Soviet Russia with a mixture of condescension, pushiness and opportunism. This has been hard to stomach and Russia has real grievances and insecurities. But so does every country, to a greater or lesser extent. Most move on. Russia does not. Such a country is not destined for global influence and greatness, and may well condemn itself to remain a source of instability in its region (this is explored in greater detail in Chapters IV and V).

## EXTRAORDINARY CHINDIA

The two countries that stand out from all other developing countries are India and China. Both, despite formidable challenges, appear destined to play greater roles in the world owing to the sheer size of their populations and their internal capacities to innovate and create wealth. Indians used to quip that the people of the subcontinent were successful wherever they lived; except in India. That has now changed and India's economic success over the past two decades has been a bottom-up story of how the inherent capacity for wealth creation can be unleashed once the dead hand of the worst kind of statism is removed. The country's creative chaos and new-found cultural self-confidence have combined to allow it to deal with modernity very much on its own terms—from software and steel to cinema and dance music (a big past and the prospect of a big future make it, to my mind, the most fascinating country in the world to visit). Its expansion, moreover, appears more firmly rooted than that of many other developing nations—it has a low foreign debt, a relatively solid banking system, limited dependence on volatile exports and a flexible exchange rate régime.

But if creative chaos rules its economy, a less positive dynamic rules its politics. The conventional wisdom—that India's democracy gives it the political flexibility that China's autocracy does not—has much to it. But that may not continue as the nature of the country's democracy changes. Sociologists do awful things to language, and Ronald Dore with his 'second generation indigenisation thesis' is as guilty as any. But his idea on how countries evolve after their colonisers leave is powerful: in the first generation after independence, elites cleave close to the coloniser's ways; but by the second generation, alien values wane and underlying indigenous values wax. This appears to be happening in India in a number of ways, and not always with positive results. In the decades after independence, India's courts exercised real control over the executive and guarded their own independence jealously. Today it is different. The judiciary has been colonised by politicians and appointments to the bench are too often determined by patronage. The result is less independence, eroding the judiciary's capacity and willingness to oblige government to operate within the law. Political practice and culture are changing too. The retreat of secularism in the face of Hindu nationalism can only breed instability in a country with more Muslims than any other in the world. If a greater role for religion in politics threatens the stability of society, fragmentation and localisation of politics are making governance and administration less effective. Building coalitions, and holding them together, has become far more difficult with the rise of caste-based parties and local and state-focused parties (the outgoing coalition as of April 2009 was composed of more than a dozen parties). The quality and focus of government, at both federal and state level, have suffered as a result.

The ineptitude of the Indian state extends even to its fulfillment of its most basic duty—providing its citizens with security. In late 2008 a handful of terrorists were able to bring Mumbai, the country's commercial capital, to a halt for days despite the full force of the military being deployed against them. The same sort of inefficiency is evident wherever the hand of the state reaches at home—in health, sanitation, education, power generation and transport—and in how India pursues its interests abroad. Its trade diplomacy illustrates this well. India is now one of the big G4 trade powers, along with China, the EU and US. But it is by far the weakest in terms of the strategic coherence of its positions and the technical knowledge of its diplomats. More generally, it is frequently obstructionist in its international positions—be it on trade, human rights or climate change—and one cannot find a single example of it providing the sort of constructive leadership that would support its claims for a seat at the top table. Its political and administrative inefficiency, tiny diplomatic corps and diffused political power structures all hinder the formulation and implementation of a strategically minded foreign policy. Although its sheer size and real economic success will ensure that it is a global player, it is likely to be a long time before India punches up to its economic weight in the world.

It is the (often brutal) effectiveness of the state in China that is its single biggest difference with India. It is inconceivable that a Chinese city would be brought to a standstill by handful of men wielding only light arms and with a few dozen kilos of explosives, as Mumbai was in December 2008. The relative effectiveness of the Chinese state can be seen not only in its security forces, but at almost every level: its infrastructure, though barely existent 30 years ago, has long since overtaken India's in breadth and quality; and educational attainment levels in basic numeracy and literacy are now far ahead. Though attempts at explanation for such differences are fraught, the respective administrative histories of the two countries, more than their current political systems, would seem to explain the relative efficiency of China. Where India before the Raj was fragmented, China's history as a cohesive entity resulted in an administrative culture which can be traced back thousands of years. This becomes clear quickly when one talks to Chinese politicians and officials. In private most are surprisingly frank. More often than not they exude a deep national self-confidence, which, at risk of generalisation, marks them out from all other developing country officials. Their highly developed sense of China as a leading world civilisation (if not the leading civilisation) gives a strategic and historical dimension to their outlook not found elsewhere. They probe, soak up opinions and ideas and are, by and large, unself-defensively willing to discuss their country's problems and failings (with the notable exceptions of Taiwan and Tibet, which trigger an often quite extreme nationalist reflex). On a foundation of the country's economic successes, China's rise to superpowerdom is probably the safest prediction one can make about the 21st century at the current juncture.

But there are no shortage of things that could go wrong. For all China's strengths, it faces about every conceivable economic, political and social problem. Its economic expansion has been centred on low-value-added manufacturing and an artificially low exchange rate. This model has real weaknesses, as the collapse in global trade is now revealing. Big falls in previously soaring asset prices are another vulnerability. Politically, governing thirteen hundred million souls undergoing the most rapid urbanisation in the history of humanity, which is simultaneously generating all manner of social and environmental ills, would stretch any form of government. The country's endemic corruption merely compounds its governance problems. Confiscation of property and evictions from homes are frequent occurrences, not only to create public goods such as roads and parks, but also for officials' private gain. Such abuses of power generate enormous resentments and are among the main reason for tens of thousands of officially documented instances of social disorder annually. To boot, China is riven by ethnic divisions. Although 90% of the country's massive population is Han Chinese, 130 million people are not. That is a lot of people, particularly when they form majorities in 30-40% of the country's remoter territory to the west. Beijing's iron fist may not always reach far enough and punch powerfully enough be able to keep them in line.

These are the knowns. There are unknowns, too. Chinese politics is a black box—not even the most gifted observer, journalist (or spy) has any real idea about its internal workings, who is up and who down, which faction is in the ascendant and which not. Pekinologists watch China much as Kremlinologists once watched the Soviet Union—they depend on speculation, rumour and interpretation of official documents and media statements for messages of intent and direction. Though succession mechanisms appear to have become smoother, with the blistering economic growth of the past three decades set to slow below the level most observers believe necessary to maintain harmony, differences among the elites, as well as among the general population, could well emerge. When such differences have come to the surface in the past, blood has flowed. There is little reason to believe it would be different now.

## DECLINISM, ENDURANCE AND THE INDISPENSABLE NATION
But it is not only the challenges of the developing world that are slowing the diffusion of global power. The enduring strengths of the west, and the absence of the sort of social and political risks faced by much of the developing world, are all too often underestimated or overlooked when the

process of change is considered. Europe's strengths and weaknesses are covered in some depth in the previous two chapters. Discussion of that continent here is, therefore, limited to the opinion that Europe is well placed to maintain a strong role in the world and is likely to manage its slow relative decline as broadly successfully as it has over much of the past century. The US is at least as well placed, despite much hand-wringing that America is falling from global grace. Such fears need to be put in perspective.

All nations with a highly developed sense of themselves tend to suffer crises of confidence when they appear to lag behind others. Britain, France and Europe collectively have all experienced such doubts in recent decades. America specialises in them. In the 1950s and early 1960s, Soviet apparatchiks were the future. Communism would bury capitalism. Paranoia reigned. In the 1970s Vietnam and Watergate rent the country, and to describe the belief in the inevitability of decline as conventional wisdom would be to understate the certainty with which most thinking Americans viewed the future of their country at that time. In the 1980s, Japan was sweeping all before it and Paul Kennedy foresaw the US overstretching to breaking point. After a long rest, from the fall of the Berlin wall to the outbreak of civil war in Iraq, the declinists are back in numbers as the US economy crashes and the country gets its fair share of blame from the rest of the world for its central part in creating the current global recession.

But despite America's many setbacks and domestic weaknesses, its not infrequent misuse and abuse of its power internationally, and the (re-) emergence of Asia, it remains by a distance the world's most powerful and influential country. This will not change soon. Even on the most optimistic forecasts, it will take China two decades to overtake the US as the world's largest national economy. America's preponderance in military affairs—in the size of its defence budget and the sophistication of its hardware—will take any comer even longer to overhaul. And as for the drivers of international influence—from its diplomatic corps to its foreign policy intellectuals to the means to project its values—it is over the horizon from its nearest rivals. The US clearly has the capabilities to lead far into the future. It is also restoring the other vital ingredient for leadership: moral authority. In a few brief months, Barack Obama has undone much of the damage done by his predecessor, in part because of his manner and (limited) policy changes, in part because of who he is not (i.e. George W. Bush), and in part because of who he is—a black man with a foreign father from a politically unconnected family with limited means. For a country with its fair share of racial divisions and a growing tendency for its politics to be dominated by the well-heeled to have elected him does a great deal to prove—to America itself and the rest of the world—what an extraordinary nation it is. How many other countries would have made a man of his profile their leader, or would conceivably do so in future?

In discussing the large developing nations and their future role in the world, an emphasis was placed on the risks they face. A further reason for the likelihood that the west will maintain its global leadership for longer than is often suggested is the risks that it does not face. The US is uniquely free of the sorts of social and political risks that threaten unrest and instability in many countries. If age is any measure of durability, the US constitutional order is by far the world's most durable. Its constitution is among the oldest in world, having been ratified as long ago as 1778. Its enduring success is illustrated by the fact that in over two centuries it has been amended a mere 26 times (some countries have had close to that number of constitutions over two centuries). Federal structures may at times have caused tensions between the states and Washington, D.C., but that system has provided the flexibility for a continent-sized country to function and it is difficult to conceive of any centrifugal force that would threaten the breakup of its union. America has its social tensions, but they are hardly of the kind that could lead to serious and sustained unrest or instability. Despite its diffused power structures and suspicion of big government, the US state can be frighteningly formidable when it girds itself: from building highways and dams to traveling into space to protecting its homeland; and from destroying European fascism and Japanese militarism simultaneously to the patient grinding of communism over decades to enduring in Iraq and learning from its mistakes there. Its politics may be corrupt and distorted by lobbying, but it can take on vested interests when pushed, as it did with the robber barons in the late 19th century, the bankers after the Great Depression and erring corporate executives after Enron (despite much suspicion that the US will resist extensive regulation of finance in the future, it is likely to be at least as tough as any other country in regulating that industry). It has endured depression and war, each time retaining its cohesion and righting itself quickly. Such a country is bound to lead for some time yet.

## THE OCCIDENT'S HOME ADVANTAGE
Slow and gradual change in the global distribution of power is likely not only because the established powers have many enduring strengths and the emerging powers face enormous challenges and risks as they modernise, but also because the functioning and the very nature of the existing inter-

national order favour such an outcome. The institutions of global governance, put in place after the Second World War, were designed and peopled by the western powers. That legacy is still to be seen today. Three of the five permanent members of the UN security council are western. The UN's three headquarters are in New York, Geneva and Vienna. The International Monetary Fund and the World Bank are in Washington, D.C. and their leaders are always from Europe and the US respectively.[12]

Even more deeply, the international system is itself a European construct, and working within one's own system is a formidable advantage, from having an education that suits its functioning to being able to express oneself in one's own language (or one that is linguistically proximate). No country provides a better example of the advantages westerners have from playing on home turf than Japan. It is the only non-western country to have modernised fully. It is the world's second largest economy. And it is leader in science and technology. But despite its achievements, Japan remains a geopolitical pygmy. Its history of aggression in the 1930s and 1940s and its subsequent dependence on the US for its security explain much, but not all, of its dwarfism. The manner of expression, debate and conduct in international affairs leave the Japanese at a disadvantage. Because modesty, restraint and blending in are their way, the Japanese do not schmooze at diplomatic cocktail parties and do not do win arguments and gain influence with soaring rhetoric. It is easy to see why so many people in so much of the world feel the deck is stacked against them. But regardless, these factors that favour the western world will continue to exert an influence in the decades to come, and probably for far longer.

## MESSY MULTIPOLARITY, DISUNITED NATIONS AND THE NEED FOR GLOBAL GOVERNANCE

Managing the global power shift, no matter how gradual, is proving difficult. This is unsurprising. History shows that shifts in power tend to be accompanied by conflict. Those staring at relative decline are defensive and have an interest in slowing change, while the risers are impatient to see their growing economic clout reflected politically and suspect that foot-dragging by the decliners may be, or become, obstructionism. In addition to such problems, which have always made adjustments in relative power prone to conflict, today's changes are complicated by the number and heterogeneity of the participants in the expanding international system. During the bipolar Cold War era there was a single central relationship, but today as the number of players rises, co-ordination becomes ever more problematic.[13] This is to be seen in world trade negotiations. Now 150 states participate in these discussions, far more than in the past, and it is no coincidence that the current round of talks, still far from conclusion in early 2009, after nearly eight years, have lasted longer than any other in the post-Second-World-War era.

The United Nations not only provides another example of how serious the co-ordination problem is in a world of proliferating states, but its functioning provides ample evidence of the practical problems of running international governance institutions. Any bureaucracy whose recruitment and promotion procedures require it to have quotas for all its member countries is sure to be chronically inflexible. Any big organisation that dispenses largesse in great quantity under difficult circumstances will inevitably have a corruption problem. And any entity with ideals as lofty as those of the UN will more than occasionally be let down by staffers who do not live up to those ideals. But for all the UN's faults and problems, if it did not exist, would it be created? This is the first and most basic test of any public institution. The UN passes this test easily (even if many of its institutions and agencies do not) because an interconnected world will always need fora in which states can interact and attempt to reach consensus on security and other issues.

In the short to medium term, the global economic crisis will place huge stresses on all forms of government—national and international. Yet it may also provide the spur to change radically existing mechanisms so that they can deal more effectively with the challenges the world faces. As Auguste Comte observed almost 200 years ago, societies throw up the institutions they need to function effectively. International society is no different. The rapid emergence of the G20 in the months after the eruption of the global financial crisis in late 2008, as a structure to co-ordinate responses to global economic challenges, is almost certainly such an example. The best example, over a much longer time scale and covering a far wider set of issues, is the European integration project—the most effective international governance mechanism thus far invented. Its emergence may well come to be seen in the future as equal in importance to the emergence of the modern state.

If structures and mechanisms of global governance do not widen and deepen, it is difficult to see how the world can function as it has in recent decades. Commerce, climate, crime and contagion require ever more co-operation among states so that the benefits of cross-border interaction can be maximised and its downsides mitigated. Ad hoc co-operation is useful, but coalitions of the willing cannot bear such a load. Rules-based multi-lateral mechanisms provide the only durable solution. Such mechanisms establish rights and obligations, enforce commitments and resolve disputes. As human interaction increasingly extends beyond national borders, rules-based mechanisms must follow suite. If they do not, the world will likely be derailed from its current globalising trajectory.

Even more seriously, without a willingness to deepen some forms of global political integration, humanity's very existence may be imperilled. The ongoing financial and economic collapse is appalling and will result in misery and insecurity for hundreds of millions of the planet's people. But for all its awfulness, it will pass, and recovery will eventually take hold. It is not, therefore, an existential threat to humanity. Climate change is. Environmental catastrophe is a real, if unquantifiable, risk. The only hope of addressing it in any meaningful way is for a global accord, involving a sharing of the burden of adjustment with real enforcement mechanisms. Such an accord has never been agreed before. Its achievement faces near-insurmountable obstacles. Human society's greatest challenge will be to overcome these obstacles. It cannot afford to fail.

> *'In the past, the political fragmentation of mankind has been a great blessing: the multi-state system ensured that the whole of mankind did not ever make the same mistake at the same time. The ecological problem, and the consequences of the development of military technology, may oblige mankind in the future to abandon this 'insurance through political diversification'. Perhaps one can reach a point of least evil by combining world government [], with the maintenance of the maximum possible cultural independence of the constituent units.'*
>
> ERNEST GELLNER

> *'Power is too difficult to assess, and the willingness to vindicate it too various, to permit treating it as a reliable guide to international order. Equilibrium works best if it is buttressed by an agreement on common values. The balance of power inhibits the capacity to overthrow the international order; agreement on shared values inhibits the desire to overthrow the*

*international order. Power without legitimacy tempts*
*tests of strength; legitimacy without power tempts*
*empty posturing.'*

HENRY KISSINGER

'*Without free, self-respecting, and autonomous citi-*
*zens there can be no free and independent nations.*
*Without internal peace, that is, peace among citizens*
*and between the citizens and the state, there can be no*
*guarantee of external peace.'*

VÁCLAV HAVEL

———

## THE BATTLE BETWEEN WAR AND PEACE (BOOK REVIEW)

*8 August 2000*

War is man's natural state and peace decadent. Conflict is dynamising and harmony will-sapping. Such were the beliefs that undergirded the conduct of human affairs until relatively recently. How these ideas have come to be considered barbaric is the central theme of this extended essay by one of Britain's foremost historians. As he approaches his 80th year, Michael Howard sums up a lifetime's thinking in a valedictory volume as thought-provoking as it is slim. In wide-angle, and with a lightness of touch rarely found in historiography, he charts the path to peace in Europe over a millennium and more.

Sir Michael's starting point is the establishment of feudal order after the collapse of imperial Rome. This order, dominated by Christendom's fiercely independent warrior caste, endured well into the Middle Ages. But its feuding aristocrats were weakened by constant fighting—against infidel and each other—and eventually brought to heel by centralising monarchs, whose writ widened with the use of fortress-destroying firearms.

In turn, monarchs gradually ceded power to the middle classes, whose ascent was largely attributable to wealth-creating commercial endeavours. The result was a swelling of the ranks of the educated, non-aristocratic and increasingly secular minority 'aware of the imperfections of their societies as measured by standards of divine or natural justice'. From these minds came a torrent of new thinking about man, God and government. And from the finest of these minds came the invention of peace. Immanuel Kant, a colossus of his enlightening times, believed perpetual peace to be the inevitable end-point of international society.

Kant maintained that this would happen in three steps. First, democracies would become the preferred system of governance throughout the world. This would give those who fight and risk their lives in wars a say in their declaration, thus curbing the belligerent impulses of often remote leaders. Second, as states developed their technologies and economies, the destructiveness of war, and hence its cost, would increase. Man, imperfect but rational, would fight fewer wars as a result. Finally, in order to solidify peace, states would accept the authority of an international body which would adjudicate in disputes, thereby circumventing the need for war.

Most of Howard's historical evidence would seem to support this happy Kantian outcome. But in his concluding chapter, when the author turns his attention to the future, he seems to see an internal contradiction in Kant's theory. He suggests that peace contains the seed of its own destruction, because once it is well established (as it is now in western Europe) the fellow-feeling and common purpose born of collectively facing an enemy is lost. For Howard, it is the shared sacrifice of wartime, more than anything else, that creates the glue that binds societies. Without war, societies, and states along with them, may unravel, leading to what that doom-monger of the 17th century, Thomas Hobbes, considered to be man's ineluctable fate; the anarchy of 'war of all against all'.

Kant may indeed be proved wrong about the inevitability of peace, but it will not be for lack of the camaraderie created by war, as Howard suggests. While the shared experience of life-threatening conflict may be a factor in forging and maintaining national identity, it is hardly more important than all other institutions and values, unrelated to fighting, that cement and give legitimacy to states. Take Sweden. It has remained uninvolved in conflagrations of any sort since 1814, but is among the most cohesive societies in the world, with its national self-image built on civilian achievement and pacific internationalism. Moreover, no country in which individual freedom has been meaningfully realised has ever disintegrated into chaos.

Some questionable conclusions aside, there are insights in spades on matters historical. Howard's conventional account of the emergence of the international state system after the destruction of the Thirty Years' War is deliciously clear and concise. On colonialism, he deftly rubbishes in a single paragraph the reductionist view that Mammon alone was the motive for the subjugation of non-Europeans.

The brushstrokes of a master are also evident in observations on, among others, secularisation, Napoleonic expansion, the rise of nationalism and the factors that led to the 'second Thirty Years' War' of 1914–45. But these are a mere taste of the subjects covered in a book so rich in ideas that it will delight anyone with the slightest interest in how the world has reached its current juncture.

*Originally published in the* Irish Times

———

## JUST WAR PRINCIPLES REMAIN THE BEST GUIDE TO THE USE OF VIOLENCE

*3 March 2006*

The resort to violence is never uncontentious, as ongoing controversies over the 1916 Rising and possible military action against Iran's nuclear programme attest. Helpful in clarifying both cases is the centuries-old just war tradition. Though in all its intricacies it can fill tomes and includes multiple criteria, its essence can be boiled down to two tests: is the use of violence proportionate to the injustice suffered or threatened? and have all other options been exhausted?

Consider first Iran's nuclear ambitions. By just war's two central tests—proportionality and last resort—how does the case for forcibly halting its nuclear programme measure up? The first test requires an evaluation of the extent to which the theocratic state's acquisition of nuclear weapons would increase the prospect of millions of innocent lives being lost in a nuclear holocaust. The risks come less from its often belligerent leadership deploying such weapons—the knowledge that retaliation in kind could in minutes obliterate 5,000 years of Persian civilisation is almost certainly deterrent enough—but from two other sources.

First, the UN's nuclear Non-Proliferation Treaty is fraying. North Korea has breached the treaty and built a bomb. Three non-ratifying countries have already gone nuclear. A review of the treaty's functioning failed last year. If Iran crosses the line the treaty will be a dead letter. The result would be rapid proliferation, centred on the Middle East, a tinderbox region where multiple nuclear hair-triggers could cause a cataclysm.

Even more serious is the risk of 'loose nukes'. The Iranian régime is divided, unstable and domestically unpopular. The risk of nuclear know-how, material, and/or ready-to-deploy bombs making their way into the hands of terrorists via the régime's extreme or rogue elements is consider-able. That risk would multiply if the régime were to collapse—an outcome that is, sooner or later, inevitable. Given the magnitude of this threat, the use of limited military action to destroy Iran's bomb-making capacity would, therefore, pass the proportionality test.

It remains, however, a long way from passing the last-resort test. A process of sanction is about to begin at the UN security council. This will involve a ratcheting up of diplomatic and economic pressure on Iran. To these sticks, a carrot will have to be added. Realpolitik dictates a recogni-tion of Iran's security interests as legitimate, no matter how illegitimate its illiberal and anti-democratic régime. Because the US is the dominant power in the region, it is the only country that can give Iran the security guarantees that might possibly persuade it to step back from the brink. Reluctant though the US is to offer such guarantees, for reasons both good and bad, it will have to do so if military strikes against Iran's nuclear facilities are ever to be justified. And while the matter has inevitably become linked to the conflagration in Iraq (the invasion of which, incidentally, emphatically failed just war tests), its gravity means that the case will ultimately be treated on its own merits.

If the possible resort to military action in the Middle East will top concerns for the international community in the near future, the con-sequences of the use of force in the past continue to have repercussions in Ireland. Again, just war thought helps clarify the issues. First, was resort to violence a proportionate response to the injustices associated with British rule in the early 20th century? Though historians differ on many issues relating to the period, none maintains that there was anything more than minuscule support for a violent response in 1916. This strongly suggests that most people at the time did not believe that the injustices they endured warranted a violent response. (It is often said the subsequent and rapid change in public opinion vindicated the decision to stage the Rising, but the just war tradition excludes retrospective justification as this could allow anyone to use violence and claim the future will vindicate them.)

If the Rising did not pass the proportionality test, it failed the last-resort test by an even wider margin. Those involved had made little effort to convince public opinion that their vision trumped the devolution on offer at the time, even though the many non-violent tactics deployed by their contemporaries—from trade unions to the Suffragettes—were untried. It is unsurprising, therefore, that the organisation most closely involved in refining the just war doctrine over the centuries—the Catholic Church—was among the sternest critics of the 1916 Rising.

*Originally published in the* Irish Times

———

## THE GULF BETWEEN THE IRAQ AND IRAN CRISES

*21 May 2006*

As international tensions mount over Iran's nuclear programme, there has been much superficial comment about recent history in Iraq repeating itself. But the fundamentals driving this crisis are as profoundly different as the conduct of the main players. The outcome, too, will be different.

First, the fundamentals. Those countries that opposed war with Saddam certainly believed him to be a threat to regional security. But, crucially, they believed that the threat he posed was containable. It was for this reason that they believed war an excessive response. The nature and magnitude of the Iranian threat is entirely different. Iran has an advanced nuclear power programme, and its claims that this is for purely peaceful purposes are no longer believed by anyone. It is now moving towards becoming an uncontainable threat. So grave is the matter, and so repeated Iranian transgressions, that the UN's 35-member nuclear watchdog gave up trying to make it comply with its commitments earlier in the year and sent the matter upstairs to its highest authority, the security council.

The manner in which Iran conducts itself is also very different from the Iraqi dictatorship. Iranians are infinitely more skilful and subtle in statecraft than Saddam's ham-fisted and fear-stricken minions. These skills mean that the Iranians are far less likely to make the sort of miscalculation that caused Saddam to believe he would not be overthrown.

Another factor making this crisis different from that of Iraq is that the conduct of the other main actors has, for different reasons, changed since the US-led invasion. The Europeans are at one in how they view the Iranian nuclear threat, in stark contrast to their different assessments of Saddam's capacity for menace. This can be seen in their cohesion in dealing with the matter. The smaller EU members have been (unusually) willing to let the big three—France, Germany and the UK—take the lead in mounting the bloc's most concerted common diplomatic effort ever.

us conduct now and then is even more different. It has reverted to the more conventional approach of doing business, using multiple means and exercising a tactical flexibility absent in the run-up to the Iraq war. But that is not to say that Americans have converted to pacificism. The us deems the threat to its security of a nuclear armed Iran unacceptable. It will take whatever measures necessary—including the resort to force—to prevent such an outcome, even if the consequences in the region would probably be appalling. In short, if it boils down to a choice between the unacceptable and the appalling, the latter will win out, as it always must.

There is yet another difference between the current crisis and Iraq. If it does come to war, the nature of the conflict will be more similar to the first Iraq war (in 1991) than the second. A targeted attack to knock out nuclear facilities would be the (limited) objective, rather than régime change, not least because post-2003 Iraq has disabused all but the most ardent ideologues of the belief that stable democracies can be socially engineered.

Mercifully, though, conflagration is still some way off and diplomacy could still triumph. The Europeans continue to plug away doggedly. They offered Iran yet another package of incentives this week. But, yet again, this was spurned, and the Euro route looks all but at an end.

Sanctions are now looking increasingly likely, even if agreeing a régime will not be straightforward. Russia is the pivotal power here, but it is hard to predict how it will behave. In the four years since the build up to the Iraq war began, the former superpower has changed. Emboldened by the clout its huge energy resources are giving it, it is asserting itself more aggressively in international affairs and is at pains to make sure no one takes its support for anything for granted. This new-found assertiveness has already seen the thwarting of efforts at the security council to agree a sanctions régime, and if it does so again, focus on bilateral relations between the us and Iran will intensify.

Increasingly it appears that a 'grand bargain' between the two offers the only real prospect of a solution. This would involve, at its core, Iran giving verifiable guarantees about its nuclear programme in return for the us giving the Islamic Republic commitments on regional security. However rational a solution this appears, lamentably it may not be achievable.

*Originally published in the* Sunday Tribune

# THE MIDDLE EAST'S UNENDING CONFLICT

*20 August 2006*

'Abandon all hope ye who enter here' was Dante's bleak warning to those descending into the seven circles of Hell. It is hard not to think of his *Inferno* when considering the Middle East today. For those unlucky enough to inhabit the region the future holds the prospect of continued conflict with little hope of a better life. For those sitting far from the firing line, future events in the Middle East are likely to have inescapable implications for security and economic wellbeing.

A good starting point for thinking about the region's outlook is the Levant, where dust began settling this week after a month of violence. Although the loss of life was tragic, this should not obscure the fact that the conflict was little more than a protracted border skirmish. Nor should it obscure the region's bigger issues, a perennial danger when Israel is involved because of the tendency of both its critics and defenders to over-state the significance of the Jewish state's existence and conduct in the region.

Panning out from the hotspot in Lebanon and northern Israel allows a wider view. The vista that comes into focus is as unpleasant as it is messy. The region has many serious political, security and diplomatic issues playing out simultaneously on many levels. To say that fear, suspicion, resentment and ancient hatreds inform the posture of the players towards each other is an understatement. It is a statement of the obvious that these players pursue multiple priorities: power, security, honour and the avoidance of humiliation. Peace may also be an objective, but, crucially, it is only one among many and certainly not the overriding goal. (This latter point, however obvious, is often forgotten by outsiders involving themselves in the region. They tend quickly and bloodily to be reminded of it after they have waded in.)

Adding to complexity is the nature of the region's régimes, which range from resolute secularists to Islamist theocrats, and its ethno-religious breakdown: Shia, Sunni, Arab, Jew, Turk and Persian. Adding to the region's fragility are almost infinite internal divisions. Minorities abound: Kurds in Turkey, Iraq and Iran; Copts in Egypt; a *mélange* of groupings in Syria; a 50:50 split in Jordan between Bedouin and Palestinian Arab; and Lebanon's patchwork of frequently warring communities.

Régimes survive by using varying degrees of repression against these groupings. The maintenance of order through fear (never conducive to creating a stable equilibrium) also means that states are doubly militarised, once to face external threats, and again to quell domestic unrest. All of this makes the dynamic in the Middle East today akin to Europe in the aftermath of the wars of religion, with a large dash of 19th-century nationalism added to make the cocktail all the more combustible. And as in Europe before peace and prosperity became the shared and overriding objective of states, a grand, solve-it-all conference in the region, as some are advocating, would be doomed to fail.

Understanding the limitations of what is achievable and prioritising objectives is crucial to containing conflict in the region and limiting spillover into the rest of the world. Top of the list of priorities is Iran's attempts at acquiring nuclear weapons. Persian imperial ambition has a long history. It now threatens the balance of power in the region and, it is worth noting, this causes far more alarm among the other big players—Turkey, Saudi Arabia and Egypt—than anything Israel does, including its excessive use of force against their coreligionists.

But because nuclear proliferation has a global security dimension the rest of the world is also involved. As the world's leading power, the US will inevitably be central to this crisis. No one else can play the role of global policeman, as it does in Europe and Asia—from the Aegean to the Taiwan Straits, a big American stick and soft voice keep conflict at bay and contain rivalries.

The US once played such a calming role in the Middle East. From the Suez crisis 50 years ago to the first Gulf War, the US slapped down aggressors and underpinned some semblance of order. But stability and democracy are now wrongly viewed as conflicting goals by many in the US administration. Miscalculation made on the basis of this thinking has reduced the US's capacity to supply global security by undermining the two things it needs to lead—moral authority and military capability.

Failure in Iraq has hugely weakened its moral authority and overstretched its armed forces, limiting the credibility of its position on Iran. There is a growing risk that the Islamic Republic will make its own miscalculation by underestimating the seriousness of American intent. This would be a grave error. The US believes that a nuclear-armed Iran would increase the threat of nuclear terrorism and trigger global proliferation. It appears ready to do whatever it takes to prevent such an outcome.

The chances that the stand-off will end in military intervention are rising. The implications of this are profoundly serious: death on a large scale; more Islamist terrorism; and a real risk that oil prices well above

$100 a barrel for a protracted period could cause global recession, adding tens of millions to the ranks of the jobless.

*Originally published in the* Sunday Tribune

———

## STRANGLE FINANCE TO SAVE CAPITALISM

*21 December 2008*

It is now clear that the global economy is in recession. It is probable that the downturn will be deeper and more protracted than any slump in living memory. It is possible that recession could turn to depression. These awful realities, and the even more awful risks, are the result of the failure of the global financial system as it has operated in recent decades.

The broad, if imperfect, consensus that had existed on the efficient and stable functioning of the international financial system—among governments, policy-makers, bankers, financiers, market participants and economists—has been proved wrong. This consensus was based on a belief that the world could sustain historically high levels of debt because sophisticated institutions using sophisticated models could price risk accurately and spread it in such a way that it posed no overall systemic risk. The consensus appeared until recently to be supported by three developments over three decades of economic history.

First, since the early 1980s, world economic growth has been strong and increasingly spread across almost all of the planet. Second, many financial crises had little or no impact on the real economy, such as the market crash of 1987 and the collapse of the hedge fund, Long Term Capital Management, in 1998. Third, when economic and financial crises did occur, most countries suffering them rebounded quickly. When the dotcom bubble burst in the early part of this decade, the downturn proved relatively mild and the countries which bounced back fastest—the US and UK included—were the ones with the most sophisticated financial systems. Those economies that did suffer profound financial crises—Mexico, a string of east Asian countries, Russia and Argentina—all recovered relatively rapidly to return to high rates of economic growth.

The consensus was strengthened by the benefits generated by financial innovation, such as securitisation at the wholesale level which allowed financial institutions to reduce risk by diversifying the asset side of their balance sheets; hedging products at a corporate level which allowed businesses greater certainty in dealing with trading risks; and equity extraction at a retail level which allowed income-poor individuals to live more comfortably while retaining their homes. It goes almost without saying that the consensus was also actively supported by the great many people who made a great deal of money in the financial services industry.

But it is now increasingly clear that innovations in the sector (they can be grouped into three broad and interconnected forms—changes in the business models of commercial banks, the rise of new kinds of financial firms and the proliferation of new financial products) have generated far greater costs than benefits.

An estimated $1.4 trillion has been lost as a result of the first wave of the crisis associated with the US mortgage market. A second wave of losses is now rippling out across the system since banks and institutions started to fail in large numbers three months ago. A third and probably larger wave will break over the course of 2009 as the effects of the financial crisis cause business and individual bankruptcies to rise across the world. Taxpayers' everywhere are picking up the tab. They will continue to pay the price for years, if not decades to come.

If the current catastrophe is a global system failure, rather than a run-of-the-mill banking crisis, the implications are enormous. In the medium term, and perhaps even longer term, the world will undergo a period of deleveraging to bring credit levels back down to a point at which they are sustainable. The best policy-makers can aim for in this context is that the unwinding is gradual and orderly to allow some new lending. The avoidance of drastic deleveraging is imperative so that a depression can be avoided. The coming Great Deleveraging will have the biggest impact on those countries where the innovations mentioned above were most advanced.

A second conclusion that seems increasingly inevitable from recent events is that the financial services industry as it currently exists simply cannot be regulated effectively. No increases in regulatory resources and manpower, no matter how great, could possibly match those of the financial sector. Regulators are condemned to remain many steps behind those who are usually smarter and better educated, vastly better incentivised and far greater in number than the civil servants who attempt to regulate them. (The same point, incidentally, extends to credit rating agencies, which cannot hope to evaluate effectively the vast number of instruments that they now rate).

If one accepts that the costs and risks of the sort of financial innovation seen in recent year are unacceptably high and that regulating it is impossible, the inescapable conclusion is that some kinds of activities and products must be outlawed, and that the onus shifts to institutions to prove that innovations are safe before being brought to market (the pharmaceutical industry could be a model).

For anyone with a liberal bone in his body, banning people from doing things goes against the grain and can only be a last resort. But we are now at that point. The financial system has foisted recession on the rest of the well-functioning market economy. Internationally, the chances of a protectionist backlash against free trade and investment are almost certain to grow. Domestically, opponents of business and markets see an opportunity to stamp on free enterprise. The conclusion seems unavoidable: strangle finance to save capitalism.

*Originally published in the* Sunday Business Post

 

 

——

## THE FINANCIAL CRISIS IS AN EARTHQUAKE, NOT A STORM

*22 January 2009*

The gravity of the crisis in global finance cannot be overstated. It can, however, be mis-described, as frequent allusions to storms attest. For analogies, it is to geology, not meteorology, that we must look in order to understand what is happening. Tectonic movements are now taking place in international finance. These shifts are causing the global economic landscape to change. Most obviously, the financial services industry itself is in a state of collapse. The contraction of a major economic sector is having, and will continue to have, a direct impact on employment and output. A second and even more important change for the wider economy is that this collapse precludes a return to 'normal' bank lending. It is understandable that businesses and consumers, many of whom are in difficult and even desperate situations, clamour for the normality that they have come to know. But any hope of this is forlorn. Banks' loan books will now shrink. This very painful process must take place if the threat finance poses to prosperity is to be contained.

What can any government do at this time of acute crisis? At the risk of over-extending the metaphor, it is helpful again to think of violent geological change. Formulating and implementing a policy response to the financial crisis is akin to trying to traverse a landscape undergoing an earthquake: the ground underfoot is unstable, reference points are moving and chasms are opening up. The extreme difficulty of attempting to respond is evident from the lack of successes in any country in restoring some semblance of stability. Despite the many policy measures put in place across the world, not a single country can claim to have succeeded in placing its financial system on a firm footing. Developments over the past week in three of the world's largest economies illustrate this.

The US's Troubled Asset Relief Programme, which has been changed almost on a weekly basis since it was set up in the autumn, is proving ineffective, as the continuing, slow-motion implosion of two financial services behemoths—Bank of America and Citibank—demonstrates all too clearly. When Britain rolled out its recapitalisation scheme in October it was hailed as a model for others. Within weeks that view was held by no one. One Monday morning, a second round of capital injections was announced and more taxpayers' money will almost certainly be poured into the system in the weeks and months ahead. Germany, with its large state-owned banking sector and absence of any domestic credit boom, has fared little better than the countries whose banks were at the root of the problems. Last week its second largest bank, Commerzbank, required a second messy infusion of public money to avoid collapse and a string of other banks are negotiating the terms of life saving capital injections.

These examples, and many others, demonstrate that there is no road map to be followed that would allow a way out of the earthquake zone, never mind a definite set of policy measures that would halt the tectonic movements themselves. Under the circumstances, policy-makers are limited to trying to mitigate the effects. They must make up responses as they go along. Flexibility and creativity are indispensable. For those of us who comment from high perches in the media or academia it is necessary to acknowledge the enormity of the challenges facing those who have to make the hard calls.

The Irish government deserves excoriation for its economic mis-management and complacency over many years. There are also questions about what precisely were all the reasons behind the government's decision to nationalise Anglo Irish Bank. But all that said, and on balance, the decision was the lesser of two great evils. To see why, we must look beyond Ireland's shores. In September some of the finest minds in the world of economics judged that the investment bank Lehman Brothers was not systemically important and could be allowed to fail. To say that that judgment has been proved wrong does not begin to describe a decision which may come to be seen as triggering a second Great Depression.

Given the impossibility of untangling banks' connections with each other, the effects of the collapse of a bank on the rest of the financial system are unknowable to anyone. Aware of this, policy-makers everywhere have since avoided taking chances and propped up all financial institutions. Not a single bank anywhere has been allowed to fail. A second reason that may have influenced the government in its decision to nationalise Anglo Irish Bank was the possible international effects of allowing the bank to collapse.

In these pages on Tuesday, UCD's Morgan Kelly proffered the view that Anglo Irish Bank's bondholders, who are mostly foreign, and the insurers of those bonds (likely to be overwhelmingly foreign), should be made take the hit for the bank's recklessness and the regulatory failures of the Irish authorities. While it is very tempting to agree, other countries' governments might well have differed—recall how Britain reacted when it believed its citizens were victims of Iceland's blunders.

In addition, given that the value of the insurance contracts taken out on those bonds, in the form of credit default swaps, is likely to be in multiples of their value (because the market for those products is wildly out of control), it is perfectly possible that default of those bonds could have caused new fissures to open in the extremely fragile international financial system. Could Ireland afford to be seen as a country adding to the crisis rather than taking its responsibilities seriously? Hardly. And all the more so because soon the country may need others' solidarity. The Irish economy is moving rapidly towards the abyss. It may even be too late for any domestic action to prevent it going over the edge. If this proves to be the case, Ireland will require all the help it can get from others.

*Originally published in the* Irish Times

—

# MODERN DEMOCRACY'S ELECTORAL DYNAMICS

*7 July 2006*

The world is shrinking. The same trends—social, technological, political and economic—are increasingly at play in every country. While every democracy's politics still has unique features, the big issues are increasingly similar. So, too, is the manner in which these are presented and debated. Nowhere is this more the case than in western Europe's mature democracies. In our calm corner of the world, war among neighbours is all but inconceivable and the big, divisive social and constitutional issues are mostly settled. This is the age of the politics of contentment. The reasons for its rise and the features of its conduct are many and varied.

**The growing middle-class majority:** The established democracies have enjoyed 60 years of rising prosperity, improving access to education and widening opportunities. During this time class divisions have blurred to the point of meaninglessness and a growing majority of voters have come to share the same characteristics, aspirations and concerns. They have a stake in stability and the status quo, seek gradual improvements and are suspicious of grand schemes and visions. The expanding middle-class majority is sophisticated and assertive. Its members are demanding and increasingly promiscuous in their political choices, being less loyal to political parties, less inclined to vote for them and far less likely to join them.

**The listening imperative:** Political parties have had to adapt to voters' changing tastes and interests. Despite the current faddish obsession with leadership, modern politicians need to be better at listening than leading. This is very different from the paternalistic past when stern, detached and aloof father-figures were trusted to know what was best. Today's voters demand deference and humility from politicians, not vice versa, and want their elected representatives to reflect their values, aspirations and lifestyles and be capable of articulating and amplifying what they think, believe and want. If statesmanship remains an appealing characteristic in a politician, being a man of the people is now far more likely to win votes.

**The feminisation of politics:** Today there is no country in western Europe in which public services have not come to dominate elections. This has changed the characteristics and skill sets that make for success in politics. While politicians continue to need to show toughness and resolve, projecting power and strength is less important today as the focus of government has moved away from the provision of physical security (as wars and civil strife have become rarer) and towards provision of services (as greater wealth exists to pay for them). Child care, health care and care of the elderly are major issues everywhere. A politician who cannot demonstrate a strong caring capacity—a virtue traditionally associated with women—will not go far today.

**It's about more than the economy, stupid:** It is no coincidence that the by-now hackneyed phrase 'it's the economy, stupid' was coined in the US. There, the state is far less involved in the provision of services than in

Europe. On this side of the Atlantic, sound economic management is, of course, a central issue, but not quite as dominating. Recent elections across the continent illustrate this—in Norway and Greece parties who presided over strong economies were voted out of office, while those who oversaw slumps in Germany and Italy were not given the routing they might have expected.

**The end of ideology:** In the realm of ideas nothing has changed politics more than the end of old-style left–right ideology. The failures of state-centred socialism and the limits of the market in providing social services and economic stability are accepted by the moderate majority. There is no longer any serious intellectual debate about the need for both efficient markets and an effective state to make societies successful. To a considerable extent the new pragmatism is nothing more than political parties catching up with ordinary folk—the majority never concerned itself much with ideology and has always been perfectly happy to hold left- and right-wing views simultaneously.

But old mindsets linger. While the thinking left has abandoned its prejudices against profit, business and the rich and its counterpart on the right has given up its visceral hostility towards welfarism and state inter-vention, many political activists still cling to the old ways and past obsessions. This has thrown up one of the quirks of modern politics—political parties are becoming less representative of wider society and party leaders spend nearly as much time winning over their members as they do winning votes.

**The rise and rise of evidence-based policy-making:** One of the con-sequences of the end of ideology (as well as being one of the reasons for its demise) is a shift towards formulating policy on the basis of evidence about what works. On health, education, transport and crime, policy formulation has never been so sophisticated. Think tanks, academic institutions and international organisations, peopled by ever more specialised policy experts, are increasingly the sources of solutions to the problems of modern society. The internationalisation of thinking on policy continues apace.

**The phenomenon of rational ignorance:** There are downsides to the more scientific approach to policy-making. It is esoteric, detailed and very complex. Evaluation of policies requires a degree of expertise that even today's educated voters don't have. Moreover, in a world where people are choice-rich and time-poor, voters are understandably reluctant to devote hours to the study and evaluation of alternative policies which usually differ more in nuance than substance. As differences are small and because the cost in time and energy of fully informing oneself is so onerous, the pay-off for earnest study of manifestos is limited. Voters with busy lives thus behave rationally by remaining ignorant. This phenomenon of 'rational ignorance' is perhaps the central concept in understanding how voters choose parties and how parties target voters today.

**The centrality of spin:** Rational ignorance leaves voters needing short cuts to weighing up their options at election time. Though 'spin' is often derided, it is really just effective and informative packaging and labelling—a means of communicating succinctly and concisely what parties are offering voters. But it does not only inform about specific policies. Even more importantly it has become a proxy for measuring political parties' general ability and competence. Voters calculate that if a party is not adept enough to sell itself and its ideas effectively, it is probably incapable of governing effectively. In modern politics, he who can't spin, or does so ineptly, is doomed to perpetual opposition.

**The gauging of the zeitgeist:** In order to generate ideas that appeal to voters and sell themselves effectively, political parties need to gauge the collective mood at any given time and understand as precisely as possible what people want of government and the state. While intuitively interpreting the zeitgeist remains the essential art of politics, a more scientific approach to understanding voters' hearts and minds is evolving rapidly. Focus groups and detailed and extensive polling have become indispensable tools of political parties.

The politics of contentment is well established in Ireland and next year's election will share many of the features of contests in other democracies. And, as is the case elsewhere, those who can best gauge what voters want and prove their competence in providing it are likely to come out on top.

*Originally published in the* Irish Times

———

# LOW-KEY BAN KI-MOON COULD REDEEM UN

*7 July 2007*

The job of UN secretary general is among the world's most prestigious. It is also one of its hardest. Ban Ki-moon, the Korean diplomat who replaced Kofi Annan at the UN's helm at the beginning of the year, knew this when he campaigned for the post. Speaking in London on Wednesday, he gave no indication that his first half-year as the world's highest-ranking civil servant has caused him to think otherwise.

How has he measured up to his new role? Ban's early days in the job did not inspire confidence. In the words of one senior security council diplomat, he hit the ground stumbling. His unceremonious clear-out of Annan's top layer of officials suggested that he lacked people skills. His appointment of an unknown as his deputy raised questions about his managerial abilities. His familiarity with policy was thrown into doubt within days of his taking office when he said that the death penalty should be a matter for individual member countries, contradicting his predecessors' position.

His first weeks did nothing to endear him to UN staffers. Unlike Annan, he is not one of their own, coming from the Korean civil service, not the UN family. He is neither as charismatic nor as cosmopolitan as his predecessor—he does not electrify with his oratory and his claim to fluency in French was embarrassingly exposed early on at a press conference. Because it was Asia's turn for the top job, some cruelly claimed that he would not have been appointed if a wider pool of non-Asian candidates had been eligible.

But not all insiders' criticisms are valid. For many on long-term UN contracts his decision to push ahead with a plan to rotate staff more frequently has caused self-serving grumbling by too-cosy officials. Moving staff around is among the most effective ways of limiting opportunities for graft, and that is sorely needed following a series of scandals in recent years that have badly damaged the organisation. If the UN is to have any chance of avoiding scandal in the future, the corrupt and incompetent will have to be leveraged out of their comfort zones.

If his manner of handling internal UN matters has not always been smooth, he has been more sure-footed with those who really count: the member countries (there are, de facto, two UNs: Ban's relatively powerless institutions and the intergovernmental forums—such as the security council—where the real clout is wielded). Humble and modest in his ambitions, he understands the limitations of the job, which is crucial if he is to have any genuine sway over the members, particularly when dealing with the planet's trouble spots.

Of the most pressing security issues in the world today, Ban has prioritised the one where he is most likely to have an influence—the continuing genocide in Darfur. He has gently pushed the Sudanese government to accept the intervention of a hybrid force of UN and African Union peacekeepers, while at the same time avoiding any falling-out with China, its protector on the security council. He has also managed to raise the $1.5 billion needed to pay for the peacekeepers' deployment.

If a criticism can be levelled at him in his dealings with the great powers it is that he has been too timid. Although this may be more to do with the fact he is still finding his feet, some have detected excessive deference towards the big boys. On this charge, Exhibit A for the prosecution is the resignation of Alvaro de Soto, the UN's point man on the Israeli–Palestinian conflict. De Soto's leaked end-of-mission report suggested that Ban was less than impartial in dealing with the parties because he was too ready to bend to the will of the US, Israel's protector on the security council.

If dealing with governments externally and staff internally is tricky enough, effecting change when both the institutions and member countries are involved is even more difficult. This is the case on reform of the UN's basic structures. With 192 members keeping a hawk eye on their position in the pecking order, a proposal to make even the slightest change is guaranteed to generate controversy. Nowhere is this more obvious than in the unending debate over reform of the UN's most important body, the security council.

Its composition is woefully outdated, reflecting the global distribution of power in the first half of the 20th century. Most egregious is Europe's over-representation. Britain and France, with 120 million citizens between them, have two of the five permanent seats. India, Africa and Latin America, whose combined population is 22 times greater, have not one. Unsurprisingly, such an imbalance undermines the legitimacy of the body, particularly among the G77, the increasingly assertive bloc of 132 developing-world nations.

But no matter how justifiable a change would be, the 'permanent five' are not about to dilute their own influence by making real change. Ban recognises this and has wisely avoided pushing a position on security council reform. Instead, he has dedicated himself to more achievable ambitions, already succeeding in splitting the secretariat's peacekeeping division into operational and logistical units. Although such a change may seem piffling to outsiders and will certainly not bring heaven to earth, by UN standards it is a considerable achievement, and most agree that it was a sensible move, particularly given how overstretched it had become.

Though it is much too early to say how Ban will compare with his predecessors, he is likely to be a safe pair of hands at the very least. He could be much more if he plays his hand well because trends in world affairs give reason to believe that the challenges to be faced in the future will increasingly require his organisation to solve them. To say that a globalising world needs ever more globalised solutions is beyond cliché. But that makes it no less true. A shrinking world is throwing up more transnational challenges—global climate change, diseases spreading more rapidly across borders, increased competition for natural resources, nuclear proliferation, international terrorism, people-trafficking and many more besides. If Ban avoids damaging clashes with the big powers, chooses his battles carefully and continues with his patient persuasion, the UN could become more indispensable than it has ever been.

*Originally published in the* Irish Times

# NOTES

## Chapter 1 (pp 1–49)

1. Canvassing is far less common in democracies with electoral systems based on national lists.
2. Malta uses the same system, but as only two parties ever win seats and the threat of independents is non-existent, it produces outcomes far closer to a first-past-the-post system.
3. The weakness of the electoral system is exacerbated by the very unusual constitutional requirement that all ministers be members of the Oireachtas, shrinking the pool from which ministerial talent can be drawn.
4. See: http://www.irishtimes.com/newspaper/opinion/2008/1230/1230581467055.html
5. One frequently hears comment to the effect that Irish politics is a blood sport. Anyone who says this is unfamiliar with politics elsewhere. I know of no other country where politics is as genteel.
6. See: http://www.oecd.org/dataoecd/37/59/40192107.pdf
7. See: http://www.eurofound.europa.eu/areas/qualityoflife/eurlife/index.php?template=3&radioindic=54&idDomain=5
8. See: http://www.eurofound.europa.eu/areas/qualityoflife/eurlife/index.php?template=3&radioindic=69&idDomain=6
9. Some powerful intellects, such as historian Roy Foster, sociologist Tom Inglis and commentator David McWilliams mentioned the index in subsequent books. None offered any evaluation.
10. See: http://www.irishtimes.com/newspaper/weekend/2000/0617/00061700218.html
11. See: http://epp.eurostat.ec.europa.eu/cache/ITY_OFFPUB/KS-QA-08-046/EN/KS-QA-08-046-EN.PDF
12. See: http://www.rightscom.com/Portals/0/European%20Book%20Publishing%20Report.pdf
13. Respondents had lower levels of knowledge about the EU in only four of the 15 long standing members, according to the Spring 2008 Eurobarometer survey. http://ec.europa.eu/public_opinion/archives/eb/eb69/eb_69_first_en.pdf
14. See 'Society and political culture' in *Politics in the Republic of Ireland,* 4th edition, Eds John Coakley and Michael Gallagher.
15. See Chapter 11 for further discussion.

16. It is not for want of press freedom. Reporters Sans Frontières ranks Ireland as having among the highest standards of press freedom in the world according to its 'Worldwide Press Freedom Index'.

17. One could argue that this insularity was advantageous in this case as it prevented the importation of anti-democratic ideas, of which there were so many in the 20th century.

18. The murder rate in Ireland was 55th out of 62 countries surveyed, according to the seventh United Nations Survey of Crime Trends and Operations of Criminal Justice Systems, covering the period 1998–2000 (United Nations Office on Drugs and Crime, Centre for International Crime Prevention).

19. See: http://www.homeoffice.gov.uk/rds/pdfs2/r188.pdf

20. See: http://www.driveandstayalive.com/info%20section/statistics/multi-country _death-rates_1988-2001.htm

21. According to Friedrich Schneider and Christopher Bajada, the Irish black economy was smaller than the average among 21 OECD countries and far below the global average. See 'An International Comparison of Underground Economic Activity', in *Size, Causes and Consequences of the Underground Economy*, edited by the same authors.

22. When adjusted for income, Irish giving came second only to the US among a group of 12 countries, according to the Charities Aid Foundation. See page 13, http://www.cafonline.org/pdf/International%20%20Giving%20highlights.pdf

## Chapter II (pp 50–102)

1. Of 25–34 years-olds, 55% of Canadians have a third-level qualification, 54% of Japanese, 53% of South Koreans and 44% of New Zealanders, according to the OECD's 'Education at a glance, 2008'. The data are for 2006.

2. The longer Ireland's recession lasts compared to the rest of the world, the greater these leakeages will be. This is but one of many reasons why front-loading all necessary reform measures is desirable.

3. Source: OECD online database.

4. Data sources on FDI are difficult to work with. There are many methodological issues too technical to delay even readers of footnotes. It suffices to say that balance of payments data include merger and acquisition activity, which does not have the same additionality for an economy as 'greenfield' projects of the kind Ireland has become well known for. The source for the data cited is UNCTAD's World Investment Report, 2008.

5. The numbers from 2003 to 2007 inclusive are 136, 130, 196, 146, 114. In 2008, there were 130 new projects according to IDA Ireland (UNCTAD's data are sourced from IDA Ireland).

6. The data here and in the following two paragraphs come from Forfás's 'Annual Business Survey of Economic Impact'. My thanks to Andrew Stockman and Debbie Quinn at the agency for providing the data in user-friendly format at short notice.

7. Foreign companies' services exports grew by 78% between 2000 and 2007, to reach just under €30 billion.
8. OECD, 'Main Science and Technology Indicators, 2008'.
9. Source: Forfás, 'Research and Development Performance in the Business Sector in Ireland, 2005/06'.
10. OECD, 'Main Science and Technology Indicators, 2008'.
11. See table 6, 'Building for the Future? Interpreting an "Irish" Current Account Deficit', Martin O'Brien, Economic and Social Research Institute, Quarterly Economic Commentary, Winter 2007.
12. Some readers might point to the Global Entrepreneurship Monitor, compiled by a network of academics, which finds that Irish people are among the most entrepreneurial in the world. But valuable and all as this report is, its findings are impossible to tally with the best single measure of success for companies in a small open economy: exports.
13. Export growth in nominal terms was 30% and 48% respectively.
14. Eurostat data on housing stock relative to population have been interpreted to show that Ireland is underhoused. The relevant figure for gauging oversupply is the stock of housing relative to the number of households (not the number of people). Using 2007 Eurostat data on housing stock and 2001 UN data on household size, which show Irish household size to be the biggest in western Europe, my rough calculations suggest that are approximately 1,260 houses in Ireland per 1,000 households, compared to an EU-13 average of 1,200.
15. Such politicisation could widen and become even more damaging. Consider FDI. Heretofore, the political class has not succumbed to the temptation to exert undue pressure on the IDA to channel jobs-rich investment to politically preferred locations. Given the gravity of the employment crisis and the very large declines in support for the party currently leading the governing coalition, how long before that boundary is crossed?
16. At time of writing, in May 2009, it is impossible to assess the handling of the banking crisis. The central question is the extent to which the cost is distributed between those whose business decisions proved incorrect (property developers and, ultimately, bank shareholders and bondholders) and the taxpayer. It will be years before that question can be answered definitively.
17. Those of us in the economic forecasting business have not had a good crisis. I will candidly admit that I did not for a moment think the international financial system would collapse as it has. That said, and for the record, I did highlight domestic and external risks, for instance during a TV debate in April 2006 with Seán Fleming TD, chairman of the Oireachtas finance committee. Readers, with the benefit of hindsight, can judge my before-the-fact analysis for themselves. It can be viewed via the following link: http://www.rte.ie/news/2006/0413/primetime.html
18. Germany has both, as successful consolidation up to 2008 demonstrated. Britain has one, but not the other. Its public finances rules in recent decades

have incorporated the best economic thinking, but the political will to maintain sound finances was absent after 2001.

19. In order not to appear to be wise after the fact, it is necessary here to make reference to past writings. In an article as long ago as August 2006 ('Fiscal ineptitude carries costs', page 82) I set out how comparatively badly Ireland's public finances were managed and stated that Ireland risked a return to 1980s-type fiscal chaos.

20. In mid-2007, the European Commission published its annual 'The Public Finances in EMU' report. The report contained an index aimed at measuring the quality of public finances management. By a distance, Ireland came last among the 18 EU countries measured. On the sub-index covering prudence, the Commission officials could find not a single measure in place that would protect the public finances from crisis.

21. Adoption of the euro took place with little understanding or appreciation among the political class that effort had to be made to minimise the risks of 'asymmetric shocks', that is, changes in economic conditions felt in one part of the currency union but not in others. Without interest rates and a currency, fiscal policy becomes the only macroeconomic lever to cushion a shock of this kind. Fiscal policy in Ireland since 2008 has been less of a cushion and more of a spike on which the economy has been impaled. The comparison with Finland is stark. It is most similar to Ireland within the euro zone in economic size and structure. The downsides of the euro were at the forefront of Finnish minds at the time of joining the currency and have remained there since. The country is riding out the current crisis relatively well.

22. Cited in the National Competitiveness Council's 'Annual Competiveness Report', Volume I, 2009.

23. *Ibid.*

24. This absence of proactivism is bad, and its costs are likely to rise in the future as the importance of smart government grows. But there is also a positive flip side to lacklustre leadership—the absence of excessive and meddling activism. The costs of too much government can be seen elsewhere. Over the decades, many continental European countries made their labour markets too inflexible and committed to universal pensions at high levels. The results respectively have been persistently high levels of unemployment even during boom years and unsustainable fiscal implications of too-generous pensions. Reforming these areas of policy has proved enormously difficult for the countries concerned. Ireland avoided both errors. Many other countries also heaped red tape on businesses, where Ireland has been more cautious, as the World Bank's *Doing Business* database attests. This is one reason why Ireland remains a good place to operate.

25. The number of public servants as a percentage of total employment is below the OECD average in Ireland. Thus, talk of a 'bloated' public service is not accurate on this level. Between 1995 and 2007, the number of state employees

rose by 30%, while the population increased by 21%. Nominal general government spending increased by 224% in the 12 years from 1995. This compares with 55% across the euro zone in the aggregate. The Irish public sector has been infused with increases in resources greater than 28 of the 30-member OECD.

## Chapter III (pp 103–50)

1. The decline in conflict and violence, and the reasons for this trend, are discussed in Chapter VI.
2. Source: Economist Intelligence Unit, *Countrydata*.
3. It should be added that wider changes in international affairs were also relevant. With the ending of the Cold War, the over-riding priority for the US of containing the Soviet Union disappeared. This allowed space on its agenda for other priorities, including those which risked irking allies. This is exactly what happened in relation to Northern Ireland, when the US intervened despite British protestations. It is very unlikely that the US would have involved itself in what Britain considered to be its internal affairs if the Cold War had not ended when it did.
4. As a member of the European Free Trade Association it does not have *locus standi* at the European Court of Justice.
5. See page 31, http://ec.europa.eu/public_opinion/archives/eb/eb69/eb69 _globalisation_en.pdf
6. Source: Department of Foreign Affairs/Millward Brown.
7. See http://www.irishtimes.com/newspaper/frontpage/2003/1217/107161628 9075.html
8. This idea came from Daniel Keohane of the European Union Institute for Security Studies in Paris.

## Chapter IV (pp 151–216)

1. At time of writing, the European Central Bank, the International Monetary Fund and the World Trade Organisation are all led by Frenchmen.
2. Germany, Italy and Spain.
3. According to researchers at investment bank Goldman Sachs, these first releases on average showed the US economy expanding at 3.1% in the 1999–2006 period, well over double the rate of the euro area and considerably ahead of the UK.
4. Even among countries usually lumped together in one European model or another, differences are often considerable. The Nordic social model often crops up in debate, not least because of the social, political and economic strengths of northern European countries. But it is less usual that differences between, for instance, Sweden and Denmark are acknowledged. The former has tighter laws on hiring and firing workers; considerably more liberal immigration laws; more onerous financial market legislation; and

more price controls (with the notable exception of its currency, which floats freely). Equally, differences are as big between other countries that are often lumped into the same 'social model': Britain and Ireland; Austria and Germany; Spain and Italy. Scratch the surface of these countries and these differences quickly become apparent.

5. The Fortune Global 500 list of the world's largest companies for 2007 gives Europe a higher weighting, with 161 compared to 162 for the US. The FT list is subject to more in-depth analysis here because its publication over a dozen years allows patterns over time to be considered.

6. As is the case with economic performance, corporate success varies across the continent. Britain, France and Germany had 13, 13 and 12 companies respectively in UNCTAD's 2007 top 100. Italy and Spain had just three each.

## Chapter v (pp 217–51)

1. A further reason for the often anodyne coverage is that many of those in the Brussels press corps have a strong attachment to the integration project. Because they do not wish to give ammunition to those who oppose integration, they do not subject it to the same rigorous scrutiny as they might their national politics.

2. There may be partial exceptions. The Mediterranean countries' pension systems need reform if there is to be any hope of longer term fiscal stability. For these countries, credible reform plans may be the price of bailout. Ireland's corporation tax régime may also be vulnerable if the country has to be rescued. It has long been viewed by some member states, and Germany in particular, as an unfair form of tax competition which erodes the tax bases of other members.

3  Financial services regulation, of which a large amount is already enacted at EU level, is likely to change in the future, probably fundamentally.

4. In theory all member countries of the WTO have vetoes. In practice, smaller members have less scope to exercise their vetoes than the big trade powers.

5. Although the European position has been undermined by many members not meeting the targets set out in the Kyoto Protocol, no region of the world has given the threat a higher priority.

## Chapter vi (pp 252–86)

1. See the Seventh United Nations Survey of Crime Trends and Operations of Criminal Justice Systems.

2. Steven Pinker marshals the evidence superbly in his book *The Blank Slate*. See in particular chapter 17.

3. See Manuel Eisner, 'Long-Term Historical Trends in Violent Crime'. http://videojuegosycultura.files.wordpress.com/2008/01/long-term-historical-trends-of-violent-crime.pdf.

4. Since reaching all-time lows in the 1950s and 1960s, levels of violent crime have risen in many developed countries. In the US, where levels of violent crime reached the highest levels in the developed world by the late 1990s, there has since been a dramatic decline. The reasons for this remain subject to intense debate.

5. The Centre for Systemic Peace at George Mason University is one of a growing number of research organisations empirically analysing conflicts across the world. Its database is available at http://www.systemicpeace.org./conflict.htm

6. *Ibid.*

7. The Economist Intelligence Unit's Index of Democracy provides one wide-ranging measure of the state of the global democratisation process. http://a330.g.akamai.net/7/330/25828/20081021195552/graphics.eiu.com/PDF/Democracy%20Index%202008.pdf

8 See: http://www.wipo.int/pressroom/en/articles/2009/article_0002.html

9. A wider conclusion is that capital and labour, what economists call 'factors of production', can cause enormous instability when they move freely. This is hardly disputed in the case of labour—no country in the world has complete free movement of labour for all nationalities. A return to some curbs on cross-border movement of capital seems inevitable, if not wholly desirable.

10. From the moment infants watch a cake being cut and divvied out, their instinct to view the world as a zero sum game is reinforced. Some argue that we evolved this instinct over tens of thousands of years when humans made little and depended on what was available in their environment for survival.

11. Only the populations of Bulgaria, Latvia and Ukraine are forecast by the Economist Intelligence Unit to shrink more rapidly.

12. In their end-of-summit communiqué on 2 April 2009, the G20 group of nations indicated that the monopolisation of the leadership roles of the IMF and World Bank by Europe and the US would end.

13. An arithmetic increase in the number of participants in any system generates an exponential increase in the number of relationships: with two participants, there is one relationship; three participants, three relationships; four participants, six relationships; and so on.

# INDEX